ARYAMEHR: THE SHAH OF IRAN

A POLITICAL BIOGRAPHY

His Imperial Majesty

THE SHAH OF IRAN

RAMESH SANGHVI

STEIN AND DAY/*Publishers*/New York

First published in the United States of America in 1969
by Stein and Day/*Publishers*

© Ramesh Sanghvi 1968
Library of Congress Catalog Card No. 69-17944

Produced in Great Britain by Transorient Books, London
and printed by R. and R. Clark, Ltd., Edinburgh

Stein and Day/*Publishers*/7 East 48 Street, New York,
N.Y. 1017

Contents

v

Contents

Contents

DOCUMENTS

Illustrations

Acknowledgements

A STUDY of this nature could not have been undertaken without the willing and unsparing co-operation of His Imperial Majesty Mohammad Reza Shah Pahlavi, Aryamehr, Shahanshah of Iran. Before I began work in the summer of 1965 I had made a specific request of the Shah : that I should have easy and unrestrained access to him whenever I needed to discuss problems arising from this study. I am happy to record that over these long months, during which the Shah himself has been deeply involved in the problems of national reconstruction in Iran and of growing conflict in west Asia, I have had the privilege of immediate access to His Majesty, as well as candid discussions.

I have relied essentially on Iranian sources. Indeed, I have received assistance from so many friends in Iran that it is impossible to acknowledge my debt to all of them individually. I am certain that they will appreciate this problem, and recognise in this expression of collective gratitude my acknowledgement of their aid and advice. However, it is essential for me to record that I would have never understood the basic orientation of the revolution of the Shah and the people but for the affectionate insistence of my friend Seifollah Rashidian who, as a participant in all the events of political life in Iran during the last thirty years, was in a position to direct me to the sources that could yield valuable and as yet unrecorded information. I am also indebted to General Hassan Pakravan, who spent innumerable hours filling the large gaps in my knowledge of the modern history of Iran.

It was my particular desire to receive an interpretation of his policies from Dr Mohammad Mossadeq. I therefore made several approaches to him through his friends. Dr Mossadeq was at that time unwell and relatively old, having celebrated his eighty-sixth birthday. He sent me a message stating that he would be happy to receive me but, so that the discussions could be really fruitful, I should first read all his speeches delivered in the *majlis*. By the time I finished this work, Dr Mossadeq was already very ill, and died soon after. However, I must acknowledge my debt to several scholars and politicians who were his colleagues during the

Acknowledgements

period of his two premierships for their assistance to me. I also received valuable help from several former members of the Tudeh Party.

The first outline of this study, and later the several drafts of the manuscript, were discussed with many friends in Iran, India and the United Kingdom. I was fortunate in receiving many suggestions for their improvement. I express my sincere thanks to all those friends who pooled their information and set me right on several points of fact. The manuscript in its final stages was carefully read and improved by my friends and colleagues, David Missen and Richard Barber. They were so closely linked with me in this work that I hesitate to thank them specifically, because I have come to consider them as joint authors. I particularly express my gratitude to Miss Helen Blakesley and Miss Rosemary Payne who willingly and cheerfully underwent the physical and mental torture of taking dictation and typing the manuscript for six long weeks.

I am also indebted to Clifford German, Financial Correspondent of *The Daily Telegraph*, London, for his two synopses on the new industrial revolution and on profit-sharing which appear as Documents III and IV, and to David Missen for his synopsis on the work of the three Corps, Document V.

Finally, I should like to express my thanks to J. C. E. Bowen for his kind permission to reproduce, as introductions to Parts II–V, four translations of Iranian classics from his collection, *Poems from the Persian*, John Baker, London, 1964.

Needless to say, all these friends and colleagues share with me the virtues, if any, of this study, and I alone am responsible for its weaknesses.

R. S.

Introduction

1

THIS study was undertaken three years ago, both as a political biography and a biographical history. The exercise was inspired by a natural instinct of search on the part of an Asian student of political philosophy, and by a desire to analyse the Iranian contribution to the fascinating phenomenon which Jawaharlal Nehru once described as ' The Revolution in Asia '. This revolution has meant the end of colonialism, ' the crumbling of those positions of power which the western nations had conquered in Asia, and in consequence, the disintegration of one of the foundation stones upon which the predominance of Europe in the world had rested '.[1] It has thus altered not only the political and military equation between Asia and the west, but also their moral relationship. In the ultimate analysis ' The Revolution in Asia ' may also have grave consequences for the rest of the world, for it is here that ' space, natural resources, great masses of men aspiring to the satisfaction of their elementary needs, are just beginning to use political power, modern technology, and modern moral ideas for their ends '.[2] Those who yesterday were still merely objects of the policies of others have now begun to play the role of active participants in shaping the world.

[1] Morgenthau, Hans J., *American Foreign Policy* : A Critical Examination (London, 1952), pp. 64–5.   [2] Ibid. p. 67.

Introduction

The most dramatic feature of this revolution has been the rise of nationalism in nearly every Asian country. Western scholars have often equated Asian nationalist values with those which were evolved in Europe after the French Revolution. Indeed, some of them have extended this analogy to suggest that the birth and growth of Asian nationalism was a direct benefit arising from the so-called western mission to the east, and that had it not been for the western concept of a right to self-determination, Asian nationalism would have no real content.[3] Without disputing the admittedly considerable influence of the west in Asia over three centuries, it may be stated that the western military conquest, and western political and economic dominance, merely intensified the historic nationalist fervour of Asia. This conquest and dominance aroused indigenous nationalist feelings to near fanatical pitch in almost every Asian country, just as was the case in several European countries whenever they felt subjugated to foreign influence, especially during the Second War. One has only to examine the heritage of each of the Asian countries to realise that their nationalist attitudes developed simultaneously with the growth of each Asian civilisation. Neither Iran nor India, to give only two examples, should be accused of having derived their respective concepts of nationalism as benefits from those who subjected them to temporary overlordship.

For at least half a century before 'The Revolution in Asia' unfolded itself in its growingly complex and painful pattern after the First War, the Asian intelligentsia believed that, under conditions of western dominance, the foundation of nationalism must be political freedom to determine the future

[3] This approach is not limited just to the believers in the myth of the white man's burden : it is observed, though decreasingly, in several western works on Afro-Asian countries : for example, see Tinker, Hugh, *Ballot Box and Bayonets* : People and Government in Emergent Asian Countries (London, 1966), pp. 8–11.

of their own society. No progress towards the renaissance of Asia could be made unless the control of foreigners over domestic, political and economic institutions — which was being used solely for the furtherance of their alien interests — was finally ended. Indeed, the leadership of ' The Revolution in Asia ', despite the diversity of its ideological outlooks, held it in common that the battle for national independence, and victory in this struggle, were prerequisites for the transformation of their ancient societies.[4] They made liberal use of several specifically western concepts to strengthen their ideological arsenal, but in appealing to their own people, by whose response the result of the struggle would be principally determined, they hardly ever referred to such niceties as those which President Woodrow Wilson zealously distributed during the Peace Conference at Versailles. Indeed, this could scarcely have been otherwise, for Wilson's principle of self-determination was actually practised solely in Europe. Even the famous Atlantic Charter, fashioned by President F. D. Roosevelt and Winston Churchill in 1941, was destined to remain a creation of the west, for application in the west, and for the benefit of the west. Churchill, therefore, felt no moral shame when, asked to extend this principle to India, he hypocritically announced his unwillingness to preside over the liquidation of the British Empire. The same liquidation, to which fate decreed he was to be an angry and powerless witness, was itself primarily brought about by Britain's inability to hold the Empire together militarily, as an honest Clement Attlee candidly admitted in the House of Commons. The west may choose to

---

4 For example, Bal Gangadhar Tilak, one of the major forerunners of Mahatma Gandhi, said : ' We want freedom. We must have in our hands the right of carrying on our affairs. If you do not get these things, no reform will be fruitful to you. That is the root of all reforms.' See Mackenzie Brown, D., *Indian Political Thought*, from Ranade to Bhave (Bombay, 1964), p. 91.

forget these facts, but the leaders of ' The Revolution in Asia ' have not. Despite the persistence of the myth of western ' abdication of power ' in Asia, first authored by Harold Laski in 1946, the Asian people and their leaders have not over-looked the harsh reality that the revolution was fought and won by millions of citizens, to whom the pristine, but selective, political concepts of the west were unintelligible, mysterious and remote.

Though national independence was its primary aim, the positive content of the Asian revolution lay in the solution of the problems which arose partly from Asia's own defeat and decay, and partly from the consequences of western conquest and the west's successful conversion of Asia into an agrarian appendage to the vast industrial complex which had grown up in Europe and the United States. The most obvious symp-toms of these difficult problems were poverty and ignorance ; but these were only symptoms. The problems themselves were more complex, and their solution infinitely more difficult to find. The belated entry of Asia into the modern age ; the collapse of the structure of, and faith in, ancient Asian societies ; and the need to overcome internal class, caste, re-gional and religious conflicts in every Asian country did not lead to congenial conditions for their speedy solution.

At the heart of all these problems lay the compelling need for basic social change, and this was to become the main feature of the Asian revolution. In its turn, the achievement of this goal was directly dependent upon accurate evaluation of the effect of western dominance on the traditional and historic way of life in every Asian country which had previously sustained its own civilisation. The new system of society and the social values which grew within each country's traditions during the period of enforced subjugation needed to be evaluated and then adapted to suit the ultimate aims of social change. Finally, unless realistic and rewarding choices were made, in the acceptance of new ideologies, new political insti- tutions, and new forms of leadership, consistent with the condi- tions and demands of each country, the process of social change would lead to even greater miseries, even more intense poverty, and would enmesh the country in a web of new superstitition.

It has been said, with some justice, that the Asian revolution really consists of two revolutions : the nationalist revolution and the ' revolution of rising expectations '.[5] It may also be said that the second of these revolutions has achieved minimal results, whereas the nationalist revolution has triumphed in almost every part of Asia. It cannot be denied that the Asian leadership in many countries is today faced with the grim prospect of failure in its search for effective social change. We have witnessed this general failure in Asia during the two decades since the end of the Second War. The older respected nationalist leaders, young enthusiastic Army Colonels and sincere patriotic professionals appear uniformly to be losing the battle of the ' revolution of rising expectations '. It has been established time and again — and most recently in a study by a team of economists and sociologists headed by Professor Gunnar Myrdal — that the essential cause of this failure lies in the collapse of the social revolution in Asia.[6]

[5] During this struggle even the influence of the Russian Revolution was marginal in most Asian Countries. Jawaharlal Nehru, asked about it, replied : 'Those were the days in the early 'twenties when we had our first experience of prison. Now I refer to that for two reasons. First of all, we were intensely occupied with our own struggle. Everything else was interesting in a distant way only. And, interesting experiences apart, only in so far as it applied to India. But we were very conscious of ourselves, so confident in ourselves, that external occurrences did not disturb us.' Mende, Tribor, *Conversations with Mr. Nehru* (London, 1956), p. 19.

[6] For a detailed discussion of this thesis see Halpern, Manfred, *The Politics of Social Change in the Middle East and North Africa* (Princeton, New Jersey, 1963).

Introduction

It is with this understanding of the semantics of ' The Revolution in Asia ' that, in the summer of 1965, I undertook the present study. At that time, as now, Iran was engaged in translating, in terms of Iranian values and needs, the historic task in which Asia as a whole was involved. The initial successes were impressive. However, what attracted me most, as a student of the Asian revolution, were these two features of the Iranian experiment : clarity of thought and dynamism of leadership. It was easy to learn, even on a first visit, that the author of the ideological content of the movement which the peasants described to me as ' the revolution of the Shah and the people ' was the Shah himself as, indeed, he was the organiser of the forces which had been mobilised to implement the goals then adopted. In the course of this study I have found that no individual was more intimately linked with this fascinating movement of twenty-five million people towards their own destiny than the *Aryamehr*, as his people affectionately call the Shah. He is the only binding thread in the recent historic annals of Iran. It was clear, therefore, that unless his thought and work were kept in the centre of this study, it was likely to lose its perspective. The best method to adopt, in these circumstances, was to use the revolution of the Shah and the people as the setting for a study of its leader as a statesman. This study thus inevitably becomes at the same time a biographical history and a political biography.

II

This study deals with the two political revolutions in Iran led by the two Pahlavi monarchs, and the major social revolution now in progress under Mohammad Reza Shah Pahlavi. It deliberately avoids the wider background of the long period of western dominance beginning in the Napoleonic era when

Iran first became involved in European politics. By the treaty of alliance of 1807, Fath Ali Shah had hoped to obtain arms with which to defend Iran against Russia. From 1813, when he lost his poorly prepared campaign against the Czarist forces and Iran was compelled to sign the Treaty of Gulistan, until the liberation of Azerbaijan in 1947 by Mohammad Reza Shah Pahlavi, the political and economic life of Iran was dominated by the European powers, especially Britain and Russia, except for a short period of two decades when Reza Shah almost succeeded in making Iran independent. The present study could not embrace the vicissitudes of this period and its pervasive effects on the early years of the life of Mohammad Reza Shah Pahlavi. Yet, to understand his life and work it is essential to grasp the basic historical characteristics of his people. There has been an organised state in the area now called Iran for 2,500 years. This remarkable record of the Iranian people was primarily due to the geographical position of their homeland as a bridge between the steppes of inner Asia and the high plateau of Asia Minor with its links to Europe. This physical situation made Iran the outpost of the Asian world and brought her people in contact with the various phases of western civilisation. She thus played 'the glorious role of defender of the treasures of ancient and oriental civilisation' and also proved to be a carrier of those western values compatible with Asian conditions. Geography thus compelled her people to develop what later became their two chief traits : the organisational capacity to build a unique civilisation and a genius for military affairs.[7]

This exceptional role enabled Iran to survive many vicissitudes. In Professor R. Ghirshman's words : 'They were able

---

[7] For the views of Mohammad Reza Shah Pahlavi on this subject, see his two books, *Mission for My Country* (London, 1961), pp. 16–26 ; and *The White Revolution of Iran* (Tehran, 1967), p. 9.

to adopt and assimilate the great urban civilisations of the land of the two rivers ; and after the Macedonian conquest they experienced an impact of a powerful western influence, but although drawing largely on this foreign civilisation, they remained Iranian ; in the face of the later invasions of Arab, Turk, and Mongol, they had the strength not only to survive but also to absorb the foreign talents.'[8]

The resilient character of the Iranian civilisation is an exceptional example in western Asia of a nation which refused to lose its identity even when it accepted an extraneous religion. The sweep of Islam from Arabia into Iran was a major encounter between ideals. Other west Asian peoples could not withstand the impact of the challenge of Islam on their indigenous civilisation. Egypt, for example, was absorbed by the new Islamic civilisation despite its ancient traditions. 'Neither the Pharaonic nor the Graeco-Roman civilisations of ancient times can claim to be represented in Egyptian life today. Egyptian civilisation during the last 1200 years is predominantly Arabic and Moslem. Similar is the case with the great civilisations which had flowered in Roman and Christian nations in Africa on the northern littoral of the Mediterranean, and today they are Islamic with hardly any important cultural roots in their pre-Islamic past.'[9] Iran was the one exception to this rule.

As a result, Iran's leadership in cultural and philosophical matters was acknowledged as far afield as Egypt and India. Students of this period of Iranian history have seen the rise of Sufism, 'a Persian product', as Iran's revenge for the military defeat her armies suffered at the hands of the Arabs and the consequent imposition of the conqueror's language for all

[8] Ghirshman, R., *Iran From the Earliest Times to the Islamic Conquest* (London, 1965), p. 357.

[9] Pannikar, K. M., *The Foundations of New India* (London, 1963), p. 12.

religious and judicial purposes. 'The tide of Sufism swept throughout the vast areas of Islamic civilisation and this over-powering influence persists even today. In this way Persia had conquered a spiritual domain far more extensive than any won by the armies of Cyrus and Darius and one which is still far from being a thing of the past. Indeed one might say that through this mystic law in an incomparable medium Persia found herself discover something like a true spiritual vocation among the peoples of the world, and that her voice is now only to make itself heard to win the delighted approval of all these seekers and connoisseurs whose souls are attuned to perceiving the message of *ustad i azal* (the Eternal Master), to use Khoja Hafiz's phrase.' [10] This appreciation by Cyprian Rice may appear to be an expression of his own admiration for the *sufi* school of Islamic philosophy and its lyrical expression in Iranian literature. However, to an Indian in whose land litera-ture in all the fourteen major languages bears the indelible imprint of *sufism*, it seems only just. It underlines the essential reality that the Iranian response to foreign challenge was never subservience nor the submersion of Iranian values.

III

The seeming anachronism of a monarch leading a popular revolution can also be explained by the specific traits of Iranian civilisation. Monarchy has been the most ancient and con-sistent institution in the civilisation of Iran. 'Though the history of Iran is long and complex', Sir Roger Stevens, who studied Iran from an ambassadorial vantage point between 1954 and 1958, has written, 'its shape is determined by the rise and fall of successive dynasties — with intervals of chaos

[10] Rice, Cyprian, *The Persian Sufis* (London, 1964), p. 11.

and confusion.'[11] This view is supported by the nature of Ferdowsi's national epic, the *Shāh-nāma*. This is a history of Iran in verse related as the record of the national dynasties from the creation of the world to the fall of the Sassanians and the Arab conquest. Ferdowsi spent thirty-five years of the eleventh century composing this great classic. He worked on the basis of an established tradition which equated the history of the life and civilisation of the people of Iran with their institution of monarchy, probably contained in prose and verse histories.[12]

This also explains the exceptional development of early political science in Iran. Nizam al-Mulk wrote his treatise the *Siyasat-Nama* during the same century as Ferdowsi. The *Siyasat-Nama* is an outstanding treatise on government. Its official title has been translated as 'the Book of Government or Rules for Kings'. The author acted as Prime Minister to two successive rulers of the Seljuq dynasty for thirty years. Though the kings whom he served belong to the tribes which had emigrated into Iran from central Asia, the opening paragraph of this treatise summarises the principal character of the institution of Iranian monarchy thus : 'In every age of time God (be He exalted) chooses one member of the human race and having adorned and endowed him with kingly virtues and entrusted him with the interests of the world and the well-being of his servants, he charges that person to close the doors of corruption, confusion and discord and he imparts to him such dignity and majesty in the eyes and hearts of men that under his just rule, they may live their lives in constant security and ever wish for his reign to continue.'[13] Though as an Iranian Nizam al-Mulk

[11] Stevens, Roger, *The Land of the Great Sophy* (London, 1965), p. 8.

[12] *The Epic of the Kings, Shāh-nāma, The National Epic of Persia*, trans. Reuben Levy ; 1967, p. xvi.

[13] Nizam al-Mulk, *The Book of Government or Rules for Kings*, trans. Hubert Darke, intro. Reuben Levy (London, 1960), p. 9.

reproduced in this definition of kingship the pre-Islamic values, as a Moslem he was fully conscious that the advent of Islam had merely broadened and strengthened the basic Iranian concept of monarchy. Imam Ali, whose authority the Shi'an Moslems of Iran accepted as second only to that of the Prophet, underlined in a message to a Caliph of Egypt, Malik Ashtar, Islam's principles of equity for rulers : 'Mete out equal justice to all. Give preference to the will of the majority as the dissatisfaction of the many invalidates the satisfaction of a few ; while the dissatisfaction of a few does not affect the satisfaction of many. This means that if the public supports you the enmity of a few will be of no avail and vice versa. The acquiescence of a few never justifies the disapproval of the public.'[14]

The enduring nature of Iranian monarchy over a period of two and a half millenia has little relevance to the rise and fall of kings in Europe during the feudal period. The classical feudal system as instituted in the west never existed in Iran though relationships of a feudal type lasted until as late as 1963, and even today their vestiges can be observed. This is an important feature of the socio-economic history not only of Iran, but also of western Asia, which needs to be borne in mind if one is not to fall a victim to the prevalent unjustifiable trend of disdain for the institution of monarchy. Professor Ann K. S. Lambton has set out the chief distinction between the classical feudal order in Europe on the one hand, and the system of feudal relationship in Iran on the other : 'Whereas the power and privileges of the land-owning classes have been relatively constant over a long period its composition has undergone many changes. . . .' The chief trait of the Iranian system of feudal relationship lies in the fact that it never permitted a stable landed aristocracy 'transmitting its estates in their entirety from

[14] Quoted in *The White Revolution*, p. 8.

generation to generation'[15] to establish a feudal pyramid with the king at its apex. Thus the feudal lords of Iran bore no resemblance to their counterparts, aristocrats, Junkers, or squires, whose nobility depended on their status as a class entitled to traditional territories as inheritance. Similarly, the king had little in common with the medieval kings of Europe in as much as he was never dependent upon these lords, and his own links were not with them but with the people over whom he ruled. This special character of the Iranian kings was equated by Professor Christensen, the Danish orientalist, with the role of a teacher who leads his people in spirit, thought and heart.[16]

Here lies the explanation of Reza Shah's initially reluctant decision in 1925 to continue the tradition of monarchy when the *majlis* expelled the Qajar dynasty. Reza Shah himself was typical of the new Asian leaders, and indeed fully comprehended the problems involved in setting up a new system of government in Iran. He was greatly influenced by the political philosophy of Kemal Ataturk, who had abolished the Ottoman dynasty to found the Turkish Republic. On the other hand, Reza Shah was an intense patriot steeped in Iranian traditions. He knew that the historical concept of monarchy and popular adherence to it would enable him to achieve tangible results much more rapidly than conditions under a republic. Mohammad Reza Shah Pahlavi had already become an Iranian intellectual who was fully familiar with western democratic thought before his accession, and like his father he valued the monarchy as an institution for the tremendous possibilities of rapid advance which were inherent in it. Of this he has written: 'This possibly makes plain why a monarch, if he has the full

15 Lambton, Ann K. S., *Landlord and Peasant in Persia* (London, 1953), p. 259; also quoted by Halpern, *Politics of Social Change*, p. 44.
16 *The White Revolution*, p. 2.

trust of the people and uses his great influence, could achieve so much without having to rely on totalitarian measures or wait for slow evolutionary processes to achieve his aims.'[17]

Within the framework of this tradition, a special kind of democratic procedure was evolved. True, it is hardly akin to those of a republic ; but it compares favourably with the un-happy experience of many Asian countries who attempted to imitate the European model of parliamentary democracy. This failure is written large in most countries, with the exception of India and to some extent Ceylon. The collapse of the parlia-mentary system in present political conditions is manifest. In west Asia, with the possible exception of the Lebanon, power has invariably gravitated towards individuals or groups ; hence on the failure of any European-type party system, individuals or groups have succeeded in acquiring dictatorial powers. This fact of political life has its origins in the peculiar social and economic conditions of the various segments of the Asian civilisation. To condemn it implies a belief in the exclusive sanctity of western democracy.

The modern Iranian monarchy is thus consistent with his-torical national traditions on the one hand, and in conformity with the contemporary Asian pattern of political power on the other. While the debate on its theoretical aspects may con-tinue, it has shown in practice that it can pave the way for out-standing material and cultural achievements.

IV

During several long discussions over a period of two and a half years, I have examined these ideas and many other matters with the Shah who himself was aware of the need to understand

[17] Binder, Leonard, *Iran : Political Development in a Changing Society* (Cambridge, 1962), p. 228.

them fully in their Iranian perspective. The Shah, proud and happy as he is with the progress of the revolution he has introduced, is under no illusions as to the remaining weaknesses in the political system he inherited at the beginning of his reign. Of the many traditional problems, he is particularly determined to put an end to the system of bargaining. Though it is by no means an exclusive feature of the traditional Iranian political system, it has retarded national progress. 'Bargaining is a technique of achieving co-operation between independent power structures, but in the traditional system it is also the basis of granting legitimisations.'[18]   One can terminate its practice only when its basis is destroyed. In order to be able to do so, each structure of power as an independent and self-interested unit has to be transformed into a part of the general structure of national power, and its interests into national interests.

As a guarantee against administrative sabotage, sloth and corruption, the Shah introduced administrative reforms under the additional three points of his programme. On October 6, 1967, while announcing these new points, he laid emphasis on administrative reform in these words : 'The meaning of this reform is that any person employed in administration and working in Government agencies, whether in high or low position, should discharge his duties with complete honesty, sincerity, and responsibility. The spirit of time-wastage, paper work and bureaucracy should be eliminated. Every worker should know that in the first place it is his duty to attend to callers who approach him with work and help solve their difficulties quickly, through correct interpretation of law and without personal bias.'[19]   Anyone who is familiar with the administrative pattern and the Civil Service in Iran would

[18] Binder, p. 24.
[19] See Document II.

immediately recognise the shortcomings which the Shah has attacked here.

I have had occasion, after visiting various parts of Iran, to congratulate the Shah on the progress that has been made. On each occasion the Shah, having thanked me with inimitable Persian politeness, has answered that much more could be done but he was handicapped by lack of people able, as well as sufficiently sincere, to keep pace with the needs of the changing society in Iran.

The Shah has an unenviable job. He has to live up to the very high standards of leadership set up by the traditional concept of a king in Iran, who must lead his people in heart and mind, as well as guiding them through the various conflicts of the moment. The Shah's personal convictions on this intricate task are firm. He is a leader who will lead and not merely follow the dictates of the crowd. He will not act alone according to his own lights and permit himself to be cut off from the very persons whom he is trying to lead. He will not lower himself and be untrue to his own ideal, by compromise and bringing himself down to the same level of understanding as others, since he is aware that the path of compromise is slippery. Nor will he isolate himself from the understanding of the common people. His is the role of a leveller. In fact, he represents a generation of Iran, as its leader, which is ordained by fate to level the fortresses of privilege and power built by individuals and classes, and secure a uniform rise in the prosperity and happiness of the common people. Its success will surely affect the thinking and future of nations besides his own.

London
April 1968

RAMESH SANGHVI

Dedication

RETURNING from the idyllic coast of the Caspian to Tehran via Rasht on my first visit to Iran in the summer of 1965, I met, by accident, a peasant in a village near Qazvin. He was old and impressive. He was also poor, as his tattered clothes clearly showed. I spent an hour talking to him. Like his father and grandfather before him, he had worked as a serf on the lands of a feudal lord who owned several villages besides his own. The feudal lord was gone, and his vast lands had been distributed among his former serfs, but my friend had not been allotted land and his life continued to be poor. 'What will you do now?' I asked him. 'I am not worried,' he replied with a smile, 'the Land Reform Commission is due to arrive in a few days. I will get my land.' I was puzzled by his cheerfulness. 'Surely you cannot be so confident. The government has already rejected your claims. How can you hope to receive any land now?' His answer was simple: 'The Shahanshah will not permit such injustice. He knows the land is mine. He will see that I get it.'

This reply of the peasant from the village near Qazvin, his hope and confidence, set me to the task of this study. To me he represented not only the formerly oppressed Iranian peasantry but also the millions of men and women of my own country, and those of Afro-Asia, in his quiet and determined optimism. I also saw for the first time the bond which joins the Shah and his people.

To him, who received his land within the next twenty-seven days, and whose trust in his Shah was fulfilled, I dedicate this book with humility and hope.

PART ONE

THE MAKING OF A KING:

King Darayavaush proclaims:
King, thou shalt reign
In the days to come,
Keep and protect thyself
From insolent imposture.

King Darayavaush proclaims:
Oramazda and all other gods of the universe
Have come to my aid
Only because I was not the servant of evil,
Not a servant of imposture,
Because I have committed no act of violence,
Neither I nor any of my race.

I have chosen the way which was as straight as
*   a javelin,*
I have chosen the right way.
To no knight, to no man-servant
Have I ever done violence.
The vassal who built my house
Have I raised up as support of my house,
But the vassal who brought down my house,
Him I have punished severely according to the
*   right and law.*

Rock inscription at Bagistan
on the tomb of Darius, 521–485 B.C.

Stormy Setting

MOHAMMAD REZA was born on October 26, 1919, in a modest house in one of the older residential districts of the walled city of Tehran. The only distinctive feature of this house, which the family left after the birth of the first son and a twin sister, was its wide courtyard. It was from here that the future Shah of Iran had his first glimpses of the majestic cone of Mount Demavand, where the two ancient mountain ranges of the Zagros and Elburz join. Its snowcapped summit could be seen in the north-east, even though it was sixty miles away. Mount Demavand, the highest peak of these two ranges, fascinated the young Shah for whom, as he related later, it came to symbolise a proud and unbending sentinel guarding the greatness of his country through its ancient historical continuity.[1]

His father, Reza Khan, as the future first Pahlavi monarch was then known, was forty-one years old at the time of Mohammad Reza's birth. Reza Khan belonged to a traditionally military family of the Bayand clan from the Upper Mazanderan region of Savadkuh. The Caspian province of Mazanderan, an area of Iran which for centuries gave its name to the Caspian Sea — the Sea of Mazanderan — is one of the original homelands of the Aryan tribes which settled in Iran. Ferdowsi, in his eleventh-century epic, the *Shahnameh*, sang the glory of

[1] In conversation with the author.

Mazanderan, which even at the time of Kavus and Rustum was famous for its sturdy and fearless soldiers.[2] It was in this ancient nursery of Iranian valour, that Reza Khan had been born on March 16, 1878.

Reza Khan's father and grandfather had both been officers in the old Iranian army. His father, Abbas Ali Khan, had been a colonel in the local regiment. His grandfather, Major Murad Ali Khan, had distinguished himself by gallantry at the Iranian siege of Herat, and was killed in action in a battle against the Afghans in 1856.[3] Colonel Abbas Ali Khan died only forty days after the birth of his son in 1878. His wife decided to leave for Tehran in the winter of that year, and the baby almost perished in the intense cold of the mountain roads of Mazanderan.[4]

No alternative to that of military service was ever considered for Reza Khan in his childhood. His mother used to relate to him the many episodes of valour, and the military virtues, which constituted his sole inheritance from his ancestors. Even before he was ten, he was aware that every member of the family had spent his life as a soldier of his country. Following this tradition, he joined the Persian Cossack Brigade as soon as he was fourteen. The Brigade had been created in 1879, the year after Reza Khan's birth, by Nassereddin Shah, the Qajar monarch, after the failure of British, French and Austrian military experts to set up a European-style fighting force in Iran. It was patterned on the Russian model and instructed and commanded by Russian officers.[5] Its regiments were stationed

[2] *The Epic of the Kings, Shāh-nāma.* The national epic of Persia by Ferdowsi, translated by Reuben Levy (London, 1967), pp. 52–5.

[3] Arfa, General Hassan, *Under Five Shahs* (London, 1964), p. 90.

[4] Pahlavi, Mohammed Reza Shah, Shahanshah of Iran, *Mission for My Country* (London, 1961), pp. 35–6, cited hereafter as *Mission*.

[5] Sykes, Sir Percy, *A History of Persia* (3rd ed., London, 1963), II, pp. 369–70

at Tehran and in the northern provinces of Mazanderan, Gilan and Abzeraijan. As the best organised unit of the imperial army of the Qajars, the Brigade's attraction for the young Reza Khan was both natural and irresistible.

The recruit from Mazanderan was a tall and sturdy young man with a rugged and determined profile. He had piercing eyes which impressed everyone who met him and which 'could make a strong man shrivel up inside'.[6] His strong attachment to discipline and his refusal to compromise once his mind was made up gave him the reputation of a person to be feared. Within a few years, by the time he was twenty, he had made his name as a courageous and resourceful soldier.

At the turn of the century in Iran, education was still the exclusive privilege of the leisured classes and clergy, who were determined to see that the common people did not share this advantage. The young Reza Khan was therefore completely illiterate when he joined the Brigade. Yet he belonged to a generation of new nationalists which had made up its mind to break the hold of superstition over their people. The west, which had come to Iran and the east in search of gold and grandeur, had already shaken the foundations of the oriental oligarchy in the country. As early as 1851, the first European-style college was set up in Tehran ; seven years later, telegraph offices first appeared in Iran ; and in 1860 the Masonic cult was introduced. A girls' school was founded in 1865,[7] and by the time Reza Khan was born the urge for education had become a passion among the more sensitive young people of the towns. Reza Khan, like other young Iranians of this group, wanted above all to educate himself. His desire turned to determination once he realised how the ruling classes of Iran

[6] *Mission*, p. 36.
[7] Banani, Amin, *The Modernisation of Iran* (Stanford, California, 1961), pp. 8–9.

had gone to great lengths to keep the people illiterate and superstitious. Each day, at the end of his army duties, he sat patiently in his barracks learning to read and write with the help of one of his more fortunate educated friends. From the beginning, he aimed at a successful military career, and his entire education and outlook were to be moulded by the needs of the army. Though he joined as a private, he was determined to use his ability and force of character to achieve the goal of commanding the Brigade — a goal he set for himself the day he enlisted. He succeeded step by step during his twenty-seven years in the Brigade, and when his son was born he held the rank of Colonel and was a member of the High Command of the Brigade.

The years of Reza Khan's advance in the hierarchy of command within the Brigade were those of a gathering political storm in Iran. Caught between the rival claims of the two mighty colonial powers then dominating Asia, Russia and Britain, the short-sighted Qajar monarchs, Mohammad Shah (1834–47), Nassereddin Shah (1847–96) and Muzaffareddin Shah (1896–1907), had either lost in battle or traded away, piece by piece, large portions of Iranian territory and several integral elements of national sovereignty. At the beginning of the twentieth century, Muzaffareddin was in the process of converting Iran into a client state of the Czars.

His acts of surrender aroused considerable opposition to his entire policy of capitualtion. In 1901 yet another grant of tariff preference ceded by him to Russia finally opened the floodgates of a massive resistance movement. The commercial sectors of the population demanded a constitution, essentially to limit the absolute powers of the monarch, and the creation of a parliament. This demand found a ready response from large sections of the Muslim clergy. Since this agitation, was, at its inception, against the pro-Russian policy of the Shah, the British authorities in Tehran gave moral and material support to the Constitutionalists.

Initially, the influence of the Constitutionalists was limited to the urban population. The Russian revolution of 1905 made a deep impact on the minds of educated Asians. Indeed, the revolt against a despotic Czar found great sympathy in Iran, due to the unmistakable similarity between the two neighbouring countries, in both of which democratic processes were absent. Demonstrations in support of the Constitutionalists continued in major urban and rural centres in the first five months of 1906. In July 1906, the Constitutionalists served an ultimatum on the Shah, who retaliated by imprisoning a large number of the popular leaders. The British Legation in Tehran became a sanctuary for them. In face of the failure of the Czar, who had his own troubles, to assist him ; the open support of Britain for the Constitutionalists ; and, above all, the rising tide of popular anger ; Muzaffareddin was compelled to accept some of their demands. A national assembly — the *majlis* — was elected and met for the first time in October 1906. It drew up a constitution which was ratified by the Shah. Though Muzaffareddin had planned to frustrate the functions of the constitutional government, his death shortly afterwards prevented this.

The accession of his son, Mohammad Ali, aggravated the conflict. He attempted a *coup* and provoked nationalist retaliation.[8] At this moment the Qajar monarchy could have ended. However, much greater forces were at work in Iran at that time. The traditional rivals for domination of the country, Britain and Russia, were now faced by a new challenge from a unified

[8] References to the events leading to the first victory of the Constitutionalists are to be found in all standard works on the political history of Iran. An Iranian interpretation is given by Sahebjam, Freidoune, *L'Iran des Pahlavis* (Paris, 1966), pp. 37–46.

Germany. In face of this increasing threat, they arrived at an agreement in which Iran had a major role to play. Mohammad Ali retained his throne as a consequence of this *détente* between London and St. Petersburg, the terms of which were embodied in the Anglo-Russian Convention of August 31, 1907.

Under this Convention, ostensibly contrived to defend 'the independence and integrity of Iran', the country was divided into two spheres of influence. Britain secured for herself the south-west corner of the country, including all territory south of a line drawn from the Afghan frontier, via Gazik, Birjan and Kerman to the sea at Bandar Abbas. Thus Seistan and most of the provinces of Kerman and Makran fell within her sphere of influence. To Russia went the whole of northern Iran above a line drawn from Kasr-i-Shirin on the Turkish frontier, through Isfahan, Yezd and Kahk to the point on the Iranian frontier where the Russian and Afghan frontiers intersect. Thus almost all the major towns of Iran — Tabriz, Rasht, Tehran, Meshed and Isfahan — fell within this sphere of influence.

The government of Mohammad Ali was left with an area between the two zones, a buffer strip, which comprised the greater part of southern Iran and the whole of the Persian Gulf coast on the Iranian side. The Convention did not specify this as a third zone, and the Shah's sovereignty over it was at best dubious.[9] The reasons for this became clear in 1911. By an informal and unwritten arrangement the two powers agreed to the complete domination of the northern areas by Russia, and the inclusion of this third zone into the British sphere of influence.

The Anglo-Russian Convention created a new situation in Iran. Mohammad Ali realised that Britain would now withdraw the support previously granted to the Constitutionalists,

[9] For full text of the Anglo-Russian Convention of 1907, see Sykes, op. cit., II, pp. 410-11.

since her interests in Iran were guaranteed, at least for the time being. On the other hand, Russia was extremely concerned with the revolutionary element in the constitutional movement, with which she was becoming increasingly familiar at home. The movement itself was primarily based in the cities which fell within the Russian sphere of influence. The Czarist government encouraged Mohammad Ali to suppress the Constitutionalists. Mohammad Ali, for his own part, needed only the promise of Russian support should matters get out of hand. He therefore lost no time staging a second *coup* against the Constitutionalists, with the assistance of the Cossack Brigade. In June 1908, he ordered Colonel Liakhoff, the Russian commander of the Brigade, to mount an artillery attack on the parliament building in Tehran. On June 23, Liakhoff bombarded parliament whilst the *majlis* was sitting, and six regiments of the Brigade occupied Tehran. While the dead and injured were still in the heavily damaged *majlis* building, Mohammad Ali, in a letter to the Prime Minister, Moshir Saltaneh, accused the Constitutionalists of being solely responsible for his own *coup*, and dissolved the *majlis*. On the same day, a state of siege was proclaimed in Tehran and Liakhoff named military governor of the capital.

The Constitutionalists retaliated swiftly and effectively. An open revolt was proclaimed by the chief clergy at Nadjaf and by the *ayatollahs* * in Khorassan and Mazanderan. Tabriz, capital of Azerbaijan, became the headquarters of the Constitutionalists, who had now taken up arms. At this stage the Czar intervened with his promised support. Russian troops entered Tabriz, where their occupation of the city was accompanied by violence and cruelty. By this time the revolt had spread to Rasht and Isfahan. The re-grouped revolutionary forces marched towards Tehran where they defeated the

* Local clerical leaders.

half-hearted and unwilling soldiers of the Cossack Brigade, who were disgusted with the cruelty of their Russian commanders and Mohammad Ali. The entry of the Constitutionalists into the capital compelled Mohammad Ali to flee, first as a refugee to the Russian Legation, and then to Russia. The Constitutionalists set his corpulent eleven-year-old son, Ahmad, on the throne. Few people were then in doubt that the young Ahmad would be the last ruler of the Qajar line.[10]

Reza Khan, during these years of conflict, was torn between his feelings of support for the patriotic movement on the one hand, and his sense of discipline and loyalty as a soldier on the other. Later, when he became Shahanshah, he related to his son the agony of those years. The Shah has written at some length about his father's feelings in the period leading up to the revolution of 1921. Depressed as he was at the progressive dismemberment of Iran and the despotic and oppressive rule of Muzaffareddin and Mohammad Ali, Reza Khan suffered deeply from the 'terrible knowledge that foreign officers commanded the force to which he belonged'.[11] He realised that he marched under orders that were often dictated by the Russians rather than from the Persian capital. His patriotism rebelled against the use to which the Brigade was put by Mohammad Ali at the instance of the Czar. As the anti-imperialist character of the national movement began to dominate its other aspects, he developed 'intense feelings of patriotism and nationalism, because he knew so well the meaning of foreign domination'.

As a soldier, Reza Khan continued to fight many campaigns aimed at suppressing tribal rebels, yet the conflict in his mind was acute. There were periods when, seeing no immediate solution to the problems involved in this conflict, and unable to bear the sense of national humiliation, he recklessly risked

---

[10] For details, see Sahebjam, pp. 55–63.   [11] *Mission*, p. 37.

his life. Of one such incident, the Shah has written : 'I remember the moving story my father told me of his feelings in one
engagement against tribal brigands. Suddenly he was so con-
sumed by disgust at the whole condition of Persia, that he
deliberately exposed himself to enemy fire. Mounted on a
white horse at the time, he provided a stationary and con-
spicuous target, but none of the enemy's bullets found its
mark.' [12] On other occasions, he sat for long hours by himself seeking to discover a bloodless solution to the problems. Meanwhile, the condition of Iran continued to deteriorate.

The defeat of Mohammad Ali was a distinct setback to
Russian power, for which the Czarist government took its
revenge in 1911. St. Petersburg served orders on the Constitutionalists to terminate the services of an American financial
expert, Morgan Shuster, who was leading an official mission
sent at the request of the Constitutionalist cabinet to reorganise
the financial, economic and tariff structure of Iran. The orders
were followed by an ultimatum which in turn was followed by
an invasion, another massacre of liberals and democrats at
Tabriz, and the bombardment of the Holy Shrine of the Imam
Reza at Meshed. The government, fearing the occupation of
Tehran by Russian troops, accepted the conditions of the
ultimatum. Shuster was dismissed and Russian domination
accepted. All hopes of support from the British proved
sterile. True to the spirit of the Anglo-Russian Convention of
1907, Britain abandoned the Constitutionalists whom she had
abundantly encouraged earlier. Thus began the decade which
Shuster has described as 'the strangling of Persia'.[13] Russian
troops were still in occupation of northern Iran when the First
European War broke out in 1914.

[12] *Mission*, p. 37.
[13] Shuster, W. Morgan, *The Strangling of Persia* (New York, 1912).

The only event of historical importance which took place during this period was the discovery of oil in the British sphere of influence. In 1901, Muzzafareddin had awarded an Australian prospector, William Knox D'Arcy, exclusive exploration and exploitation rights for sixty years throughout Iran except the northern provinces bordering the Czarist empire. The D'Arcy concession also included the right to build pipelines to the Persian Gulf. In 1906, the Burmah Oil Company and the Scottish financier, Lord Strathcona, formed an oil syndicate to assist D'Arcy for a period of three years. In 1908, oil was at last discovered at the site of an ancient fire temple, more than a hundred miles from the head of the Persian Gulf. Production from the first well, at Masjid-i-Sulaiman, evoked further interest in Britain and with the blessing of the British government the Anglo-Persian Oil Company was formed in London. The D'Arcy concession was taken over by the new company, which built a refinery at Abadan which came on stream in 1913. Before the war broke out, therefore, Iranian oil had begun to flow to Europe. A new factor, which was later to become crucial, had entered the complicated situation of Iran.

The years of the First War were a time of alien military occupation, untold misery and vast desolation for Iran. The government declared Iran neutral ; but this neutrality was violated first by the Russians and Turks in the north-west and then by the Turks and the British in the south-west. The activities of Wassmuss, the German counterpart to T. E. Lawrence, further complicated the situation. After the Czarist armies collapsed in February 1917 and the first phase of the Russian revolution began, northern Iran was converted into a major battlefield where the Turkish, British, White Russian and Bolshevik forces sought to settle their scores against each other, primarily at the cost of Iranian peasants. By the end of the war, the White Russian troops were in occupation of the Caspian seaboard. The rest of the country was under virtual military occupation by British forces.

The condition of Iran at the end of the war has been well described by the Shah in the context of the increasing mental conflict which Reza Khan felt at that time. 'I can visualise him now', the Shah wrote, 'as he sat astride his horse, the man whose royal bearing yet revealed the shame he felt for his country. Really it was not a country, for his once proud land now possessed no central government worthy of the name. Much of Persia was in the grip of local chieftains paying nominal allegiance to the king, thereby allowing him to save his face : actually they were doing whatever they pleased in their own regions, thus compounding the miseries of the people. There was no modern army, and none that owed allegiance to Persia ; there was no law and order ; there were no Persian courts save those of the clergy and the tribes. In most of the country it was the law of the strongest that prevailed. The pillagers pillaged and the common people suffered.' [14]

At the end of the war Iran made one last attempt to seek justice from powers which had formally sanctified the principle of national self-determination at the Peace Conference of 1919. A delegation from Tehran went to Versailles to plead the case of Iran. The government had prepared a document in which it argued Iran's case for political, judicial and economic independence, and her right to territorial restorations and reparation. Iran had requested the abrogation of the Anglo-Russian Convention of 1907 and demanded the withdrawal of consular guards and the abolition of consular courts. The delegation had been encouraged to think that, in their anti-communist mood, the victorious powers would return to Iran territories

[14] *Mission*, pp. 37–8.

she had lost during the Czarist expansion in Asia. It had hoped that reparation for the damage inflicted during the war, and in violation of Iran's neutrality, by the Turkish, British and Russian armies would also be granted.[15] The delegation never reached the stage of pleading its case, and was dismissed in a humiliating fashion. Lloyd George, prompted by Lord Curzon, was primarily responsible for this iniquity, the reasons for which became clear on August 9, 1919, when the British decision to convert Iran into a protectorate was gently announced.

On that day, Sir Percy Cox, then Minister at the British Legation in Tehran, obtained the signature of the President of the State Council of Iran, Vosough-ed-Dowleh, on a document which embodied the Anglo-Persian Treaty of 1919. This later proved to be the only British proposal to remain unratified since 1814, when the first treaty of defensive alliance was signed. It also turned out to be the spark that set ablaze the smouldering fire of Iranian nationalism. The events to which it gave rise changed dramatically and decisively the course of Reza Khan's life. Above all, they provided the stormy setting against which the life of Mohammad Reza Pahlavi, to be born seventy-eight days later, was to unfold.

[15] Sykes, II, pp. 518-20.

CHAPTER TWO

The Revolution of 1921

SIR PERCY COX, an experienced colonial pro-consul who had served for many years in Mesopotamia and on the Persian Gulf, had been appointed Minister at the British Legation in Tehran in September 1918 with a special mission. He was to secure Iranian agreement to a new Anglo-Persian treaty. For nearly nine months he laboured hard to convince the various ministers in Tehran to accept the terms of the new agreement. It was a painful process, but Sir Percy negotiated from strength. The government of Iran at that stage was completely dependent upon Britain for its financial existence. Its treasury was empty and in the prevalent conditions of anarchy and chaos it had no hope of collecting any taxes. Sir Percy was thus in a position to dictate the pace of negotiations.

The new treaty consisted of a short document containing a preamble and six articles.[1] The preamble stated the platitudes. It was essential and in the mutual interest of both Iran and Britain that the ties of friendship existing between the governments of the two countries should be cemented and 'the progress and prosperity of Persia should be promoted to the utmost'. By the first article the British government reiterated 'in the most categorical manner' its past undertakings that it would respect absolutely the independence and integrity of

[1] For text, see Appendix A.

Persia. Having stated this, the British government in the remaining articles acquired for itself complete control over the Iranian army and finances. British military experts were to reorganise and equip Iranian armed forces at Iran's expense. British financial experts were to reorganise the revenues, customs and other sources of income at Iran's expense. British technical experts were to construct railways and other forms of transport at Iran's expense. In return for all this, Britain was to advance a loan, the terms of which were defined by a second agreement. A sum of £2,000,000 at 7 per cent redeemable in twenty years, was granted as the amount of this loan. A commission was to be appointed for the reorganisation of the Iranian army in which Iranians were allowed to participate.

As soon as Vosough-ed-Dowleh put his signature to this treaty, and even before the Shah or the *majlis* had ratified it, several of its provisions were put into operation. A financial commission headed by the British expert Sydney Armitage-Smith arrived forthwith at Tehran to prepare for the reorganisation of the Iranian financial system. General Dickson, whose troops had occupied eastern Iran during the First War, headed the military commission, and British engineers began a survey for building a railway.

The terms of the treaty irritated other western powers who considered that they too had some right and interest in the internal affairs of Iran. The government of the United States was more forthright than others in registering public protest. The implicit provision in the treaty that Iran should not engage experts from any other country but Britain debarred American financial experts from the country. The French were unhappy because many French nationals were engaged as teachers in Iranian schools. The White Russians in Iran claimed to represent the continuity of the Czarist government, and were very upset at the complete elimination of what they considered to be

Russian interests. They argued that Britain was bound to protect these. That they were sadly mistaken was subsequently shown by the exchange of two letters between Britain and Iran as part of this agreement, the effect of which was to abrogate the 1907 Anglo-Russian Convention. Britain had realised by 1919 that the empire of the Czars had fallen for good.

The treaty of 1919 was, in a sense, the culmination of a policy which Britain had pursued over a long period in Iran, the Persian Gulf and India. It was the handiwork of Lord Curzon, who never concealed his belief that British supremacy in Iran and the Persian Gulf was unquestionably bound up with British supremacy in India. 'If we lose control of the Gulf', Lovat Frazer, one of Curzon's most ardent disciples, had stated, 'we shall not rule long in India.'[2] Every effort of other European powers to gain a foothold in the Gulf was treated as a 'menace to India'. The specific interest of the British in India, according to the Curzon school, was not confined to the Gulf coast, but extended over the whole of Iran. Lord Curzon had been a bitter critic of the Anglo-Russian Convention of 1907 in which, according to him, Britain had sacrificed her own interests. He had been awaiting the opportunity of putting into effect his scheme for the conversion of Iran into a client state, and that opportunity came with the final overthrow of the Czar in November 1917.[3]

The acceptance by the central government of the humiliating treaty of 1919 was the turning point in Reza Khan's life. That he was opposed to the terms of the treaty was known to his friends. The *majlis* was not in existence at this time, since the government had not called new elections since 1915. Had it been in session, it could easily have served as the forum for national feeling, and opposition to the treaty could then have

[2] Frazer, Lovat, *India Under Curzon* (2nd ed., London, 1911), p. 112.
[3] Marlowe, John, *Iran, a short political guide* (London, 1963), p. 44.

been organised on constitutional lines. There was widespread discontent with the government's policy of capitulation, which Ahmad Shah was believed to be backing. The treaty had exposed the inherent political impotence of the central government by showing in an unmistakable manner that it was really an appendage of the British Legation.

This realisation had influenced others besides the politically conscious sections of the Iranian population. Among them was the leadership of the Bolshevik party in Russia. The Bolsheviks had made three earlier approaches to the government of Iran. Immediately after their seizure of power, Lenin had made a general statement of policy towards those countries in which the Czarist government had claimed extraterritorial powers. In January 1918, the Bolshevik government had addressed a Note to Tehran renouncing all Czarist privileges and denouncing the Anglo-Russian Convention. In June 1919, a further Note was delivered. In this the Bolsheviks declared that all Iranian debts to the Czarist government were cancelled; all Czarist privileges in respect of Iranian customs, posts and telegraphs were ended; all public and private concessions acquired by the Czarist government were renounced; and all property belonging to the Russian state in Iran was made over to the Iranian government. Finally, the Bolsheviks had expressed both officially and unofficially a desire for a treaty of friendship, for which preliminary negotiations had already commenced.

It was against this background that the Bolsheviks suddenly landed troops on the Caspian coast. The apparent cause of this extraordinary step, which was bound to revive the dreaded memories of decades of Czarist aggression, was the Bolshevik desire to eliminate the remnants of the White Russian forces of General Denikin. When the Russian fleet arrived at Bandar Pahlavi, then called Enzeli, these White Guards had left several weeks earlier. Bandar Pahlavi was still at that time under British occupation. The Bolsheviks demanded that Brigadier Bateman-Champain and his detachment should evacuate the port. When this demand had been complied with, the Bolsheviks marched south through Gilan, and joined hands with the rebel forces, headed by Mirza Kuchik Khan who had earlier risen in revolt against the Tehran government. The formation by Kuchik Khan of a 'Soviet Republic of Gilan', and Bolshevik assistance to Shaikh Mohammad Khiabani in Azerbaijan, renewed the threat from the north.[4] By June 1920, the Communist party of Iran had been founded as a section of the Communist International, with political and material assistance from the new power centre of international communism.

Reza Khan made his first cautious move at the beginning of 1920. The Brigade was still commanded by the Russians. Nominally, they were all White Russians but some of them were sympathetic to the new rulers in Moscow. When the Brigade was sent north to fight against the Bolshevik forces, some of the officers had crossed over to the Red Army. Reza Khan decided, as a first step, to eliminate the Russian officers, about seventy in all, from the Brigade, in order to convert it into a truly Iranian force. The final dismemberment of Iran appeared to him to be imminent. The terms of the treaty of 1919 securely tied the political, administrative, military and economic limbs of the central government to Britain. British troops were in occupation of large areas in southern and western Iran and the Persian Gulf. The Red Army in the north had proved its superiority over the British occupation forces by dislodging Brigadier Bateman-Champain from Enzeli. The formation of the Soviet Republic of Gilan and the Communist

---

[4] For analysis of Soviet policy, see Laqueur, Walter Z., *The Soviet Union and the Middle East* (London, 1959), pp. 29–32.

Party of Iran appeared to him to be part of a scheme to convert the entire country into a Soviet republic.

Who was to prevent the end of the ancient Iranian state? The Qajar monarch was a mere figurehead. The Constitutionalists had dissipated their patriotic fervour and energy in endless internal quarrels. Reza Khan had to make his decision, of which his son was to write later : 'The era, the people, and the necessities of a nation demand that at a certain time the right man be found in a particular position ; such a man as will profoundly affect the fate of the country and modify the course of history.' [5] There were several precedents in Iranian history. In the eighteenth century, for example, Nadir Shah had lifted Iran from the depths of decay and degeneration which followed the end of the Safavid dynasty to great heights of national prosperity and international glory. In 1920 there was no-one but Reza Khan who could play a similar part.

Reza Khan moved swiftly to effect the removal of Colonel Clergé, the Russian commander of the Brigade. The operation went smoothly and successfully, as did most of his military and political exercises in the next twenty years. The climax was described by a contemporary in these words : 'While the unsuspecting Clergé was having his evening tea in his house, the premises were surrounded by Iranian Cossacks, Reza Khan entered the room and, quite politely, invited him to take his place in a carriage waiting at the gate. This carriage took the Russian under escort to Enzeli. From there he sailed for Russia.' [6]

Reza Khan was promoted to the command of the Cossack Infantry regiment as a Brigadier-General, and began to collect about him a group of Iranian officers whom he wished eventually to take over all leading commands. His efforts were speedily successful, for these officers felt a deep sense of shame

[5] *Mission*, p. 38.   [6] Arfa, p. 91.

at the state of affairs then prevailing in the country, and even more so at the fact that they themselves were under foreign command. An incident took place on the first day of the Iranian New Year, March 1, 1920, which helped the hesitant among them to make up their minds.

On that day Lieutenant-Colonel Fazlollah Khan was found dead in his room, in full ceremonial uniform, revolver in hand. The Colonel was a member of the joint Anglo-Iranian military commission appointed under the unratified treaty of 1919. He had left a letter stating that it was against his conscience as a patriotic Iranian officer to agree to the subordination of the Iranian army to a British command, and that he preferred to die. Naturally the letter was destroyed, but not before the news of its contents spread.[7] The sacrifice of Colonel Fazlollah dramatically underlined the crisis of conscience which afflicted many Iranian officers.

The way was now clear for Reza Khan's rise to the position of supreme command. By August 1920, the Brigade had wiped out the last vestiges of the forty-one years of domination by the Russians. The central government was a mere witness to this development, as it was now powerless to intervene in the affairs of the Brigade. The group which had grown around Reza Khan elevated him to the overall command, and the central government merely endorsed this promotion. The British authorities in Tehran accepted this new turn of events, seeing it as a reaction against the White Russians who were already an obstacle to the safe fulfillment of Britain's aims. The rise of Reza Khan was also felt to be a guarantee against the spread of Bolshevik influence within the ranks of the Brigade. General Dickson thought very highly of him as a soldier.

By this time, London had decided upon new tactics, on which the Legation had already begun to act. Reza Khan, it

[7] Arfa, p. 91–2.

was believed, could contribute to the success of their new plan. The author of this plan was Lord Curzon, then Foreign Secretary in the Lloyd George government, which had left Persian affairs in the hands of the former Viceroy of India. According to General Arfa, who was then in close contact with the British Legation, the premise of this plan was Britain's realisation that the *majlis* would not ratify the treaty of 1919.

'On the other hand', wrote General Arfa in 1964, 'it was obvious that if Iran was abandoned to its own devices, without money or military force and with a weak central government, it would become the prey of anarchic forces represented by well-armed predatory tribes and leftist revolutionary elements, and would drift towards Bolshevism and eventually would become engulfed in the wave of the Communist advance towards India and the Arab Middle East.' The solution of this situation lay in 'the coming to power in Iran of a strong government friendly to Great Britain but not compromised by the 1919 treaty negotiations, which could be helped to apply piecemeal certain of the stipulations of the treaty after they had been watered down'.[8] It was as part of this plan that Syed Zia ed-din Tabatabai was suddenly propelled to the forefront. Syed Zia, as he came to be known, was a young man of thirty-three at that time.

Syed Zia was the son of a respected *mullah*. As a journalist he had been a courageous and uncompromising critic of the sad state of the government and of national affairs in Iran.[9] His name was known not only among the nationalist groups in the country but also among the foreign embassies and legations. A strange story came to be told in later years about his association with the British authorities in Tehran before the revolution of 1921. He had appeared at Baku in 1919 as leader of a delegation which had come from Iran to fraternise with the British-

[8] Arfa, p. 109.   [9] *Mission*, p. 39.

supported anti-Bolshevik governments in Russian Azerbaijan, Georgia and Armenia. Afterwards, it was said that Syed Zia's main task was to open negotiations with the leaders of the short-lived government of Azerbaijan on behalf of the Anglo-Persian Oil Company, to try to bring the Baku oil industry into the company's sphere of influence. These negotiations proved fruitless because the Red Army occupied Baku early in 1920, whereupon the Bolsheviks accused Syed Zia of being a British agent. He returned to Iran and continued his crusade against the government. He was constantly in touch with the British Legation and, after the return of Sir Percy Cox to London, appeared to have become particularly close with the new Minister, Herman Norman, and with General Dickson.

At this stage Syed Zia became a convenient instrument of British policy. According to contemporary Iranians he was brought into the political picture by those who wanted to set up a strong government in Iran, 'friendly to Great Britain, but not compromised by the 1919 treaty negotiations'. The original British nominee to lead this government had been Prince Firuz Mirza Nosrat ed Dowleh. However, the British authorities in Tehran believed that Firuz Mirza had already been compromised in the eyes of the Iranian nationalists, since he was one of the principal negotiators on the Iranian side for the treaty of 1919. The British Minister and General Dickson therefore chose Syed Zia in place of Firuz Mirza to set up the new government.[10]

As in all revolutions, so in the case of Iran : unexpected developments completely changed the course set for it by its

---

[10] Most Iranian authorities suggest that Syed Zia was a British protégé at this stage. I have placed reliance on General Arfa's interpretation of events since he had met Syed Zia at Baku and also because he was one of the few nationalists who maintained close contacts with the British Legation throughout this period.

backdoor architects. Syed Zia, originally the chosen instrument for furthering British interests, after Reza Khan's success, nevertheless set in motion the movement which finally made Iran independent of British influence. It may be that Syed Zia, true to the recognised pattern of Asian nationalists, had always intended to use British power to further the cause of his country. In any event, his comrade-in-arms, Reza Khan, was unaware of the arrangement between him and the British Legation. He knew Syed Zia by reputation as a well-meaning, if volatile, revolutionary. There could be no objection to an alliance with him. When Syed Zia approached Reza Khan to seek military assistance from the Cossack Brigade, Reza Khan himself was ready to act.

Soon after removing the Russian commanders of the Brigade, Reza Khan had decided that the time had come for decisive and immediate action. He realised that any delay on his part would strengthen British and Bolshevik schemes to an extent which would make it impossible for him to secure the overthrow of the central authorities in Tehran without bloodshed. Recent events in Turkey, where Mustafa Kemal had unfurled the banner of resurgent nationalism, had deeply impressed him. He had also seen the first signs of the great transformation to come in India, where Mahatma Gandhi had challenged British supremacy. After his talks with Syed Zia, he took half a dozen of his comrades into his close confidence and outlined his aims to them. He wanted to place in power a homogeneous, disciplined military force, and see that the government put into practice a policy of nationalism and non-engagement towards Russia and Britain alike. Such a move would create a strong central government able to withstand both external and internal dangers and capable of introducing revolutionary reforms.

The Brigade was then stationed at Qazvin, north of Tehran. Under Reza Khan they began their famous march on Tehran

on February 16, 1921. Within four days, by the night of
February 20, they had reached the outskirts of the capital.
Ahmad Shah and his supporters learnt that morning that Reza
Khan was on his way to Tehran, and had therefore ordered
troops to guard the western approaches of the town from the
Qazvin gate to the Bagh-e-Shah gate. By 11 p.m. it was all
over. Reza Khan, with his Cossacks, entered the town through
the Gomrock gate, where the defending troops surrendered,
and occupied the town. The local police made some show of
resistance, but quickly abandoned the fight.

A new government was immediately formed, headed by
Syed Zia. General Reza Khan was appointed Minister of War,
granted the title of Sardah Sepah, and presented with a jewel-
studded gold sword. He also became the supreme commander
of the Iranian armed forces. His first act was to issue a proclamation to the army, explaining the reasons for his revolution.
The intention behind the revolution, he said, was to save the
country from traitors, and to establish a strong central government which would uphold the independence and dignity of
Iran and work for the prosperity of the nation.

That Reza Khan would not permit the new revolutionary
government to become subservient to any western power
became clear on the occasion of a formal ceremony at the
Gulistan Palace, where there was to be a parade before Ahmad
Shah. All the units which were to march past the Shah were
drawn up in the palace courtyard when Reza Khan, Sardah
Sepah, entered. He passed in front of the senior officers.
General Westdahl, the Swedish Chief of Police, was obviously
insolent and, though he saluted, his fingers did not quite touch
his sheepskin cap. 'You are a General, but you do not know
how to salute,' said Reza Khan and, angrily seizing Westdahl's
hand, he pushed it towards the sheepskin cap, which fell to the
ground. It was evident to everyone present from this action

that the Sardah Sepah was determined that the foreigners were to lose their privileged positions.[11]

The young Mohammad Reza, then five months old, had already become the only other focal point in Reza Khan's life beside his dedication to the cause of his country. Mohammad Reza was born at the fateful point in his father's career when Syed Zia had approached Reza Khan with the plan for the revolution. At this juncture, Reza Khan had not only to take the most important decision of his life, but also to conduct very guarded talks with his colleagues. The winter that year was extremely severe, and Tehran was covered with snow during the five months in which Reza Khan prepared for and won his battle.

His only moments of joy and relaxation were those when, late in the evening, he came home and visited his infant son. He was a different man with his heir when he sat by the wooden cradle and sang little lullabies. He laughed and played with the child, and his forbidding sternness, with which others were so familiar, melted into love and kindness. This relationship matured in the course of time, and Reza Khan became the dominant influence in his eldest son's life. 'All over the world', the Shah was to record forty years later, 'the father helps shape the character of the son. In my case, my father influenced me more than anyone else'.[12]

[11] Arfa, p. 111.   [12] *Mission*, p. 45.

CHAPTER THREE

The Crown Prince

EVENTS moved with great speed once the revolution had taken place. Syed Zia fell out with Reza Khan almost immediately by beginning to promote measures that alienated the wealthy conservatives of the country. While Reza Khan did not disagree with Syed Zia's political and economic ideas, he felt that the latter's tactics and timing were unwise. He considered that such measures, at that stage, were likely only to divide the country further. Instead he wanted to give priority to the task of national unification. These differences led to the removal of Syed Zia from the post of Prime Minister and his ultimate exile to Baghdad.

Reza Khan reorganised the armed forces and then launched an offensive against Kuchik Khan and the 'Soviet Republic of Gilan'. His lightning victory over Kuchik Khan strengthened his position in the government and among the people. He now began to assert his influence and insisted that the new Prime Minister, Qavam os-Saltane, must engage only those foreign experts who had no connection with either Russia or Britain. This was accepted. Reza Khan's next and much greater achievement was the suppression of tribal revolts and restoration of law and order throughout Iran. One by one he brought Azerbaijan, Luristan, Kurdistan, Fars and Khorassan under the control of the government at Tehran. He conducted these campaigns as Minister of War and Commander-in-Chief of the Iranian armed forces. Qavam os-Saltane was replaced early in 1923 by Mostowfi ol-Mamalek. By this time Reza Khan was, in reality, the moving force in the government, a position which was regularised a little later with his appointment as Prime Minister. He still retained the portfolio at the Ministry of War and supreme command over the armed forces. Three months later, Ahmad Shah Qajar packed his bags and departed for an indefinite stay in Europe.

During this period Reza Khan had come into conflict with the dominant leaders of the *majlis*. The Fourth *majlis*, elected in the summer of 1921, was crowded with 'a majority of selfish, jealous, reactionary and defeatist landlords and clergy, and it was dominated by Modarres of Isfahan, an egotistical *mullah* who had no aims beyond self aggrandisement and the acquisition of power'.[1] This situation led to a deep-rooted distrust and contempt for the *majlis* in the mind of Reza Khan, a significant development, since from then on he never permitted himself to be dominated by the *majlis*.

By December 1924, Reza Khan had suppressed the most serious of the tribal revolts, that of Shaikh Khazal in Khuzistan. This was not only his greatest military achievement but also a national victory. Khazal was known to be a British protégé and at one stage had even been considered for the new Iraqi monarchy about to be established.[2] He worked under the protection of the unquestioned British supremacy in southern Iran, and the Anglo-Persian Oil Company had paid some royalties to him. The defeat of such a powerful chieftain, who had only nominally accepted the sovereignty of the central government, aroused tremendous admiration for Reza Khan. Thousands of

[1] Banani, p. 41.
[2] Marlowe, John, *The Persian Gulf in the Twentieth Century* (London, 1962), pp. 46, 64.

people welcomed his return to Tehran. On February 14, 1925, the *majlis* put its stamp on the recognition accorded to the Sardah Sepah by the people in a special Act by which it recognised the supreme command of the country's defence and security forces as the special domain of Reza Khan. 'He shall exercise his command with complete authority, within the frame of the Constitution and the laws of the land. This command may not be removed without the approval of the *majlis*.'

Though Reza Khan himself did not set much store by the *majlis* resolution, within months popular demand for the termination of the Qajar monarchy brought about a completely new situation. On October 31, 1925, the *majlis* finally and formally ended the rule of the Qajars. It entrusted the provisional government to Reza Khan Pahlavi, and resolved to convene a constituent assembly to determine the final form of the new government. It was at this stage that the question of establishing an Iranian republic came to the fore.[3] Of this period, and the eventual decision to continue with monarchy in Iran, the Shah has written: 'The year before my father became premier, the Turks had abolished their archaic Caliphate and soon afterwards they established a republic under the dynamic leadership of Ataturk. Some Iranian circles, influenced by these events, leaned towards the idea of setting up a republic in Persia too. I am sure that my father for a time preferred the concept of a republic. But the tide of opinion now shifted back towards the idea of continuing the monarchical system which, after all, had for years been our tradition.'[4]

Thus, when, in December 1925, the Constituent Assembly met in Tehran, the die was cast. The Assembly revised Article 36 of the Supplement to the Constitution to read: 'The Constitutional Monarchy of Iran is vested by the Constituent

[3] Sykes, II, p. 546.   [4] *Mission*, p. 39.

Assembly on behalf of the nation in the person of His Majesty the Shahanshah, Reza Shah Pahlavi, and shall remain in his male progeny generation after generation.' [5] On April 25, 1926, the formal Coronation, a great event lacking nothing in pomp and grandeur, took place. At the same ceremony, Mohammad Reza was proclaimed Crown Prince. 'You can imagine', he later wrote, recalling his reaction to the event, 'the awe it inspired in a six year old like me.' [6] Born the eldest son of Iran's most outstanding commoner, the young Crown Prince now became a link in the long chain of his nation's tradition of twenty-five centuries of monarchy. This meant a completely different childhood.

Until now, the Crown Prince had lived in the family house with his mother, his brothers and sisters. There were also several half-brothers and half-sisters, since Reza Shah had more than one wife. The family was a close-knit unit and was to remain so even later. Reza Khan's heir had been its centre of attention. He was not considered strong in health but was very lively, running, jumping and climbing trees all the time. Even at this early age he had taken to the Iranian national sport of wrestling; and in winter he would go out and have fierce snow fights with his brothers and neighbours. A love of sport and adventure was thus imbibed in his early childhood.

Reza Khan had become Minister of War soon after his heir's birth. His large and imposing figure and his deep love for his son were landmarks in the son's infant world. He would wait in the morning to see his father being driven from home to work, and waited once again, late in the evening, for his father to return. On reaching home, Reza Khan would devote some time to his family and especially to his heir, a rhythm of life which continued even after he became Prime Minister.

[5] Banani, p. 45.   [6] *Mission*, p. 52.

Suddenly this whole pattern of life changed completely when Reza Khan was proclaimed Shahanshah, and Mohammad Reza Crown Prince. Now began a training designed by Reza Shah to enable his son to discharge his duties when he became the second Pahlavi monarch. After the coronation, the Shah was therefore separated from the rest of his family. His father decided that the son must receive 'manly education'.

A new elementary military school was established by Reza Shah for the Crown Prince, and his four brothers and half-brothers were placed with him, as well as twenty-one other, carefully selected, pupils. These were the young sons of those government officials and army officers who had actively worked with Reza Shah during and after the revolution of 1921. The boys wore military uniforms and followed a rigorous curriculum. Drill and military subjects constituted an important part of the programme.

In the hours that the young Crown Prince had to himself, he developed a special liking for building, which was to provide some of his most pleasant memories of those days. 'Beautiful mountain-fed streams flowed through the grounds of the summer palace at Saadabad (in Shimran, a suburb of Tehran), and across the streams my companions and I used to build dams that in their way were miniature prototypes of the dams that Iran is now constructing for irrigation and hydro-electric power. Alongside, we would build small houses of bricks and pieces of wood. In winter, particularly, I would spend long hours making mechanical models with my Meccano construction set.'[7] This system of education continued for the next five years until the Crown Prince left the elementary military school in May 1931.

The primary influence on his life during this important formative period was Reza Shah. The Shahanshah was 'patriotic almost to excess . . . so complete was his dedication to his

[7] *Mission*, p. 53.

country that he believed the Persian culture surpassed all others in every respect'.[8] Though the Shah has never taken a provincial view of accomplishments outside Iran, he shared with his father this deep sense of patriotism. He learned eagerly the history of his proud and ancient land, and especially of the endeavours of great Iranians. Avicenna, whose knowledge of medicine was accepted as authoritative in medieval Europe, and to whom Sir Alexander Fleming later paid tribute as a pioneer of what came to be antibiotic medicine, was one of those he much admired ; and he was proud of such Iranian achievements as the development of the sundial, made possible by the work of one of the first observatories in the world, and their invention of the calibrated clock dial.

Among his political heroes, the great Achemenian kings were always a source of inspiration. The establishment by the Achemenians of a system of imperial administration by provincial satraps ; of lines of communication based on a network of postroads which enabled royal couriers to reach the farthest ends of the empire from the capital within fifteen days : the romance involved in all this, fascinated the Crown Prince. He was taught that the empire founded by Cyrus the Great was not based on territorial acquisition alone but also on international tolerance and understanding : the rights of all subject nations were upheld and their laws and customs respected. No trace of national chauvinism darkened the story of Iranian greatness for the Crown Prince.

When the Crown Prince reached his ninth birthday, a system by which he lunched each day with his father was introduced. Reza Shah wished his son to know what was being done in his country, and the son himself was keen to become acquainted with everything that his young mind could absorb. Naturally, there were as yet practically no specific political questions

[8] *Mission*, p. 47.

which Reza Shah could discuss with his young son. He talked to him mainly on more general aspects of life. The virtues of sobriety and hard work, of speaking in good faith, of friendship, of observance of order and of care in every undertaking were thus inculcated in the character of the Crown Prince through his close association with his father. The essential simplicity of an Emperor who continued to wear an ordinary army uniform, home-made stockings and well-worn short boots, inevitably made an indelible impression on his devoted heir.

In 1956, the Shah was to write a short biographical appreciation of Reza Shah. In this, a portrait of his father — with whom he became so intimately familiar between 1926 and 1931 and later between 1936 and 1941 — was drawn by him for the younger generation of his people. His example, wrote his son, showed that 'it is every man's duty to prefer manliness and perseverance to fear and timidity ; not to choose untruthfulness and meanness in place of truth and courage ; to confront difficulties fearlessly and overcome them and take a pleasure in so doing ; to realise the shamefulness of idle habits and to regard work as his highest goal ; to know that work . . . is the highest tribute of a man and gives him justifiable pride'.[9] It was these central values of Reza Shah's character which he did his best to instil in his son.

One other person besides Reza Shah influenced the Crown Prince. When he was separated from his family, he had been placed under the care of a French governess who took charge of his life at home. Madame Arfa, who was married to an Iranian and whom Reza Shah had carefully selected to look after the Crown Prince, was to open a completely new world for him with which his father was not very familiar. 'To her I owe', the Shah wrote later, 'the advantages of being able to

9 Pahlavi, Mohammed Reza Shah, Shahanshah of Iran, 'Biography of Reza Shah', in *Self Made Man*, a collection of biographies (Tehran, 1956).

speak and read French as if it were my own language ; and beyond this she opened my mind to the spirit of western culture.'[10] The immense consequence of this initial step of introducing the young Crown Prince to the world of western culture was to mature during the years when he was a student in Switzerland. Reza Shah himself knew that the future second Pahlavi monarch must have the benefits of a proper appreciation of the west from childhood, and it was this that led him to employ a foreign governess.

The third lasting influence of this period has been described by the Shah as his religious awakening. Soon after his investiture as Crown Prince he had fallen ill with typhoid fever, common in Asia at that time, and his life was in danger. His parents sat by his bedside, not knowing whether he would survive. Then the fever-ridden Crown Prince had a dream about Ali, chief lieutenant of the prophet Mohammad. In his dream the Crown Prince saw Ali, with his two-pronged sword, sitting on his heels on the floor and holding in his hands a full bowl. Ali told him to drink from the bowl, and this he did. The next day the critical stage of his illness had passed and he was on the road to rapid recovery.

He did not speak of this dream to anybody. He was then only seven years old, but even so he recognised that the dream and his recovery were not necessarily connected. During the same year, however, two similar events followed, both concerned with visitations from the spiritual leaders of Islam.

In the summer of the year of his illness, the Crown Prince went on an excursion to Imam Zadeh-Dawood, a beautiful spot in the mountains north of Tehran, which the family usually chose as a summer resort. It was difficult to reach Imam Zadeh-Dawood since one had to follow a steep trail on foot or on

[10] *Mission*, p. 52.

horseback. The Crown Prince, being too young to walk or ride by himself, was being taken up the mountain by an army officer seated in front of the saddle, when the horse slipped and he was thrown. Though he fell head first onto a jagged rock and fainted, he did not have even a scratch on his body. The astonishment of his family at this miraculous survival was increased when he told them that as he fell, he felt he was held up by one of the Shiah saints, Abbas, who had prevented his head from hitting the rock. Reza Khan, when he learnt about this vision, sought to dismiss it, and there was no point in arguing. The Crown Prince, however, never doubted its reality.

The third experience occurred as the Crown Prince was walking with his guardian near the royal palace in Shimran, along a picturesque cobbled street. Suddenly he saw before him a man with a halo round his head. As he passed the stranger, he recognised him as the Imam Mehdi, the last Imam who, according to the Shiah faith, had disappeared but was expected to return to save the world. Moved immensely by this experience, he asked his guardian whether he too had seen the Imam. The guardian had seen nothing. The Crown Prince told nobody of this experience, not even his father.

The dreams of childhood often leave a lasting impression and such spiritual experiences, at so early an age, especially for a boy from the east, were bound to influence him. He has written : 'Nevertheless, from the time I was six or seven I have felt that perhaps there is a supreme being who is guiding me ; I do not know. Sometimes the thought disturbs me because then, I ask myself, what is my own personality, and am I possessed of free will ? Still, I often reflect if I am driven — or perhaps I should say supported — by another force, there must be a reason.'[11] The spiritual experiences of his childhood bred

[11] *Mission*, p. 55.

in him a strong religious faith. This in turn was later considerably strengthened in the years after 1948 when four incidents occurred in which he came close to death. The three influences of this period together led him, even before he went to Switzerland for further education, to think of the part he had to play in the destiny of his nation. 'I have known since my early childhood', he has admitted, 'that it was my destiny to become a king, and to preside over a land whose ancient and often magnificent culture I venerate. I want to improve the lot of my people, especially the common folk, and feel that my faith supports me in this difficult task. Indeed, I should consider it arrogant to believe that I could accomplish my life's work without God's help.'[12]

In May 1931, the Crown Prince left the special elementary military school in Tehran. By this time his father was engaged in the monumental task of the modernisation of Iran. It was logical for the Shahanshah to want the heir to his throne to become more familiar with western civilisation and absorb some of the secrets of western progress. On the one hand, Reza Shah had not forgotten the experiences of his people in their unfortunate relations with the west : on the other, like all true Asian nationalists, he admired the fruits of western civilisation and yet had no faith in foreigners in general, and Europeans in particular. This contradiction came to the fore when a European school for the young Shah had to be chosen. Reza Shah finally decided on Le Rosey, near Lausanne. More than the school, it was the country that led to this decision, as Switzerland was not competing with other European powers for Asian domination. Also, Reza Shah had been told that the cold and healthy climate of Switzerland offered a good atmosphere for serious study.

After the summer vacation, the Crown Prince left for Switzer-

[12] *Mission*, p. 58.

land in September 1931. He was accompanied by his personal physician and guardian, Dr Moadeb Nafici, and his Persian teacher, Professor Mostashar, who was to continue teaching him the history of Iran and the Farsi language. So that his son should not feel lonely at school, Reza Shah decided to send his second son, Ali Reza, and a couple of friends from the elementary military school with him. Having said farewell to his parents and the other members of the family at Bandar Pahlavi on the Caspian shore, the Crown Prince and his party sailed to Baku, and reached Switzerland by way of Russia, Poland and Germany.

CHAPTER FOUR

The Growing Intellectual

THE Crown Prince spent his first few months in Switzerland at a private school in Lausanne. He and his brother, Ali Reza, went to live with M. Mercier, whose large Swiss family included three sons and two daughters. Here the Crown Prince met for the first time a middle-class European family. Though M. Mercier knew that his two boarders were the sons of the Emperor of Iran, he chose to ignore the rules of protocol. The boys were allowed to mix freely with his children and an easy, informal relationship with the family developed. This was the first change in the Crown Prince's way of life : the walls of exclusive upbringing which had surrounded him since 1926 began to collapse.

In 1932, Reza Shah decided to move the boys to their boarding school, Le Rosey. The Crown Prince was to remain there until the spring of 1936, when he gained his diploma and returned to Tehran. During these four years, away from the direct and overpowering influence of Reza Shah, his individuality found scope for natural growth. It was at this time also that he began to evolve his design for a new Iran. It was to be a difficult road that he had to travel before he could give concrete shape to this design, but nevertheless the first ideas germinated at Le Rosey.

The Swiss climate, and the enthusiasm for sport at Le Rosey,

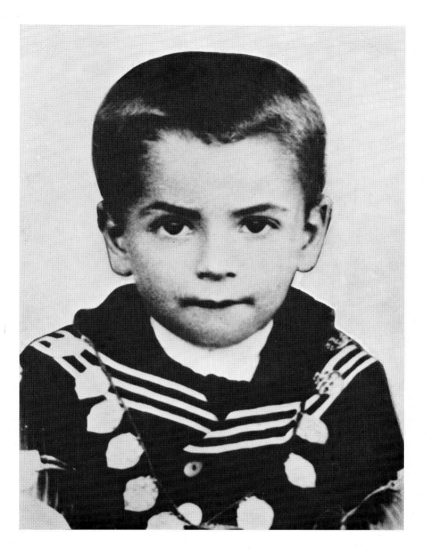

The young Mohammad Reza

Crown Prince

led the Crown Prince to become a keen sportsman. Soon the physical frailty of his childhood disappeared and he began to compete in various athletic events — throwing the discus, putting the shot, throwing the javelin, high and long jumps, and the hundred metre sprint. He won several individual prizes, and also captained the football and tennis teams of the school. The various silver cups and medals which he won during these years were to remain his proud possessions for life.

This physical development was accompanied by an intellectual and social growth which came to him naturally in this new environment. His special interests in the academic field were geography, history and natural science, as well as French literature, which he enjoyed all the more easily because of the good grounding in the language he had received from Madame Arfa. He also liked algebra, trigonometry and analytical geometry although, strangely, he found no attraction in plane geometry. He was a good student and usually secured excellent marks in all examinations.

The contrast between Tehran and Le Rosey was expressed most markedly in social life. For the first time, the Crown Prince was being judged by his companions on his own merits and not because he was the heir to the throne. The other boys found in him a good student and a first-class sportsman, whom they admired for his own achievements. His room became a meeting place for them, often crowded beyond capacity. The character of these student friendships bore no resemblance to royal or palace etiquette, and it was this that the Crown Prince enjoyed the most.

The effect on the Crown Prince of the atmosphere within the school was parallelled by the influence on him of its setting — Western Europe. In strong contrast with the feudal way of life to which he had been accustomed in Tehran, the routine at Le Rosey was based upon discipline with freedom, discipline

E   *39*

combined with the democratic exercise of their rights by the students. With discipline he was familiar, but the freedom that accompanied it at Le Rosey was a new experience. Gradually he realised, as he later recorded, that 'discipline without democracy is authoritarianism, and that democracy without discipline is anarchy'.[1]

Despite the large measure of disciplined freedom that the Crown Prince enjoyed, his life remained different in one respect from that of the average boarder at Le Rosey. He was still the future monarch of Iran. His academic programme included the Persian studies on which his father was especially keen. Professor Mostashar made him work hard, for the Professor knew that he would have to render an account of his pupil's progress to the Shahanshah. Dr Nafici limited the Crown Prince's activities. The physician could not perhaps get over the importance of his position as guardian, and was conscious all the time of his responsibilities. These, unfortunately, he discharged by trying to keep the Crown Prince almost like a prisoner. One of his strictest rules for him at Le Rosey was that he should not leave the school grounds, though his friends were allowed to go into the town in their free time. During the Christmas and New Year holidays there were parties and balls in some of the local hotels, which were eagerly anticipated by the other boys. The Crown Prince was not allowed to join them and sat painfully alone by himself in his room, with only the consolation of a radio and gramophone which Dr Nafici had given him.

Of these long enforced periods of isolation the Shah has written : 'I suppose this isolation helped to make me serious'.[2] There was nothing else to do but to read and to think during those long evenings and empty days, and there was much to think about in the letters which Reza Shah wrote regularly every

[1] *Mission*, p. 61.   [2] *Mission*, p. 62.

week. Each of these was a major event. Reza Shah wrote about the progress of the great task he had undertaken. It was an exercise based on three ideals : a complete dedication to the idea of a national state ; a desire to assert this nationalism by a rapid adoption of the material advances of the west ; and an assault on the traditional power of religion accompanied by a growing tendency towards secularism. At the centre of these ideals was Reza Shah, guiding, and goading when necessary, his people towards a new life.[3] In his letters to the Crown Prince he drew a distinction between the complete emulation of, and identification with, the west, and the adoption of ideals and activities inspired by the west. Each letter was a ringing reminder of the future task for which the Crown Prince was being trained.

As a student of history, the Crown Prince rapidly became familiar with the changing pattern of the grandeur and decline of Europe. He learned of the rise and fall of Napoleon, of Metternich and of the Year of Revolutions. He realised more clearly than ever that the history of Europe, from this period, had become enmeshed with the history of Asia in general, and Iran in particular. In the free and unobstructed Swiss political climate, he had ample opportunity to study not only the liberal democratic ideas of such men as de Tocqueville and President Wilson, but also those who proclaimed that the spectre of communism was haunting Europe. The ideology of Marx and Engels, and its application and further evolution by Lenin and Stalin, came under analysis by the growing intellectual that the Crown Prince was then becoming.

Whilst he was at Le Rosey, Hitler came to power and, with Mussolini, became the symbol of a new kind of leadership in Europe. The Crown Prince was keenly interested in German history. Reza Shah had throughout his reign chosen to associate

[3] Banani, p. 45.

with Germany in preference to the old imperial powers of Britain and Russia. The fall of the Weimar Republic and the rise to power of the demagogues of national socialism were events which the young student at Le Rosey examined carefully. He was seeking to draw lessons from these European developments which could help him to reign wisely over his people when the time came. For even though he mixed freely with his fellow students and enjoyed this democratic association, the Crown Prince was always conscious of his destiny. At Le Rosey, he grasped for the first time the full significance of the anatomy of power, and also saw that the regeneration of Iran was a task which could not be accomplished in one man's lifetime.

Reza Shah was, above all, a man of the people. He rose from among them, though later chosen Emperor by them. He continued to instil in the Crown Prince a sense of deep love, concern and identification with the common people of the country. Of those fateful processes of thinking which were ultimately to lead to the Revolution of the Shah and the People in 1963, he has written: 'I also began to think about the specific policies that I might adopt when I became king. Already I had acquired a special concern for the common people of the country, and especially for the peasants.' In this lay the key to the future political ideology of Mohammad Reza Shah Pahlavi. Even at the age of sixteen he had realized that the centre of political gravity in his country rested with the long-oppressed peasantry.

The basis of the Crown Prince's new design, which began to emerge clearly during his last year at Le Rosey, was a scheme for agrarian revolution. It had become clear to him that landowner–peasant relations in Iran had to be changed. The peasant, once liberated from the yoke of sharecropping, had to become an active participant in every sphere of national life. The ideas were tentative and the institutional framework required to put them into practice as yet not thought out.

This cardinal phase in his thinking he has described in these words : 'In my young mind the idea now evolved that when I assumed the throne I would for two or three years declare a moratorium on receiving any proceeds from the labours of the thousands of peasants who worked our royal estates. I would let each peasant family amass a little fortune which it could use to build a house or buy new cattle or do other things which were usually difficult with their meagre incomes. This youthful thinking and dreaming eventually led to my present plan . . . for partitioning my lands among the peasants.'[4]

As part of this new design the Crown Prince evolved another plan based on his desire for identification with his people. 'Another idea that came to me in those days', he has written, 'was that when I became king I would establish a public complaint box. If anybody had any complaint, no matter of what kind, he could write it and put it in the box, to which I would have direct access.' The idea, of course, was partly inspired by the example of Naushirwan, the greatest emperor of the Sassanian dynasty, who ruled between A.D. 531 and 579. The young Crown Prince was a fervent admirer of this monarch, to whom the people had given the affectionate title of Naushirwan the Just.

Naushirwan had a bell put outside his palace. Any citizen who had a complaint to lodge with him could ring the bell at any time of the day or night and the Emperor would appear in person to listen to his grievances. The influence of Naushirwan the Just also extended to the Crown Prince's thinking on the plight of the peasantry. Naushirwan had also encouraged education. He had been a scholar of Greek and Sanskrit

[4] Banani, p. 63.

literature and had had the classics of these two languages translated into Persian. He had also been a very tolerant monarch : in an era when Christianity was considered heresy he had allowed its practice, and adopted a rational approach to the whole question of religion.

In the earlier period of his stay in Switzerland, the religious fervour of the Crown Prince had ebbed. There were so many new things to absorb that he did not think much about religion. During the last two years, however, he returned to religious life with greater interest and dedication than before. He began to recite his daily prayers regularly. This was no mere formality : his religious obligations were now dispatched with zeal and conviction. This also formed a part of his growing conscious-ness of what he would do when he came to the throne. 'I was determined that when later I came to the throne', he had already resolved in 1934, 'my conduct would always be guided by a true religious sense.'[5]

Even though deeply involved in his academic work and in the search for a design for the new Iran, the Crown Prince could not but take an interest in the affairs of the western world around him. It was of great importance to the evolution of his ideas that, as a growing intellectual, he should have been at Le Rosey during the four years of the thirties which produced a climate of dissent and search. The established order at that time appeared to him, as well as to others, to be crumbling. Between 1929 and 1933, free enterprise economy was failing, and a sense of insecurity spread to every country. The new world across the Atlantic, which the Crown Prince had been taught to accept as the most stable centre of economic pros-perity, was as much afflicted as the old. The spread of un-employment and want in the traditionally opulent societies of the west shook his faith in the durability of the *laissez-faire*

[5] Banani, p. 62.

system. During these years, the privations of large masses of people had effectively unmasked the existing system, which, while providing for formal political equality, had hidden social and economic inequality. The ebb of prosperity in the west left behind a tidemark of dirt and squalor and helped the Crown Prince to appreciate Reza Shah's rigid opposition to a blind imitation of the western way.

While the spectre of slump haunted the lands of free enterprise, a neo-colonial Japan had invaded Manchuria in 1931. The massacre of democrats in Spain went unchallenged two years later. The tragic farce of disarmament was played out at Geneva in 1932 and 1933 and ended only when, on Hitler's instructions, the German delegation walked out. The faded memories of the First War still lingered in 1936 as shadows of the Second War began to lengthen.

New struggles for national freedom had shaken the foundations of western imperialism in Asia in the early thirties. From Turkey to western Asia, to India, Indo-China and Indonesia, and then to distant China, the movement had spread. It aimed at compelling the west to return to its natural and national boundaries and in the process was instrumental in awakening the political consciousness of millions of men and women. Gandhi had already led his second non-violent revolutionary movement against British power. China was on the eve of another revolutionary upheaval. Many countries, large and small, were about to rise against the dominance of the west over Asia, and the age of colonialism seemed to clear-sighted observers to be entering its twilight.

Such were the forces that helped to mould the mind of the Crown Prince. Though no single idea dominated his thinking, he was part of a generation which grew up on disillusionment and dissent with the existing order, and which was thereby compelled to evolve a new way of thinking. The Crown Prince, despite his great admiration and reverence for Reza Shah, now fully realised that he could not be the mirror image of his father. His individuality was already asserting itself and his outlook was being forged in a different intellectual climate. The values which motivated his thinking were different from those which guided the limitless energies of Reza Shah. And yet there was continuity, for the Crown Prince shared with the Shahanshah an uncompromising loyalty to his people and the Iranian way of life.

The new intellectual who returned to Tehran in the spring of 1936 was scarcely a European in any sense of the term. He was an Iranian intellectual who, unlike Iranian intellectuals of the previous generation, was in a position to analyse and assess the strength and weakness of western civilisation.

CHAPTER FIVE

Royal Tutelage

THE Crown Prince returned to Bandar Pahlavi by the same
route which he had taken for Lausanne. The first impression that he gave to those who had come to meet him at the
harbour, was that he had changed. Even Reza Shah had some
difficulty in recognising him. The great transformation in his
outlook became apparent as the days passed. The country he
returned to was also greatly altered. His pleasant surprise at
the degree of the change in Iran began when his boat arrived at
Bandar Pahlavi. 'When I left', he later wrote, 'it had resembled
a Persian village; but when I returned it seemed like a modern
European town. That was merely one instance of the vibrant
process of change that had been going on while I was away.' [1]

After a short holiday, he plunged into the work that awaited
him. Reza Shah wanted to have his son fully trained in military
matters, so he enrolled at the Military College in Tehran. Reza
Shah had engaged French military advisers, with the idea of
eliminating British and Russian influence in the armed forces,
and the Military College had been established on the model of
St Cyr. The Crown Prince joined the standard course and also
began to take a special advanced course in strategy. This was
only a part of his training. His major occupation in the succeeding five years was that of understudy to Reza Shah. He

[1] Banani, p. 64.

47

was personally interested in military affairs and awareness of his future responsibilities made him a keen student of the national and international policies of Iran. It was during these five years that he became first familiar with and then part of that 'vibrant change' which he had observed with happiness on his return home.

Within two years the Crown Prince graduated from the Military College, with the rank of a second lieutenant. In the spring of 1938, he was appointed an inspector in the army. His duties in his new post were many. They called for his presence in the field to observe the troops, assist them in their manoeuvres and direct their operations and training. He spent each morning and afternoon on the training ground, and often took part in night manoeuvres as well. Besides this field work, he had considerable paper work to do. Though this part of his assignment was not very absorbing in itself, his concern with the immediate and future organisation of his nation's armed forces made it deeply interesting to him.

In his second and more important role, the Crown Prince came into further and closer contact with Reza Shah. Every morning the Shahanshah met him half an hour before lunch and the old practice of discussions over lunch was revived. Later in the afternoon they met again for a further hour. Reza Shah familiarised the Crown Prince with every aspect of the domestic and foreign policies of Iran, and the Crown Prince accompanied his father on field trips to different regions and provinces. Reza Shah was determined to show his heir the people, geography, and special problems of each area. He believed that he had a complete grasp and understanding of every problem involved and during these meetings and tours his main consideration was the education of his son rather than any discussion. Of this royal tutelage the Shah has written : 'The word "discussion" is really a misnomer. I and all the officials of my father's government had such respect for him and were so much in awe of him that "discussion" with him had nothing of the give and take the word implies. I advanced my views and my hints and suggestions, but discussion in any usual sense was out of the question.'[2]

Reza Shah had then been in power for more than a decade and a half. He was in full command of the country, loved and feared at home and respected abroad. Yet he realised and accepted that the Crown Prince was a changed man. The son frequently spoke his mind to his father, and the father was willing, contrary to his psychological make-up and lifelong practice, to listen to him. In his zeal for law and order, Reza Shah was accustomed to arrest and imprison people he considered to be troublemakers. On several occasions, however, such persons were released from prison on the intervention of the Crown Prince. Fate played a strange trick in this context. One such person was Dr Mohammad Mossadeq, 'the man who later bankrupted the country and almost ended the dynasty'.

Mossadeq had been arrested on the orders of Reza Shah, and sent to a particularly unpleasant prison in a remote and isolated corner of the country. Even in those days he was an old man who enjoyed indifferent health, for which he became famous in later years. It was clear that, if he were kept in such a prison, he would have died in a short time. The Shah pleaded with his father a number of times for the release of this old man. Reza Shah, shrewd as he was, was unwilling to free Mossadeq. Finally, after the Crown Prince had raised the matter yet again with him, he issued orders for Mossadeq's release. This was one of the rare cases where a man who owed his freedom and life to the Crown Prince became his bitter enemy. In most other cases, the prisoners given liberty through the Crown Prince's intervention rallied round the banner of Iran in the

[2] *Mission*, p. 64.

difficult days during the Second War when the Crown Prince
ascended the throne and faced a period of problems even more
critical than those which had led to the revolution of 1921.

As he became increasingly familiar with the process of
'vibrant change', the Crown Prince came to understand the
two ideals which had made the transformation of the country
possible. These were nationalism and secularism. In the eyes of
his people Reza Shah had come to symbolise these two values.
Though nationalism as a reaction to foreign dominance had
come to Iran at the turn of the century, Reza Shah was the first
leader to weld it into a single territorial and spiritual force. His
nationalism was not the product of the study of learned books
written by Europeans. Nor was it merely a product of mis-
trust and anger at the humiliation of his country. Its deter-
mining factor was his pride in his national heritage and his
faith in the capacity of his people to rise once more to the
glorious heights which Iran had achieved time and again in her
long history. Secularism was a corollary of his nationalism. He
believed firmly that religion was a matter of conscience and that
it should exclusively remain so. The use of religion as an
instrument for political ends, as it had been exploited in Iran
for thirty years before the revolution of 1921, was, according
to Reza Shah, a violation of the injunctions of religion itself.

The Crown Prince, much as he revered the great personality
of his father, also realised that Reza Shah had been greatly aided
in the task of modernising Iran by a dedicated group of men.
These men represented a new force in national life — a breath
of fresh air after the earlier, suffocating and depressing climate
of intrigue and self-interest. Most of them had their origins in
the middle class or the lower orders of the clergy. Syed
Hassan Taqizade, son of a *mullah*, was one such revolutionary
who refused to be a *mullah* and secretly studied the language
and political institutions of France. He was already a leader

of the constitutional movement when Reza Shah rose to power. After the revolution of 1921, he served in several cabinets and later represented Iran in the League of Nations. Mostafa Adl was another outstanding figure who also came from the poorer sections of Iranian society. He became one of the most outstanding jurists of his time and later came to be known as the father of the modern judicial system in Iran. Mirza Mohammad Sa'ed, son of a merchant, served his country as Reza Shah's emissary.[3] These and other men, such as Ali Akbar Siyasi, Ali Dashti, and Kazmezade-Iranshahr were striving to break the stranglehold of the 'oligarchy of the thousand families' and bigoted clergy which had brought Iran to the brink of ruin and disaster. They worked under the leadership of Reza Shah and represented a new wave of nationalist thought, tending to secularism and, in some cases, downright anti-clericalism.

During these years of royal tutelage the Crown Prince realised the enormous size of the task undertaken by Reza Shah. His consolidation of the revolution of 1921 had ended any prospects of Iran becoming a protectorate of Britain. The defeat of Curzon's policy in Iran was his achievement. He had annulled the unratified treaty of 1919 within five days of coming to power. This action proved to be a landmark in Anglo-Persian history and sealed the end of an era. A British student of this period later wrote : 'The fate of the Anglo-Persian treaty may be taken to represent the beginning of the twilight of British imperial power, which was soon to set in.'[4] It changed the entire course of British policy. Curzon put up a last ditch fight against this change and, as his biographer has said, 'sang a mournful requiem over his perished hopes'.

Moscow had also drawn its lesson from the events leading to the rise of Reza Shah. The U.S.S.R. agreed to enter into a treaty with the new government and, significantly, the

[3] Banani, pp. 48–9.   [4] Marlowe, p. 44.

Iran-Soviet Treaty was signed on the day that Reza Shah put a match to the treaty of 1919. By the terms of the new treaty, the Bolshevik government confirmed all its renunciations of the Czarist gains and interests in Iran which had earlier been outlined in the Soviet Note of June 1919. The Treaty, signed on February 26, 1921, also referred to an agreement between the parties to prohibit the establishment on the territory of either of any organisation hostile to the other. It further contained a provision for the entry of Soviet troops into Iran in the event of Iran becoming a base for attack against the Soviet Union. This vague provision was specifically clarified through an exchange of letters between the parties, which made it clear that it related only to the then prevalent conditions of the war of intervention against the Bolshevik state, and specifically to the presence of White Guards and their European supporters on Iranian territory.

The Crown Prince, as he moved from one province of the country to another, saw how his father had made a territorial unity of a land which had been the victim of a century of balkanisation. Reza Shah had succeeded through a series of hard-fought campaigns against tribal and provincial chiefs who were usually supported by one foreign power or the other. The Shah, both as an understudy to his father, and as an inspector in the army, saw the growth of a unified system amongst the armed forces. Reza Shah had merged the various units of the armed forces soon after he became Minister of War. In June 1925, the *majlis* passed a compulsory military conscription law at his request. Conscription changed the character of the officer class. Eleven years later, in February 1936, on the eve of the Crown Prince's return to Iran, the army was further re-

5 Later claims by Stalin that he had the right to send troops into Iran were thus illfounded. This clause had become illegal and inoperative in any event after the Soviet Union and Iran signed the United Nations Charter since it was clearly restrictive of the sovereignty of Iran.

organised. New Persian names for the ranks, a revised order of battle, basis of promotion, retirement age, and pensions and insurance were introduced. In 1932, Reza Shah organised for the first time in recent history an Iranian navy based on the Persian Gulf. Four years earlier in 1928, he had laid the foundation for an Iranian air force. He had employed Swedish officers for the army ; sent the pilots to be trained in Russia and later in France; and arranged for the training of his naval officers at Italian academies. The armed forces were equipped with arms and munitions from Czechoslovakia, Sweden and Germany.

Between 1936 and 1941, the Crown Prince became familiar with each branch of the new system of government established by Reza Shah. He saw how his father had made Iran independent in financial matters. The small industrial revolution introduced by the establishment of light industries, and the beginnings of secular judicial, educational and public health service systems were other features of the transformation. When he returned from Switzerland, the construction of the Trans-Iranian Railway was about to be completed. The work had begun in 1927. It was a difficult engineering task. The line crossed more than 4,100 bridges, and passed through 224 tunnels — an aggregate length of fifty-four miles had to be bored. It was also a major achievement financially, since the nine hundred miles of line were financed entirely within Iran through special taxes on sugar and tea. Reza Shah did not want to burden his country with foreign loans, of which she had had bitter experience. The Trans-Iranian Railway was completed in 1939, and by an irony of fate became the principal reason for the Anglo-Russian invasion of the country in 1941.

Although the changes were enormous and extremely impressive, the young intellectual saw great weaknesses inherent in his father's system. He realised that the tax system bore heavily on the peasants. The agrarian structure had hardly undergone any change and the landed aristocracy and tribal chiefs still held great economic power. If they did not exercise this for political purposes, it was only because Reza Shah was powerful and popular among the common people and there was a unified modern army to face. Due to the peculiar conditions of the period, Reza Shah had ignored the growth of democratic political institutions. He had begun as a great believer in popular democracy and even supported the idea of setting up a republic in 1921. In the course of his work he had developed a dislike for the slow and cumbersome processes of a parliamentary regime. His control over the *majlis*, which continued to survive, was an indisputable fact of political life in Iran.

There were several other aspects of the situation which his heir found in need of change. And yet he realised that Reza Shah had done more than any other man could. Appraising his father's contribution to the progress of his country, he was to write later that 'it must be remembered that the situation in Iran was very different from what it is now'. But above all, he realised that his father had a distinctive personality. Reza Shah's nature admirably qualified him for the task he had to perform, within the limits imposed by the conditions of the time.

Of all the changes that characterised the rebirth of Iran under Reza Shah, the most significant was that in Iranian relations with the Anglo-Persian Oil Company. Ever since his coronation, Reza Shah had conducted, through the government, negotiations with the Company to improve the terms of the original concession granted to D'Arcy in 1901. The Company had not responded favourably and the crisis in its relations with Iran matured in 1931. For various reasons, the Company decided to offer the government an insignificant sum as royalty. Reza Shah retaliated sharply and, in November 1932, the government notified the Company that the 1901 concession was can-

With Reza Shah at Persepolis

Accession

celled. Simultaneously it showed its willingness to negotiate a new concession.

There were several reasons, other than financial, for this cancellation. The Company, by this time, had claimed rights to explore and exploit oil resources throughout Iran, including the five northern provinces which had been specifically excluded from the original D'Arcy concession. It based its claim to rights in the northern provinces on the purchase of a concession from a White Russian, to whom it had been granted in 1916. The Company had acquired this concession a year before the Russo-Iranian Treaty of 1921, by which the Soviet government had renounced all such concessions in Iran previously granted to Czarist nationals. Reza Shah was unwilling to accept the validity of this acquisition and the rights that went with it. There was also a dispute over the site of the refinery at Abadan. The Company claimed to have secured a lease from Shaikh Khazal, who had already been defeated by Reza Shah and driven out of the country. The government did not accept the validity of the lease since Khazal was in no sense a sovereign in Khuzistan.

The dispute was brought before the Council of the League of Nations in January 1933. Once the case had been argued by the parties, direct negotiations began between them under the chairmanship of a representative of the League of Nations. In April 1933, a new agreement was signed. The Company undertook to increase the size of the royalty. The British monopoly of exploration rights throughout Iran was broken and the concessionary area reduced. Its name, too, was changed. It now became the Anglo-Iranian Oil Company, since Reza Shah wanted his country to be known by its ancient name of Iran.

Apart from the direct economic benefit accruing from the new agreement, Iranian political gains were of some value.

Reza Shah had established that the Iran of the Pahlavis was in a position to negotiate successfully with an all-powerful company, backed by the British government. This meant the end of an era of external pressures and gunboat diplomacy. Various consequences of this new agreement led to increasing bitterness in Anglo-Iranian relations. These were to have much greater significance in 1941 when Britain insisted upon the abdication of Reza Shah.

By 1939, Reza Shah had begun to lean heavily on the opinion of the Crown Prince. They were together most of the time and always shared serious decisions. When the dark shadows of the coming war in Europe touched Iran, Reza Shah asked the Crown Prince to study this threatening situation. He had full confidence in the judgement of his son, who was familiar with the new pattern of politics in Europe. On September 1, 1939, when Hitler's Panzers attacked Poland and the Second European War began, Reza Shah and the Crown Prince decided to keep their country strictly neutral.

CHAPTER SIX

Invasion

IN the autumn of 1939, a major crisis had to be resolved not
only by the nationalist leaders in Iran but by nationalists in
all Asian countries. The problem which the war posed for
them was quite different from that which Europe faced.
Though Britain had belatedly entered the war against Nazism,
after Neville Chamberlain had sacrificed Czechoslovakia, and
had protested its adherence to democratic values, there were
no signs of any relaxation in its imperial outlook.[1] As Hitler's
troops cut through the Polish defences, Asian leaders observed
that British policies in west Asia, especially in Iraq, were not
undergoing the change which might have been expected of a
nation fighting to save the world for democracy. As for the
Soviet Union, the sympathetic image its anti-colonial policies
had earlier created was tarnishing badly. The sight of its troops
moving into Poland and Finland revived memories of the days
when the Czarist armies had marched under the flag of Russian
expansionism. This reincarnation of imperialist Russian policy
aroused much concern in India.[2]

The Germans reaped the harvest of this dual antagonism,

[1] This was clearly seen by the leaders of the Indian National Congress in
India, and was expressed by them. See, Nehru, Jawaharlal, *Discovery of
India* (Bombay, 1948).
[2] Ibid.

which dominated the Asian mind in general, and that of Iran in particular. This had nothing to do with any sympathy for Nazi ideology.[3] The mind of the people was subject, in 1939 as before, to the illusion that one should treat one's enemy's enemy as a friend. The scores which the Asian nationalists had long wanted to settle with their colonial oppressors were now being settled by the Germans. Vicarious pleasure inspired the celebrations which accompanied German victories. There was also a feeling of intense satisfaction that at last there was now a power that was teaching a lesson to those who had ridden rough-shod over the independence of Asian countries.

Apart from this general feeling, which he shared, Reza Shah was gravely concerned at the radical change in Stalin's policies since the Russo-German pact of non-aggression. The thrust of Stalin's armies into Poland, the merging of the Baltic states into the Soviet Federation, and the Finnish War created a considerable feeling of insecurity in Iran. The Stalinist attitude towards both Iran and Turkey had stiffened. Many Iranians felt that the Russians had decided simply to profit from the war in which the capitalist countries were engaged. Stalin seemed determined to re-establish Russian influence in all the regions which had once been subjected to Czarist dominance. Reza Shah kept in close touch with the Turkish government, which stood in equal fear of Stalin's ambitions. Iran and Turkey both decided to send special envoys to Moscow. Hamid Sayah, Reza Shah's emissary, followed Sarajoghlu, the Turkish plenipotentiary, to Moscow.

Although Hamid Sayah stayed in Moscow for three weeks,

[3] Several Asian leaders temporarily co-operated with the Nazis and later with Japan in what they believed to be the struggle against the colonial powers holding dominance over their country, including Subbas Chandra Bose of India ; the Grand Mufti of Jerusalem ; Aung San, later General and first Prime Minister of Burma ; and Dr Mohammed Hatta, later first Vice-President of Indonesia.

Stalin never found time to receive him. Discussions with Molotov, then Soviet Foreign Minister, proved fruitless. Both Hamid Sayah and Sarajoghlu had been instructed by their governments to secure a guarantee of non-aggression from the Soviet Union. This was not given, and Hamid Sayah returned from Moscow with a report which only deepened the mystery, and the fears about Stalin's intentions. It was a peculiar situation in which Iran was placed : the German radio was daily attacking Reza Shah and his government as reactionary and British influenced ; Moscow Radio followed suit ; and Britain, too, was unwilling to trust the Iranian government. These three major European powers appeared to have developed a common antagonism to Iran, caused by irritation at Reza Shah's policy of neutrality, which stood in the way of their conflicting plans.

By the spring of 1941 many Iranians were convinced that there existed a Russo-German secret agreement whereby the Germans had consented to a Soviet drive into Iran. Yet Reza Shah, attacked by both groups of belligerents and the Soviet Union, remained consistently neutral, and this was still the situation when, on June 22, 1941, Hitler suddenly turned east and quickly breached the Soviet defences on a thousand-mile front. The initial German success heartened some influential Iranians who had feared that a Soviet victory would mean the annexation of the northern part of Iran by Stalin. 'The newspapers appeared with big headlines announcing the German victories', an eye-witness has written, 'and a loud-speaker giving news in Sepah Square brought a crowd of listeners who cheered and applauded the announcement of each Russian town fallen into German hands.' [4]

Earlier in 1941, Reza Shah had ordered the Supreme War Council to prepare a strategic plan for the defence of Iranian

[4] Arfa, p. 272.

territory in case of invasion from the north. In May, however, a new danger arose in the west and south. British troops occupied Iraq, an episode which had a considerable impact in Iran. Most people were unwilling to accept the British interpretation of events and did not see the British occupation of Iraq as an 'inevitable consequence' of Rashid Ali's 'revolt'. Rashid Ali was the legally appointed Prime Minister of Iraq, which had been recognised as an independent country. He was also a nationalist who, for historical reasons, was anti-British and, in that limited sense, pro-German.

As Prime Minister of Iraq, Rashid Ali was entitled to take whatever steps he considered beneficial to his country, but the British government, by then headed by Churchill, naturally did not put much trust in him. It had therefore decided to add a further infantry brigade to that already stationed in Iraq to prevent possible sabotage of oil installations. Under the Anglo-Iraqi Treaty, Britain, though entitled to bring more troops to Iraq, was bound to consult with the Iraqi government before taking any such step. When Rashid Ali was ignored, he protested in the name of Iraq's sovereign rights and ordered the Iraqi army to resist the British action. His resistance lasted for thirty-five days, after which he fled in defeat to Iran, and thence to Berlin.

The occupation of Iraq added to the anxieties of Reza Shah and the Crown Prince. The war was no longer distant, as in the autumn of 1939. The German invasion of Russia had brought Churchill to his feet to declare in the House of Commons on June 23, 1941, that Britain would aid the Soviet Union with all the means at her disposal. A promise of support soon followed from President Roosevelt, who announced that the United States would extend the Lend-Lease Act to assist the Soviet Union.

These promises meant that Britain and the United States

would dispatch arms, munitions, raw materials and foodstuffs to the Soviet Union. There were three routes by which these materials could be sent : the Murmansk route, which passed through the north Atlantic and the North Sea ; the Crimean route, through the Bosporus to the Black Sea ports ; and the Persian route via the Gulf ports across Iran and the Caspian Sea. The dangers involved in taking the first route were soon obvious. German submarines in Norwegian waters inflicted heavy casualties on the British Merchant Marine. Turkey, which had also declared its neutrality in the war, was unwilling even to consider the passage of arms to the Soviet Union. Moreover the Bosporus route would involve the risks of moving ships through the Mediterranean. It was thus that Iran suddenly became directly involved in a war with which she wanted nothing to do.

Reza Shah had deliberately fostered very close economic relations with Germany.[5] Neither Hitler nor his ideology had been factors in the growth of this policy. The process had begun soon after the Revolution of 1921, in the days when great hopes were pinned on the rise of the Weimar Republic. By 1938, Germany had gained first place in Iran's foreign trade, supplying mainly industrial equipment and railway machinery, and importing raw wool and cotton. German engineers and technicians were engaged in the construction of ports, railways and factories. Naturally many of them lived in Iran.

Reza Shah had adopted this policy on purpose. He greatly admired both German technicians and equipment, and received excellent terms from German industrialists. Germany

[5] Reza Shah, in the years after abdication and exile, never recorded his views on the Anglo-Soviet invasion of 1941. However, they were later interpreted by the Shah, *Mission*, pp. 66 to 68 and pp. 71 to 74 ; semi-officially by Shamim, Ali Asghar, *Iran in the reign of His Majesty Mohammad Reza Shah Pahlavi* (Tehran, 1966), pp. 4–5 ; and unofficially by Arfa, pp. 273–4.

had no particular record of colonialism in Iran. She had seldom interfered in Iranian affairs and, of course, was opposed to Britain and the Soviet Union, whose histories included dark chapters of oppression in Iran. There was also another reason for Reza Shah's adherence to this policy : it enjoyed popular support. Since Hitler had come to power, Nazi propaganda had concentrated on the common racial origins of the Germans and the Iranians. The dubious concept of Aryanism had become popular. Nor did the average Iranian see why there should be anything to criticise in the German dictatorial regime since he, and generations before him, had been accustomed to authoritarian rule.

Reza Shah's own evaluation of the Germans and of Hitler was quite simple : he disliked both the German attitude towards Asians, and Hitler. Later, on the eve of the invasion of Iran, Allied propaganda depicted him as a sympathiser of the Nazis. Both Moscow Radio and the British Broadcasting Corporation made this the theme of their tirades. His son was to repudiate this charge later in the following words : '. . . contrary to the claims of some historians, my father had little use for Hitler. When Reza Shah visited Turkey in 1934, he heard stories of the arrogance of her German allies in the First World War, and as the 1930s advanced, he perceived the same sort of behaviour in Hitler and his henchmen. Moreover, Hitler's occupation policies in Europe showed my father the dangers of ever allowing Iran to become a German satellite. Finally, as a leader who himself had authoritarian tendencies, my father resented another dictator such as Hitler.'[6]

Neither London nor Moscow ever gave enough thought to the attitudes of the Asian leadership in general, and of Reza Shah in particular, towards Germany during the war. Grievous results were to flow from this blindness on the part of the Allied

[6] *Mission*, pp. 66–7.

war leaders not only in Iran but elsewhere in the Asian world. The crisis in India was delayed because Mahatma Gandhi pleaded with Britain to agree to Indian independence, so that India could co-operate with the Allies. On August 9, 1942, Gandhi and Nehru, leaders of the Indian National Congress, and twenty-five thousand other nationalists were imprisoned even though they themselves had no ideological sympathy either with Nazism or the cult of Hirohito. The situation in Iran became critical within hours of the outbreak of the Soviet-German war. The decision to use the Persian route for supplies to the Soviet Union followed inevitably, and soon other considerations, over which Reza Shah had no control, also affected the policy of Britain and the Soviet Union towards Iran.

The Crown Prince was quick to realise the implications of the new dangers which now faced his country. Reza Shah, on the other hand, believed that there was no need to make immediate changes in his foreign policy. His extreme sense of self-respect did not permit him to revise his policies to suit Allied interests. He would not be forced by any power or any set of circumstances into a sudden revision of a policy which he had scrupulously and steadfastly followed since the Revolution of 1921. The Crown Prince had succeeded in making him aware of the need for a change, but Reza Shah trusted his own judgement better than that of anyone else. Later events were to prove that he had, for once, miscalculated, and this error of judgement cost him dear.

Several new and unexpected factors, which were to change the complexion of the war and fate of Iran, were not taken into account by him when he calculated that he could maintain his nation's neutrality without provoking the aggressive attention of the belligerents. The first of these was the initial collapse of the Soviet armies. When he first heard the news of the Nazi attack on the Soviet Union, Reza Shah, like most observers, had believed that the Soviet armies would give a good account of themselves and contain the invasion at the frontier. Instead, the Germans both seized the strategic initiative and maintained it. Nazi assault groups of Panzer and motorised divisions crushed Soviet resistance and penetrated swiftly into the heart of Russia. The Soviet armies suffered heavy losses and were in retreat over the entire front.[7] As the war moved east and south, it became obvious that the Caucasus could fall into German hands unless drastic measures were adopted by the Allies. Iran therefore became a focal point for the Allies in planning their new strategy.

Churchill later analysed this situation in his history of the Second War : 'The need to pass munitions and supplies of all kinds to the Soviet Government, and the extreme difficulties of the Arctic route, together with future strategic possibilities, made it eminently desirable to open the fullest communications with Russia through Persia. . . . The Persian oilfields were a prime factor, and if Russia were defeated we would have to be ready to occupy them ourselves.'[8] Stalin's anxieties were somewhat similar. He was also afraid that a neutral Iran might prove to be a danger to his rear. This fear was later summarised by Deborin in the official Soviet history of the Second War : 'Vital communication lines crossed that Eastern country [Iran], which also possessed vital strategic materials such as oil, and bordered on the key areas of the Soviet rear. . . .'[9]

Churchill was determined to 'open the fullest communication with Russia through Persia'; Stalin eyed 'vital communication lines' which 'crossed that Eastern country'. However, neither of them considered it necessary to communicate their thinking to Reza Shah. Partly as prisoners of previous preju-

---

[7] Deborin, G., in *The Second World War, a political-military survey*, edited by Major-General I. Zubkov (Moscow), p. 155.
[8] Quoted in *Mission*, p. 71.   [9] Deborin, p. 102.

dices and policies of their countries towards Iran, and partly from panic, they decided to invade and force Reza Shah out of power. The idea was first discussed between Churchill and Lord Wavell, who was then Viceroy of India. Churchill, true to his character, followed the old British colonial system of treating Iran as part of the British-Indian sphere of influence. He also planned to use the Indian army to secure his aims. Wavell wrote back on July 11, 1941 : 'It is essential that we should join hands with Russia, through Iran, and if the present government [of Iran] is not willing to facilitate this, it must be made to give way to one which will.' [10] Churchill immediately set up 'a special committee to co-ordinate the planning of an operation against Persia'.[11]

Churchill, after issuing orders to prepare the invasion of Iran, left for Placentia Bay, Newfoundland, to meet Roosevelt. Ironically, besides the papers which dealt with plans to attack a small neutral country, he carried a preliminary brief on the rights of nations which later came to be known as the Atlantic Charter. While he was at sea, he was informed that the British War Cabinet had approved the invasion and its operational plans. How the Russians reacted to the proposal for the invasion has not yet been officially stated. According to Churchill, the Soviet Ambassador Ivan Maisky had initially expressed to Anthony Eden the inability of his country to undertake an invasion of Iran single-handed. He had also conveyed Stalin's readiness to co-operate with Churchill should the latter invade Iran. Once this was agreed, Moscow and London worked out the details of the invasion plan with extraordinary harmony.

[10] For Churchill's version of the reasons and preparations for this joint Anglo-Soviet invasion of Iran, see Churchill, Sir Winston, *The Second World War*, vol. 6, ' War Comes to America' (London, 1965), pp. 90–91. [11] Ibid. p. 91.

Some Iranian sources later doubted the veracity of this report. General Arfa, for example, had another interpretation to offer. He wrote in 1964 : 'I had always thought that it was the Soviets who insisted on invading Iran, but in 1959, during a conversation, Rushru Aras, the former Turkish Foreign Minister, who was Turkish Ambassador in London in 1941, told me that the Russians would have been content with the Iranian Government's consent to allow war material to pass through Iran, and its assurance to protect the lines of communications ; but that the British, fearing a repercussion of a possible defeat in Egypt, did not like to have a nearly 200,000 strong Iranian army at their rear. They insisted on the occupation of the country and control over the Iranian Government.'[12]

Between the time of the decision to invade Iran and the invasion itself, a little drama was played out. The curtain rose on June 26, four days after the outbreak of Soviet-German hostilities, with a Soviet Note to the government in Tehran. It dealt with the question of the presence of German nationals in Iran, and was in a sense a polite overture to the grim *dénouement*. The Germans, the Soviet Note pointed out, were busy plotting a *coup* against Reza Shah ; Moscow had enough evidence to prove this ; and, therefore, they must be thrown out. The *coup* element was the one novelty in the Soviet Note ; otherwise it followed the pattern of a series of British protests.

The demand for the expulsion of the Germans was made once again in a joint Anglo-Soviet Note on July 19. Finally, a stronger Note from the two powers was delivered on August 16. Both these later Notes were solely concerned with the question of the presence of Germans in Iran. None of the Notes referred even indirectly to the Allied need for communication lines across Iran to assist the embattled armies of the U.S.S.R. It was strange that the Allies should insist upon the expulsion

[12] Arfa, p. 277.

of the Germans, as there was an almost equal number of Allied nationals in Iran at that time. As the country had adopted a policy of neutrality, if the Allies could require the displacement of the Germans, then so could Hitler that of the British and Soviet citizens.

The Crown Prince was fully aware of the strategic needs of the Allies, as was Ali Mansur, then Prime Minister. Sir Reader Bullard, the British Minister, and the Soviet Ambassador, Smirnov, had made this point verbally, though they were unwilling to place their government's views on formal record. However, Reza Shah could not be approached by Mansur on the strength of such unofficial conversations.[13] Nobody except the Crown Prince could influence his opinion. The latter tried, as far as he could, to find a solution to the problem. Several Germans were asked to go. Only those whose presence was vital to the economic well-being of the country were permitted to stay.

In the meanwhile a major propaganda campaign had been organised both in Britain and Russia against Reza Shah. The ghost of Wassmuss had been invoked, and the possibility of German sabotage of the oil installations, followed by a march on India, had been revived. The first British reports spoke of two to three thousand Germans, many of them fifth columnists, in Iran.[14] *The Times* then reported that besides these Germans, there were others numbering four thousand who had come as

[13] It has been suggested by some Iranian sources that Ali Mansur did not convey the substance of the real Allied demands to Reza Shah, see Shamin, p. 5, and that this was Ali Mansur's great political mistake. On basis of conversations with Ali Mansur's contemporaries it appears that Ali Mansur was in no position to do so, though he informed the Crown Prince about them.

[14] This estimate was made by the British Commander-in-Chief of the Indian Army on July 29, 1941. See Skrine, Sir Claremont, *World War in Iran* (London, 1962), p. 76.

'tourists'.[15] When the final count of Germans in Iran was made in late August, it was found that there were no more than a few hundred of them with their families.[16]

Reza Shah now realised that the Allies were not giving him the full picture. He was angry as well as worried. Unable to make a full assessment of the Allies' motives, he could not take any decisive measures. Yet his instinct told him that some major crisis was about to break. Under these circumstances, he took a quite uncharacteristic step. 'Forgetting his dignity as a sovereign', the Shah later disclosed, 'he went so far as to request his Minister in London to ask the Allies if they would explain their real wants and needs. . . . My father also notified the German Minister in Tehran that Iran planned to expel all the remaining Germans. Arrangements were made for their transit through Turkey and their repatriation.' [17] Reza Shah now hoped that the Allies would place their cards on the table, and that a *modus vivendi* might be found, even at this eleventh hour, which would secure equally the honour of his country and the interests of the Allies.

This hope was wiped out at dawn on August 25, when British and Russian forces simultaneously invaded Iran. British troops attacked from the west and south-west and the Russians from the north. British and Indian soldiers of the Tenth Indian Division from Baghdad, under the command of Major-General Slim, crossed the frontier at Qasr-i-Shirin. Simultaneously, three hundred miles to the south-west, Major-General C. O. Harvey led the Eighth Indian Division from Basra and attacked southern Iran. The Russians sent a strong mechanised column from Tiflis across the frontier at Julfa, which

[15] Skrine, p. 76.
[16] According to the Shah, Iranian records showed the number of the Germans at 470 males and their dependants (*Mission*, p. 72); Britain never estimated a figure higher than 900 (Skrine, p. 81). [17] Ibid. p. 72.

passed through Tabriz and headed for Tehran. A similar column from Baku moved down the west coast of the Caspian to Bandar Pahlavi and Rasht. There was no choice left for Iran but to fight as best as she could this multi-pronged invasion.

Early on August 25, Tehran radio briefly announced that Soviet and British troops had crossed the frontier and penetrated Iranian territory : 'Our forces are defending the national territory ; fighting has started and is continuing on all fronts'. Soviet planes began to fly over Tehran. The invasion was well planned : within twenty-four hours the Soviet columns had occupied Marand, Sofian, Bandar Pahlavi, Khoi, Maku and Shahpur. The British forces under General Slim were checked at Pa-e-Tak by troops of the Kermanshah Division, but General Slim retaliated by parachuting a battalion into Masjid-i-Sulaiman. Bitter fighting continued in the south where the Iranian forces gave a good account of themselves. Meanwhile Britain had brought its navy into the Persian Gulf, and the British assault by land and sea proved overpowering. The Iranian navy in the area lost its commander, Admiral Bayndor, and it was clear that the Iranian army was not equipped to fight a combined Anglo-Soviet invasion. On the morning of August 27, it was officially announced that orders had been given to Iranian troops to cease fighting and return to their barracks.

CHAPTER SEVEN

Abdication and Accession

THE invasion had deeply wounded the pride of the Crown Prince, who was pre-occupied with the injustice of this un-provoked attack on an independent country by two great European powers. Could there have been an alternative to this military action which had violated every principle of inter-national law and canon of civilised behaviour? He thought there was. This belief was to stay with him over the years, and he was to continue to argue that there had been another course which Churchill and Stalin had refused to accept. In his view the Allied protest Notes contained 'an element of deception'. He suspected that all along the Allies had been less interested in reaching a settlement with Reza Shah than in finding a pre-text for invasion. There was no doubt in his mind that the Allies had not wanted to take Reza Shah into their confidence. Later he summarised his feelings: 'Besides being more candid with my father, the Allies should have proposed an honourable diplomatic alliance with him. Some may scoff at this idea, believing that Reza Shah's political convictions would have prevented it. But before violating my country's independence and sovereignty, the Allies should at least have made an effort. I have reason to believe that Reza Shah would either have accepted the Allied overtures or that, by resigning his throne to me, he would have allowed me to do so.' [1]

[1] *Mission*, pp. 72–3.

The Crown Prince was a different man from Reza Shah. Although he shared with his father a deep sense of nationalism, he was the product of the intellectual turmoil of the early thirties in Europe. He therefore realised that the Allies could not have read his father's secret thoughts. 'What I am saying', he stated later, 'is that before invading my country in Hitlerian style, thereby violating some of the cardinal principles for which they professed to be fighting, the Allies had the responsibility of trying to arrange an honourable alliance with Reza Shah or, barring that, with his son'.[2] He held firmly to the conviction that the Allies could have entered into some sort of alliance with Iran.

He was convinced at that time that his father, as a rational man, would have made his own country's welfare the cardinal consideration. Reza Shah would have agreed to such a military alliance if the Allies had abandoned 'their circumlocution and had given Reza Shah an honest picture of their strategic predicament in relation to Iran's interest'. By putting such a proposal to Reza Shah, wrote the Shah in 1961, 'the Allies would have avoided having to send into Iran forces which they badly needed elsewhere. We would have been spared the humiliation and chaos of the invasion and occupation, and we would have joined earlier in the common battle against Hitler's tyranny.'[3] By the fourth week of August, the Crown Prince was himself prepared to accept such a diplomatic offer.

No such offer had ever been contemplated by the Allies, who were determined to reach their objective by force of arms. Within forty-eight hours of the invasion the government of Ali

[2] *Mission*, p. 73.
[3] Shamim, p. 9. The Shah wrote about this : 'I should add that later, when I had assumed the throne, I refused to deal with any Allied representations other than their head of Government or their ambassadors.' *Mission*, p. 75.

Mansur resigned. He was replaced by Mohammad Ali Forughi, one of Iran's leading intellectuals, who was also an astute
politician. Forughi, on the orders of Reza Shah, entered into
negotiations with Britain and Russia as soon as he had been
sworn in. He also called an extraordinary session of the *majlis*
at which he gave the deputies a brief account of the events of
the previous two days, and presented the members of his
Cabinet. He told the *majlis* that the order to lay down arms
had been issued by Reza Shah himself.

Forughi also informed the agitated deputies that Reza Shah
had instructed the government to make every endeavour to
terminate the state of war. These efforts met with immediate
success. Iran signed an armistice agreement with the invading
powers, by which the Russians were to retain control over
Azerbaijan, Gilan, Mazanderan, Gorgan and the northern part
of Khorassan, as well as Qazvin, Semnan, Demdhan and Schah-
loud. The British were to remain in occupation of the whole of
Khuzistan and part of Kermanshah. Iran undertook to expel all
Germans and nationals of other states with which the occupying powers were at war, including their diplomats. Besides
providing various facilities to the armies of the invaders, the
government was to place all its lines of communication at their
disposal for the transport of supplies to the Soviet Union.

The armistice in itself amounted to no more than a recognition of the *de facto* position. Its terms precluded the occupation
of Tehran by either British or Russian troops. While Iran was
busy rounding up the Germans, who had had ample warning
of the fate awaiting them, several vanished. So much propaganda capital had already been made out of their presence, that
it was unreasonable of the Allies to lay the blame for these
escapes at the door of the Forughi government ; but they decided to seize upon this incident as a pretext for marching on
Tehran. Many Iranians at this stage believed that this further

advance was intended to create a situation in which Reza Shah could no longer continue to reign. Whether or not this was the case, that was precisely what happened.

On the morning of September 16, Reza Shah summoned the Crown Prince. It was to be the last, moving meeting between father and son. Reza Shah calmly informed the Crown Prince that he had decided to abdicate in his favour. Before the Shah could absorb the full significance of this stunning news, Reza Shah added : 'The people have always considered me an independent, determined and powerful king, and protector of their country and interests ; and because of this respect, reliance and confidence of the people, I cannot be the nominal head of an occupied land, to be dictated to by a minor English or Russian officer'.[4]

The decision was characteristic of Reza Shah. Although he had earlier thought of abdication, he had postponed his decision because of the outbreak of the war. He had never spoken directly of this plan to his son, who learned of it much later from one of his father's most trusted advisers. Reza Shah had planned to hand over the throne to his son early in the 1940s, relegating himself to the position of an elder statesman, in which role he would have been able to give the new monarch the benefit of his knowledge and experience whenever necessary. Now, of course, this decision was being put into effect under very different circumstances. The invaders knew that they could not work with Reza Shah and he in turn knew that he could not work with them. As the Shah concluded in later years, it was true that the invaders put pressure upon his father to abdicate and leave the country but, paradoxically enough, their wish and his were in a manner identical.[5] Reza Shah went into exile by mutual consent.

Soon after his meeting with the Crown Prince, Reza Shah

[4] *Mission*, p. 75. [5] Skrine, p. 85.

left for Isfahan with all the other members of his family. On September 27, he boarded the British steamer *Bandra* at Bandar Abbas and sailed for Bombay. The news of Reza Shah's imminent arrival in India quite unnerved the Anglo-Indian government in Delhi. Sir Claremont Skrine, who played a major part in this drama, later summed up the situation : 'Things were going badly for the Empire on land and sea ; nationalist Muslim agitation was at its height. There would almost certainly be riotous demonstrations if the king of the largest and the most ancient Mohammadan state in the world whom (in Muslim eyes) we had deposed in exile by force of arms, were to appear in Bombay, Calcutta, or any other big city.'[6] The Anglo-Indian government appealed to London, pleading that it was in no position to accommodate a man of Reza Shah's stature. It was for this reason that the decision was made to take Reza Shah to the island of Mauritius.

With the utmost secrecy, Reza Shah and his family were transferred from the *Bandra* to another British ship, the *Burma*, six miles out at sea off Bombay. Reza Shah's protests were to no avail. On October 6, the *Burma* began its 2,300 mile voyage to Port Louis, capital of Mauritius. Sir Claremont accompanied him on this painful journey during which, on a number of occasions, Reza Shah spoke of the mistake which the British had made in not taking him into their confidence about the strategic needs of the war.[7] The climate in Mauritius did not suit him. He stayed at Port Louis for some time, but was later taken to South Africa where he took up residence in Johannesburg.

Reza Shah kept in close contact with his son, but avoided giving advice on any particular affair of state. Instead, his constant message to the new Shah was never to be afraid of anything. He realised that the Shah was then engaged in re-

[6] Skrine, p. 83.   [7] *Ibid.* p. 85.

orienting the foreign and domestic policies of Iran, and he did not wish to prejudice their success in any way. It was because of this that he refused to entertain all requests, even from his son, to write his memoirs. Reza Shah, in exile, might have changed in some ways, but he remained steadfast to the cardinal principle of his life. His country's interests came before all else. After two years in Johannesburg, Reza Shah died in July 1944 at the age of sixty-six.[8]

Reza Shah's abdication had created a complete vacuum in the political life of Iran. The Shah partly shared the feeling which swept the country and which has been summarised by a contemporary : 'I felt as if the ground on which I stood had been taken from under me, the world foundering around us, the feeling of security given by knowing that Reza Shah was in his palace, looking after his nation, suddenly disappeared.'[9] The void created by the departure of Reza Shah appeared to be so great that many at that time believed that it could not be filled. Despite his feelings, however, the Shah knew that he must move to fill this breach without a single faltering step.

The Shah had been trained to rule his country by his father, but his character had been moulded by other factors too. During his years in Europe, he had developed a powerful, resolute and distinctive personality. At that time he had thought that the transference of power from Reza Shah to himself would be peaceful, and that he would thus have the opportunity of translating his design for a new Iran into a reality. On his

---

[8] On the Shah's orders, Reza Shah's remains were brought to Iran from Johannesburg, via Egypt to Tehran, and his nation paid its tribute to him on May 7, 1950 in a state funeral. General Arfa relates a story which underlines Reza Shah's attachment to Iran. When Ernest Perron, his Swiss personal secretary, presented Reza Shah in Johannesburg with a handful of Iranian earth, Reza Shah expressed a desire that it should be placed in his coffin if he died away from Iran. See Arfa, pp. 391-2.

[9] Arfa, p. 302.

return in 1936 and until the outbreak of the war, his ruling passion had been to acquire a deep knowledge of his country so that he would be able to realise this dream as quickly and effectively as possible. Since the unforeseen outbreak of war. his experiences had helped to mature, even if painfully, his political understanding and moral courage. He had been severely tested during the five days of crisis — when he had remained steadfastly at his father's side. Reza Shah, by temperament and policy, had not been an easily accessible man, but this had never been the case with the Shah : many patriotic Iranians had come to him during the crisis to seek guidance, and to share with him their own feelings of disgust at what they considered to be a shameless aggression against their country. In this angry political climate, there appeared on September 11 an editorial in the daily newspaper, *Ettelaat*, which blamed Britain and Russia for having violated Iran's neutrality and territorial integrity, a courageous indictment of the military occupiers of the country. The commanders of the invading armies believed that the Crown Prince had either written or inspired this challenging article.[10] The incident provoked their antagonism towards him, yet, at the same time, the first feeling of respect for Reza Shah's successor was born among his opponents.

With the departure of Reza Shah, the Shah stood alone. The umbrella of protection and guidance of his great predecessor had been furled. All his family, including his twin sister and his younger brother, Ali Reza, had left Iran with their father. Except for Forughi, there were few politicians on whom he could rely for advice. On the other hand, many politicians had already sold their honour to one or other of the occupying powers. Moral decay, an ugly consequence of alien domination, had already set in.

[10] Skrine, p. 82 ; Arfa, p. 302.

Under the Constitution, the Shah had become monarch of Iran from the moment of Reza Shah's abdication. In accordance with Article 39 of the Supplement to the Constitution, he was required to read and sign the text of the oath of loyalty. The Prime Minister, Forughi, decided that no time should be lost in going through this ceremony at the extraordinary session of the *majlis* which he had called. It was a grim occasion, described by an eye witness in the following words : 'We were standing in the entrance hall, the officers to the right of the entrance, the civilians to the left. There was very little conversation while we waited. A few civilians tried to look casual, but the majority looked subdued, and even gloomy. Then we heard from outside the national anthem being played by the band and the greeting of the Shah answered rhythmically, according to regulations, by the guards : *Javid-bad-Ala-Hazrat.* Mohammad Reza Shah Pahlavi entered the hall'.[11]

The Shah, in ceremonial uniform, looked neither at the officers of the armed forces, standing frozen to attention, nor at the civilians, bowing deeply in accordance with court etiquette. He mounted the rostrum and took his oath on the Qoran in a voice which did not falter and yet conveyed both a deep sense of tragedy and the faith and confidence essential if he was to undertake his new duties successfully. He said : 'Now that internal circumstances have made it expedient that I should assume the serious duties of kingship and, in accordance with the Constitution, take the reins of the government in my hands in such a burdensome situation, bearing in mind the principles of the Constitution and separation of powers, I deem it necessary to point out the need of absolute and constant co-operation between the government and parliament, and in order to save the high interests of the country I wish to state that I myself, the government, parliament and all citizens of this country

[11] Arfa, p. 303.

should take every care in the performance of our duties and should never show negligence in the perfect observance of the laws'.[12]

A short speech followed, in which the Shah made three points. Bearing in mind the grave dangers of anarchy and chaos in the wake of the invasion, he emphasised the need for perfect collaboration and harmony between the various departments of state. He laid special stress on the strict enforcement of laws and regulations to safeguard public welfare, particularly by the army and civil service. His next point emphasised the distinctive personality of the new monarch. He told parliament and the nation that the legal system must be reviewed in the light of the needs of the time, and that a new and comprehensive programme of social, economic and financial reform must be introduced. The legal security of the individual, he went on to say, must be considered, as a central point in this reform programme. Finally, he addressed the occupying powers. There was a need, he said, for close co-operation between Iran and those governments whose interests were particularly related to those of Iran. Of course, he added, such co-operation could exist only on condition that the interests of Iran were fully and perfectly borne in mind by these others.

After concluding his speech and taking the oath of loyalty to the Constitution, the Shah left the *majlis* building without speaking to anybody. He was then forty days from his twenty-second birthday. Never had any Shah of Iran come to the throne in circumstances such as those under which Mohammad Reza Shah Pahlavi inaugurated his reign over his ancient, proud, and yet occupied, land.

[12] Shamim, pp. 9–10.

PART TWO
THE STRUGGLE FOR SOVEREIGNTY

The sea is baying like a wolf tonight ;
 It springs in fury on the cliffs ; but soon
The waves in wild disorder will retreat,
 Obedient to the influence of the moon.

FARRUKHI (ABUL HASAN ALI)
d. 1037

CHAPTER EIGHT

A Sea of Trouble

'WHEN I took the throne at the age of twenty-one', the Shah was to write later, 'I found myself plunged into a sea of trouble.' In the autumn of 1941, this sea of trouble not only surrounded Iran but threatened to submerge her. The new monarch faced problems wherever he turned. To begin with, the Allied commands were unwilling even to recognise the succession during the first few days after he had taken his oath of loyalty.[1] This, however, only proved part of the major problem which the presence of the occupying powers posed. They appeared to believe sincerely that their victory in the unequal military battle had given them a right to treat Iran as a conquered country, and to exploit every dissident element for their own ends. They appeared to be intent upon weakening the authority of the new ruler. 'Their continual interference in political life and affairs', the Shah later wrote, ' disgusted me and my people.'

Despite such difficulties, however, the Shah had to look to the future, and establish a working relationship with the occupying powers. The pressing problem of developing a new foreign

[1] This strange attitude has never been recorded, though various sources have referred to it indirectly, see Arfa, p. 302 ; however, the Shah confirms that the Allied Commands were averse to recognising the constitutional succession for several days.

policy for the country could not be tackled unless this was accomplished. The Shah had never fully agreed with the policy pursued by his father in international relations. Reza Shah had adopted a narrow, ultra-nationalist approach which had suited conditions in the early inter-war years. He had failed to correlate the interests of Iran with the realities of international politics as practised during Hitler's rise to power. The Shah had come to the conclusion, long before the Allied armies invaded Iran, that in the last analysis his country's interests would be better served by an alliance with the anti-fascist coalition. His ideological sympathies lay with the war aims of the Allies : his outlook ran counter to the spirit of fascism.[2]

Had there been any offer of an alliance from the Allies, the Shah would have happily accepted it, as he repeatedly stated later, even if Reza Shah had personally found it impossible to be party to a coalition with Britain and Russia. Such a scheme would have been successful for, the Shah was convinced, Reza Shah would not have stood in the way of his son adopting this policy, and would have been prepared to abdicate. But now the invasion was a fact of life, and could not but shake the faith of the Shah in the democratic ideals by which the Allies swore. The events leading to his father's exile had hurt him deeply. Thus the evolution of a new foreign policy was as much an emotional test for him as it was a matter of political judgement.

It was under these circumstances that the Prime Minister, Foroughi, rendered the Shah invaluable assistance. Foroughi was a student of British policy in West Asia, and his sympathies lay with British interests in the area. Indeed Reza Shah had

[2] The Shah, in his argument with the architects of the invasion, repeatedly drew the distinction between the policies of Reza Shah and those which he would have followed if the Allies had offered an alliance to Iran. This powerful argument reveals his differences with Reza Shah over foreign policy.

appointed him in place of Ali Mansur partly, if not wholly, because of his ability to deal with the British.[3] Forughi agreed with the Shah on the fundamental promise that co-operation with the Allies was not merely a matter of necessity but was also a highly desirable move : nevertheless, reconciling himself to this new foreign policy in the light of the agony of the previous week meant a bitter personal struggle for the Shah.

The first step towards the implementation of the new foreign policy lay in the conversion of the *de facto* situation created by the invasion into *de jure* status. The Shah instructed Forughi to start negotiations with Britain and the Soviet Union for a tripartite treaty of alliance, and kept himself closely informed of their progress. It was as well he did so, for the negotiations proved tricky and on several occasions he had to intervene personally. Five months later, the Tripartite Treaty was signed, on January 29, 1942.[4]

The preamble to the treaty invoked the principles of the Atlantic Charter and assured Iran of its benefits on an equal basis with other nations of the world. By Article I, Iran received jointly and severally a guarantee on the part of Britain and the Soviet Union to respect her territorial integrity, sovereignty and political independence. By Article II, an alliance was established between the three parties. Article III comprised an undertaking on the part of the occupying powers to defend Iran from all aggression on the part of Germany or any other power. By the same article, the Shah agreed to give the Allies any co-operation they might require to discharge their undertaking to defend Iran : but the Allies stipulated that the 'assistance of the Iranian forces shall, however, be limited to the maintenance of internal security on Iranian territory'. The Allies also secured for themselves the unrestricted right to use, maintain, guard and, in case of military necessity, control

[3] Arfa, p. 299. [4] For full text, see Appendix II.

in any way that they might deem necessary any means of communication in Iran including railways, roads, rivers, aerodromes, ports, pipelines and telephones, telegraph and wireless installations. They also acquired an assurance of co-operation in obtaining materials and recruiting labour, and in the maintenance of censorship controls.

By Article IV, the Allies reserved to themselves discretion to determine the number of their troops to be stationed in Iran, while agreeing that the government of Iran should be consulted on their troop dispositions, 'so long as the strategic situation allows'. It was in the terms of this article that the Allies sought to whitewash their invasion. 'It is understood', the text ran, 'that the presence of this force on Iranian territory does not constitute a military occupation.' They also gave an assurance that they would disturb 'as little as possible the administration and the security forces of Iran, the economic life of the country, the normal movement of the population, and the application of Iranian laws and regulations.' This article also stipulated that separate arrangements would be made regarding the financial obligations of the Allied powers.

From Iran's point of view, Article V was the most important. It dealt with the vital issue of the termination of the Allied occupation. From the sad experience of his country, the Shah knew that occupying armies tended to dislike evacuations. A mere pledge, without mention of a specific withdrawal time for the British and Russian armies, would therefore be insufficient. The question of how and when the foreigners should return home had to be settled, and Article V dealt with this question. It stated : 'The forces of the Allied powers shall be withdrawn from Iranian territory not later than six months after all hostilities between the Allied powers and Germany and her associates have been suspended by the conclusion of an armistice or armistices or on the conclusion of peace between them, whichever date is the earlier.' The provisions of Article V were to be invoked later by Iran — in 1945 and 1946 — in her dealings with the Soviet Union at the Security Council: and it was this safety valve, upon which the Shah had so wisely insisted, that was to provide Iran with the necessary authority to compel Stalin to withdraw from Azerbaijan.

The Shah had also insisted upon the inclusion of a guarantee against any future partition of Iran between his new Allies. This guarantee was made explicit in Article VI (1) which stated: 'The Allied powers undertake in their relations with foreign countries not to adopt an attitude which is prejudicial to the territorial integrity, sovereignty, or the political independence of Iran, nor to conclude treaties inconsistent with its provisions.'

By Article VII, the Shah sought to secure economic security for his people. The Allied powers jointly undertook to use their best endeavours to safeguard the economic well-being of the Iranian people against the privations arising from the conditions of war, and agreed to start discussions with Iran on this subject. Article VIII further provided for making the Treaty binding as a bilateral agreement between Iran and either of the other parties. Finally, by Article IX, it was agreed that the Treaty would remain in force until the date fixed for the withdrawal of the Allied forces in accordance with Article V.

When the Treaty came into force, letters were exchanged between the British Minister, the Soviet Ambassador and the Foreign Minister in Tehran, confirming certain articles of the Treaty. The Shah was taking no chances. He instructed the Foreign Minister to seek reiteration of the obligations undertaken by the Allies in Article VI (1). As a result the Soviet and British representatives assured Iran by a letter dated January 29, 1942, that they would make no agreements at any peace conference which might be contrary to the territorial integrity, sovereignty and political independence of Iran, and that they would endeavour to facilitate the participation of Iran in international conferences and peace negotiations in so far as the interests of Iran were concerned. On the same day a further assurance was secured from Britain and the Soviet Union. In a Note, the Soviet Ambassador and British Minister assured the government of Iran that the Allied governments would not call on Iran for military assistance; and that the Treaty did not require the government of Iran to underwrite the expenses of any operations carried out by the Allies for their own purposes, and which had no connection with the interests of Iran.

To make matters absolutely clear, the Shah asked Foroughi to write letters to Churchill and Stalin, incorporating these guarantees. Stalin replied on February 1, 1942, confirming the assurances. Churchill's reply also arrived on the same day. With his usual flair for historical perspective he pointed out that for the first time Iran, Soviet Russia and the United Kingdom had joined as confederates in pursuit of a common objective. He concluded his letter by concurring with Foroughi's interpretation of the specific articles of the Treaty. The Shah thus accomplished a very intricate and difficult task, assisted at each stage by Foroughi. Later he was to write : 'I was lucky in that Mohammad Ali Foroughi, my able and scholarly new Prime Minister, wholeheartedly shared my views. He deserves most of the credit for negotiating for us the Tripartite Treaty of Alliance, which we, Great Britain and the Soviet Union signed on January 29, 1942.'[5]

The next logical step in implementing the new foreign policy was the severance of diplomatic relations with Germany, Italy and Japan. Meanwhile, United States naval units had entered Iranian waters in the Persian Gulf. American troops began to arrive in Iran to assist the British. The United States had signed

[5] *Mission*, p. 75.

no treaty of alliance or similar agreement with Iran. The Iranian government agreed to the entry of the U.S. forces solely on Washington's undertaking to abide by the terms of the Tripartite Treaty. President Roosevelt also included Iran among the beneficiary states for aid under the Lend-Lease Act. On September 9, 1943, Iran declared war on Nazi Germany.

The previous nine months had not been easy either for Iran or the Shah. Though he had evolved a new foreign policy and taken several steps to implement it, relations between Iran and its new allies remained brittle. There were constant skirmishes between the government in Tehran and the representatives of Britain and the Soviet Union. The terms of the Tripartite Treaty were bound to be unpopular. Iranians felt that they had done all they could to create the basis of good relations with the Allies, without receiving due return and recognition; and this feeling was to persist in later years. A quarter of a century later an Iranian scholar wrote : 'After bringing Reza Shah and the Iranian government and the people face to face with an accomplished fact, by means of a treaty which recognised the political independence and territorial integrity of Iran, that is to say, it recognised the natural and indisputable right of this country, they [the Allies] established control and supervision over all the economic potentialities of their ally. In fact, Iran placed whatever she had at the disposal of the Allies against their undertaking to defend the frontiers of this country in case of a hypothetical and imaginary aggression by Germany or any other country.'[6]

Interference by representatives of Britain and the Soviet Union in the internal affairs of the country took various forms. The government in Tehran was always subject to considerable pressure and the Prime Minister relied on the Shah for assistance in solving the problems this posed. The Shah stood firm

[6] Shamim, p. 21.

on several occasions and refused to accept the demands of the foreigners when he felt that they were either inconsistent with the terms of the Tripartite Treaty or plainly unreasonable. This attitude brought about a number of clashes between the Shah and his Allies. Among other incidents the Shah later recalled one specific case which clearly illustrated both the nature and extent of British interference. The Allies were paying their troops in Iranian currency. Because of the abnormal shortage of consumer goods in the country, due to the conditions of war and the abundance of Iranian currency liberally paid out to their soldiers by the Allies, Iran's economy suffered from inflation, and the cost of living suddenly shot up, leading to misery among the people. Regardless of these economic conditions, the Allies demanded that a further substantial increase of Iranian currency in circulation should be made. This demand was put to the then Prime Minister, Qavam, who replied that he was unable to comply because he knew the *majlis* would not agree and, under existing Iranian law, the *majlis* alone was competent to sanction any increase in the circulation of currency.

The British Ambassador decided to put pressure on the Shah himself, and told him that both his own country and the Soviet Union trusted Qavam, but the Prime Minister could not work with the existing *majlis*. The Shah, added the British Ambassador, should therefore dissolve the *majlis*. The Shah was extremely angry, though not surprised, at the insolence of this demand. He wrote subsequently: 'What a proposal by the representative of a foreign power ! I told the Ambassador that I and my people alone would decide when and if parliament were to be dissolved, that only the King and the Parliament of the land could trust or not trust their own Prime Minister, and that we would not be dictated to by any outsiders. Categorically, I refused his request.'[7]

[7] *Mission*, p. 76.

The Shah was learning fast. Daily skirmishes with the Allied commands; the impertinence with which the foreigners treated his government; the differences which often strained the alliance almost to breaking point; and the need to keep a cool head in the face of provocation — all helped to forge a new attitude on his part towards international relations. He had now learned by sad experience that to be the ally of great powers, even under the terms of a solemn treaty, in itself meant little. The game of power politics could be played only with some power at one's own disposal. At the time the Shah had precious little military or economic power to balance that of the Allied Command; yet he was not completely unarmed, for he had the growing support of his people to back him; and his own training, which gave him the courage to face the foreigners and defy them when necessary, was an even more potent weapon.

CHAPTER NINE

The Seeds of Dissension

THE Shah had proclaimed the second birth of constitutional democracy in Iran in his very first speech as monarch. He had also signed an amnesty for communist and other political prisoners, by which several rebel tribal chiefs confined to the municipal limits of Tehran were permitted to return to their homes. All restrictions on the formation of political parties and on the Press, inherited from the previous era, had been lifted. The Shah wanted his people to enjoy a new sense of democratic freedom, and had underlined the need to protect the legal freedom of individuals. All these measures, under normal circumstances, would have helped to usher in a new era of democratic growth.

The abdication of Reza Shah, however, and the occupation of the country by British and Russian troops had created an abnormal political situation. The *majlis* itself had become a coveted, and contested, prize for the Allies. At the Shah's accession, the term of the Twelfth *majlis* had ended. As was customary during Reza Shah's rule, the list of the deputies for the Thirteenth *majlis* had already been drawn up and their election completed. Thus the character and composition of the new *majlis* was not much different from its predecessors. It was oriented towards a particular home policy, and was designed to function under the peculiar system of security which Reza Shah had established.[1]   There had been little room for political parties on a European pattern within the state structure he had built.   He had, on purpose, always dominated the *majlis* and invariably moulded it to his own ends.

The Shah, while still Crown Prince, had known that the system his father had fostered was ill-suited to the type of demo-cracy which he had in mind.   He was not unaware that the *majlis*, as it was, symbolised the weakness of Iranian political life.   A large number of deputies were opportunist politicians, whose political loyalty gravitated towards what they considered to be the centre of power.   Most of them had therefore been loyal to Reza Shah if only because there was no other power centre in Iran between 1921 and 1941.   Only a few among them were capable of standing the test of the crisis which had suddenly descended upon Iran in the summer of 1941.

The apparent centre of power was now the Allied Command. Both the British and the Russian authorities were determined to make this clear beyond doubt.   Their dominance and inter-ference extended not only to the administration of the country, but also to its parliamentary life.   It had been customary, for both Britain and Russia in the years between 1908 and 1921, to retain the services of politicians who had succeeded in gaining seats in the *majlis*.   This practice was revived, intensified and justified on the ground that there was a pressing need to estab-lish 'political stability' in Iran.   The Shah did not accept this line of argument.

Sir Claremont Skrine, who had been appointed Consul-General at Meshed on his return from Mauritius, later described the general direction of British policy: 'I had come to Meshed under the impression that Britain was going to be not only Persia's saviour from the Nazi dragon, but her guide, philosopher and friend during the difficult war years to follow.'[2]

[1] Shamim, p. 13.   [2] Skrine, p. 168.

The Russians, for their part, shared the same feeling but were less subtle. The Russian command refused to co-operate with civil authorities in the areas under Soviet occupation. They controlled almost the entire administration, including the distribution of food and other primary commodities. The supposition that Iran was an occupied country, despite the Tri-partite Treaty, continued as the common denominator of Soviet and British policies.

The first two years following the German invasion of the Soviet Union marked a period in Russo-British relations when their underlying ideological differences were submerged by the need for a common approach in the face of danger. Several strange consequences stemmed from their alliance. British policy towards communists and their movement underwent a sudden radical change : the government in India, for example, lifted its ban against the Communist Party, and sought their assistance in fighting the war. The communists, for their part, were only too willing to co-operate. Before the Nazi attack on the Soviet Union, they had condemned the war as an 'imperialist war' and worked to convert it, in accordance with the Leninist dictum, into 'civil war in each country'. Once the Soviet Union, 'fatherland of the international proletariat' was in danger of being overrun by the fascists, who represented 'the decay of the highest form of capitalism', they had changed their policy, even in colonial countries still under colonial occupation. The 'character of the war' had undergone a 'qualitative' change, so they enthusiastically proclaimed : it had been converted from an 'imperialist war' into a 'people's war'. The energetic prosecution of such a war had become a 'patriotic duty', not only for them but for 'all patriots, in all countries'.

Britain, for her part, was only too keen to exploit the benefits accruing from this political somersault. British policy in this period, moulded by Churchill, therefore exploited the support of local communists in several Asian countries in the general war effort. There was some logic behind this apparently strange attitude : the war was at its most critical stage ; Britain was in alliance with the Soviet Union ; so if Churchill could co-ordinate his moves with Stalin, there was no reason why representatives of the British government in these countries could not adopt the same attitude towards local leaders of the communist movement. This logic had a compulsive force in countries like India and Iran. The dominant nationalist leadership had not yet endorsed the war and thrown its weight on the side of the Allies. It could not, for the simple reason that no concessions were offered by Britain. In India, Gandhi, Nehru and the entire nationalist leadership were imprisoned. In Iran, Reza Shah had had to abdicate. The communists thus appeared to be the only trustworthy allies.

The Shah received weekly reports from his security services on the consequences of this new turn in British policy towards communists in Iran. These reports pointed out that the Anglo-Iranian Oil Company was deliberately encouraging communists to set up a broad-based political party to help the Allies in mobilising Iranian popular support for the war. Mostafa Fateh, a high official of the Company, was one of the principal organisers of this new political party. He was readily supported by a group of communists and leftists who had won their freedom as a result of the Shah's amnesty. The new party was called the Tudeh party.

The Tudeh published its first manifesto in September 1941. The slogans of anti-fascism were writ large throughout. It was known that the Tudeh had the backing both of Britain and the Soviet Union. Its apparently broad-based programme, and its claim that it represented a united front of all anti-fascist and nationalist elements, sounded unexceptionable, besides being highly convenient. Many nationalists who joined its ranks did not share the Marxist convictions of its hard-core leadership, and even those who believed in constitutional monarchy saw no reason why they should keep away from its activities. Suleiman Mirza Eskandari, a former leader of the Democratic Party and well known supporter of constitutional monarchy, was chosen to head this united front. Despite all this, the Tudeh, from the beginning, was merely a revival of the Communist Partly previously banished from open political activity by Reza Shah. It held its first public demonstration on Friday, February 3, 1942, the anniversary of the death of Dr Taghi Erani, founder of the Iranian Communist Party.

In the initial stages, the Tudeh received all the encouragement it needed from the Anglo-Iranian Oil Company. The confidential reports submitted to the Shah emphasised that the first nucleus of the Tudeh was the work not of Soviet communists but of British agents. Several members of the party were given employment in the Company's service. The new newspapers which sprung up like mushrooms all over the country, and which were directly controlled by the Party, were financed by the Company. Even the organisation of trade unions on a national scale by the Party was encouraged by the Company, a step which it must have regretted in 1949–50 when the Tudeh used these very unions to destroy the Company's previously undisputed power in Khuzistan.[3]

The success of such a politically united front was inevitable while its improbable patrons dominated the country, and was accelerated by the defeats of the Nazi armies in the winter of 1942–3. Many 'hundreds of intellectuals who had been enthusiastic supporters of fascism' a Tudeh historian was to write later, 'realised their errors, and joined the Tudeh party'.[4]

[3] Shamim, pp. 22 to 25.

[4] Bozorg, Alavi, *Kaempfendes Iran* (Berlin, 1955), p. 70, quoted by Laqueur in *The Soviet Union and the Middle East*, p. 132.

The myth of Nazi invincibility collapsed in Asia in general and Iran in particular after the Stalingrad débâcle. The Tudeh reaped the harvest of the belief that the Soviets had now in turn become invincible.[5]

The Tudeh, from its inception, consisted of an inner and an outer circle. The leadership was firmly controlled by the communists. The strength and power of this leadership came to be greatly enhanced by the addition of some thousands of cadres which effectively converted the Party into a mass movement. The outer circle, which comprised a strange assortment of interests, was specifically a phenomenon of the occupation. Some nationalists who genuinely believed that the defeat of the Axis Powers would lead to real freedom and true democracy all over the world belonged to this outer circle, but the others were strange bedfellows for the communists. Their reactionary outlook was notorious : many of them were attached to the discredited Qajar dynasty ; others, such as the feudal landlords and tribal chiefs, saw the last chance of regaining their power in the conditions of anarchy which they hoped the party would succeed in creating. The existence of these two circles was to lead to important consequences for the independence of Iran throughout the next decade, and especially when Dr Mohammad Mossadeq became Prime Minister.

Although the Tudeh was the most powerful of the organised parties to appear after the occupation, some other parties are also worthy of note. The platform of both the *Eradeh Melli* and *Edelat* parties centred on the preservation of constitutional monarchy and the national constitution. They had their own newspapers ; they, too, organised demonstrations and, later, found representation in the *majlis*. Besides them, two small groups with fascist tendencies also entered the political life of the country. The rise of these political parties and increase in

[5] For further discussion on this point, see Laqueur, pp. 132–4.

the number of newspapers further unsettled the precarious stability of the *majlis*. Sharp and often unprincipled attacks on government personnel undermined popular confidence, while the newspapers secured wide circulations and influence. In a short time, senior government officials, members of the *majlis* and even Cabinet ministers, came under pressure from journalists and street politicians.

The Shah watched these new developments with growing uneasiness. He was astounded at the potential chaos they could cause if allowed to go uncontrolled. As he later wrote: 'One of my first acts as king had been to affirm the rebirth of constitutional democracy. Yet such chaos had come to the country's political life that perhaps it would have been understandable if, at that juncture, I had become permanently disillusioned with the democratic process. Fortunately, for the country and for me, my political convictions had by then become firmly rooted so that threatening developments could not easily scare me into abandoning the principles of such men as Thomas Jefferson, principles I was determined to follow.'[6]

Besides the degeneration which had begun to afflict the political life of the country, the Shah had to tackle several other problems. The war and occupation, as he had feared, had led to economic anarchy. The cost of living had continued to rise and by the end of 1942, inflation had increased prices by nearly four hundred per cent. Since all channels of foreign trade were effectively blocked by the occupation, the scarcity of goods became extremely pressing. The supply of wheat and rice from the northern provinces, which normally helped to feed Tehran, was stopped by the Russians, who quietly diverted the supplies northwards to their own country. The Allied powers had requisitioned all transport facilities for their own use so that, even when there was sufficient food in one area, a

[6] *Mission*, p. 77.

neighbouring area would starve because there was no means of transporting the surplus. Many local traders exploited this situation : the wealthy and the merchants began to hoard food and other commodities. The epidemic of greed and insecurity was bound to spread to the rural areas, where peasants with surplus grain refused to part with it, at the instigation of the Tudeh. Profiteering and speculation dominated the commercial life of the urban centres, giving rise to occasional bread riots.

That the Tudeh should seek to take advantage of this economic and political chaos was natural. However, the Shah was shocked by what could only be considered the callous attitude of his new Allies. They did little or nothing to fulfil their commitments under the Tripartite Treaty to render economic assistance to Iran. True, Britain, at least, was not in a position to do much. She could send food to Iran only from India, and some wheat did arrive from the Punjab. However, India herself was in the throes of a terrible famine and in one province alone, Bengal, two and a half million peasants died of starvation in the winter of 1942–3. The Russians were in no better position but, on the other hand, they did not seem to want to exert themselves in any manner to assist Iran at this stage. They argued that, even after the victory at Stalingrad, the Ukraine, their traditional granary, lay in German hands. Both Britain and Russia, of course, exacted first priority over what little food there was in Iran for the supply of their troops under the terms of the Tripartite Treaty.

Against this depressing background, the Allies did not hesitate to make extraordinary demands on Iran. Not being in a position to honour their commitments under the Tripartite Treaty, they did not suffer from any sense of shame in making various demands inconsistent both with the letter and the spirit of the Treaty. The Soviet command peremptorily required that Iranian munition factories should be surrendered.

The Russians wanted to dismantle them and remove the machinery to the Soviet Union. The British command, not to be outdone, 'requested' Iran in a more polite manner to hand over the Iranian army's 105 mm. artillery. The Prime Minister, not knowing how to handle these demands, consulted the Shah ; and prolonged and painful negotiations followed. Both the Russians and the British representatives brought the greatest possible pressure to bear upon him to surrender to their demands, but he refused to give in and, with great difficulty, managed to prevent these confiscations.[7]

Every attempt of the Allied powers to exact some concession or other from Iran was accompanied by unruly demonstrations organised by the political parties, mainly the Tudeh, in support of their patrons. When the Shah refused to dissolve the *majlis*, as Britain had demanded at the time of the currency incident, political supporters of Britain staged violent demonstrations. Even then the Shah would not give in : Britain, in a rather unsubtle manœuvre, took the extraordinary step of ordering troops to the capital which they had evacuated earlier under the provisions of the Tripartite Treaty. Even the simplest Iranian could see that this was an attempt to blackmail the Shah and *majlis*.

The Shah withstood these numerous and repeated pressures. He has described his feelings during this period : 'During the occupation I was full of sorrow and had many sleepless nights. I opposed it [the occupation] both in principle and practice for, to me, it seemed a wholly needless infringement of our independence and sovereignty. On every side I saw the miseries and suffering of our citizens, brought on by the economic and other policies adopted, and at the same time was revolted by the way in which some wealthy Persians became yet more bloated, in utter disregard of the welfare of their country.'[8]

[7] *Mission*, p. 78.   [8] Ibid. p. 78.

The Shah clung to his faith in the design which he had devised for a new Iran. There were moments when he was restless. The thought that he was ruler of a nation which was poverty-stricken and ridden with class privilege disgusted him. Yet his mind was constantly engaged with the problems of his people. His earlier conviction that the exclusion of the peasantry and the working people from the benefits of modern civilisation must be ended was strengthened when this exclusion became even more rigid in the years of occupation. Again and again, he returned to the fundamental problems of ignorance, super-stition and poverty among his people. His only escape to a world of hope and optimism was to perfect the design for a new Iran which was his primary passion.

CHAPTER TEN

The Tehran Conference

THE Shah watched the progress of the war closely, though his main energies were devoted to solving numerous problems posed by the policies of the British and the Russians, and the increasing internal political and economic chaos. With his military training, he kept himself fully informed of events on the four principal war fronts — Russia, North Africa, Italy and the Pacific zone. Each day, he spent considerable time poring over maps of these areas, and argued with his military advisers on the wisdom or otherwise of the belligerents' moves.

By the summer of 1943, he had little doubt as to the ultimate outcome of the war. Hitler had gambled dangerously on a lightning victory in the east and had lost. Like any losing gambler, he was now raising his stakes, and his losses increased accordingly. He had thrown more than three-quarters of his troops into a bid to stem the tide of Soviet counter-attacks. The Shah knew that the prospects of a Second Front, though agreed on by the western Allies, were not particularly bright. Yet after a study of the balance of military power, he had come to the conclusion that the situation was no longer complex or even uncertain. The end of the era of Nazi supremacy was already discernible. A new and powerful military machine had been forged by Stalin which had given the Russians new confidence and increased international prestige. Stalin was certain, sooner rather than later, to demand political dividends for his military achievements in any post-war settlement.

Western leaders *en route* for and returning from Moscow usually spent several days in Tehran. The Shah gathered valuable information either through direct discussions with them or through talks held by the Prime Minister and Foreign Minister with these visiting dignitaries on his instructions. Some of the secret information which he thus collected added to his worries. With victory in sight, the wartime Allies were now beginning to engage in a classic game of power politics. Each Ally was now exercising such power as it commanded to secure future territorial benefits. All of them proceeded on the assumption that their approaching triumph of arms over the Axis powers *ipso facto* granted them some form of divine right to decide the fate of the entire world.

The Shah knew what this meant in practical terms for the smaller nations : yet another division of the unhappy and ravaged world into spheres of influence. By the autumn of 1943, he had realised that new tensions dominated the relations between Britain, the United States and the Soviet Union. Stalin had taken the initiative in this by demanding an immediate but harsh peace with Germany. Both Churchill and Roosevelt still insisted that ' pastoralisation ', which had unleashed two world wars within a generation, was a better solution. The concept of the dismemberment of the Third Reich was already taking root in the combined diplomacy of the Allied powers. A summit meeting between Churchill, Roosevelt and Stalin appeared imminent.

The Iranian Ambassadors in London and Washington had already reported to the Shah on Stalin's agreement to meet Roosevelt and Churchill to evolve an outline plan for the future shape of the post-war community of nations. Molotov, on Stalin's behalf, had sounded out his counterparts in Britain and the United States as to the new division of Europe into spheres of influence. Stalin had already decided which countries were to fall within the Soviet sphere. Soon after the Russian Revolution, the west had created a *cordon sanitaire* of anti-communist regimes around the perimeter of the Soviet Union. To Stalin this was a scheme of encirclement. Hitler had mounted his invasion of the Soviet Union from the very countries lying in this belt, and had thereby lent credence to Stalin's charge that the whole scheme was no more than a poorly disguised threat to Russia. He now wanted to turn the tables on his anti-communist Allies from the west, and bluntly asked that these countries, bordering on the south-western frontiers of the Soviet Union, should be treated as falling within the Soviet sphere of influence. His claims extended to all the Balkan countries, and the western Allies had not rejected this proposal. The Shah knew that they were in no position to reject it since Stalin's armies had borne the brunt of the most savage fighting in the war. Churchill had, however, prepared a counter-plan for a joint Anglo-American-Soviet sphere of influence over this area. In the autumn of 1943, this had only a marginal chance of being accepted by Roosevelt.[1]

Though talks at the Allied Foreign Ministers' Conference in Moscow in October 1943 were limited to the subject of Russia's southern frontiers in Europe, according to the Shah's information, he quickly realised that the premise on which the Russian demand was founded could be dangerous for Iran. The principle of securing the Soviet Union against future invasions from the south could easily be extended to the south-eastern frontiers of Russia, in Asia. If this happened, Iran

---

1 Most of the phases of the Stalinist policies have now been documented and published. For a concise analysis of this policy, see Deutscher, Isaac, *Stalin, a political biography,* Oxford Paperbacks (London, 1961), pp. 500–502.

The Tehran Conference: with Churchill

The Tehran Conference: with Roosevelt

would be compelled to undergo partition once again. The Allies, intoxicated by victory, could easily dispense with the independence of Iran supposedly guaranteed under the Tripartite Treaty. They could either agree to her being wholly within the Soviet sphere of influence, or partition her territories. It was only natural for the Shah to remember that this had happened before, and could happen again. His task was to prevent such a calamity at all costs.

The Shah found an opportunity of bringing Iran, and his own personality, into the mainstream of international politics in November 1943, when Roosevelt, Churchill and Stalin became his guests in Tehran. The Foreign Ministers of the three Powers had met in Moscow from October 19 to 31 and had agreed upon a joint declaration concerning future Allied measures. The Shah had succeeded in persuading Anthony Eden, then British Foreign Secretary, to recognise Iran's role in the struggle for Allied victory. On his way to Moscow, Eden had publicly stated : 'In England all the people are indebted to the invaluable assistance of Iran in achieving common objectives.'[2] The Moscow meeting of the three Foreign Ministers had prepared the way for the summit. It had also, with the concurrence of the Shah and the government of Iran, decided that the conference should take place in Tehran.

The vast Russian Embassy building in Tehran became the centre of this high-powered diplomacy and the focus of attention for an anxious world. President Roosevelt chose Stalin's Embassy in preference to his own smaller and less secure building for his stay. Though Churchill stayed at the British Legation, all the plenary and secret sessions of the conference

---

[2] Eden, during this talk had also stated : " It seems that Hitler has not read Sa'adi's book in which he says : ' Human beings are all [equal] members of the same body, who have the same origin in creation ' ; otherwise he would not have fallen into the present predicament." Shamim, p. 36.

were held at the Russian Embassy. The Shah had met Churchill in the summer of 1942 when the British leader was on his way to Moscow for his first meeting with Stalin. He had stopped for a couple of days in Tehran and the Shah had invited him to lunch. The meeting had been friendly and the two leaders had had a good discussion. 'I think I should record' the Shah later wrote : 'an interesting moment in the course of our talks. We were speaking of the Allied intention to invade Europe, to crush Hitler's armies. I suggested to Churchill that the Allies should strike at Italy first, consolidate their position there and then stage a massive invasion from the Balkans. As Churchill sat reflecting upon my proposal, I saw a strange light come into his eyes. At the time he made no comment upon my idea, but it was not far removed from his later well known plan for invading Europe by way of the 'soft underbelly'. No doubt, it was a coincidence that our minds had met in the same broad strategic conception. Had the plan been followed, the history of central Europe would have been very different.'[3]

The Tehran Conference lasted from November 28 to December 1, 1943. The Shah met all three leaders during these crucial days. Stalin visited the Shah at his palace. Roosevelt, because of his physical disability, and on the advice of his security men, did not leave the Russian Embassy, so the Shah went to see him there. Though Iran was not represented officially at the summit conference, the Shah freely discussed the international situation with the three leaders. His principal purpose was to gauge the intentions of his guests in so far as they affected their commitments under the Tripartite Treaty. His doubts on this question were increased by his knowledge of the as yet unrevealed agreement between them on a new Russian sphere of influence in the Balkans. Though he could not question them directly as to Russian

[3] *Mission*, p. 79.

intentions concerning Iran, and the attitude of Britain and the
United States towards them, all three leaders knew of the
Shah's chief concern. He could only emphasise, under the cir-
cumstances, the place of Iran in the future framework of the
United Nations, which the leaders of the anti-fascist coalition
were then discussing.

Churchill, Stalin and Roosevelt were all in an extremely
polite and cheerful mood. Stalin, for example, was keen to
reassure the young monarch and win him over. He offered
him a regiment of T34 tanks, then the terror of the Nazi
armies, and a squadron of fighter planes. He made this offer
when the Shah raised the question of the desperate shortage of
modern arms from which Iran then suffered, but nothing came
of it, for Stalin's gesture was accompanied by curious terms.
With the tanks and planes, he wanted to send Soviet officers
and other ranks to Iran. The tanks could be based only at
Qazvin, and the planes at Meshed. Till the end of an unspeci-
fied training period, the units were to be under the direct
command of the Soviet Chief of Staff in Moscow. The Shah
could not accept these conditions.[4]

Roosevelt too was very affable, and discussed many subjects
with the Shah, showing particular interest in re-afforestation as
a means of protecting agricultural land against the encroaching
desert. Indeed, he even told the Shah that once his presidential
term of office was over, he would return to Iran as an adviser on
re-afforestation. The geniality and sincerity shown during these
talks convinced the Shah that Roosevelt was an extraordinary
man who certainly meant what he said at that time. Of his
impressions of one of the greatest presidents of the United
States, the Shah wrote : 'His interest in this field was, of course,
well known, and the earnestness of his tone suggested that he
really meant it. Roosevelt gave me the impression of being

---

[4] *Mission*, p. 80 ; on Iranian suspicions, Arfa, p. 324.

in the long tradition of distinguished Westerners who have become enraptured with my country and its culture. While I profoundly disagreed with him on some aspects of foreign policy, I admired him in other ways ; and I am only sorry that his untimely death prevented his following up his welcome suggestion.'[5]

The Shah moved adroitly through the labyrinth of power politics, fully conscious of the stake of his own country in this, his first experience of international diplomacy. The three Allied leaders were involved in heated discussion over such wide issues as the nature of an armistice with Germany, the timing and locale of the Second Front, the frontiers of Poland and the fate of the Balkan countries. Against this background of pressing issues, extraordinary measures were called for if concrete commitments on the independence and prosperity of Iran were to be secured.

As soon as the dates of the Tehran Conference had been finalised, the Shah had instructed his Foreign Minister, Sa'ed, to prepare a draft of the memorandum to be submitted to the three Allied leaders through their respective Foreign Ministers. While approving the Foreign Ministry draft, he had carefully shortened it to include only the basic needs of Iran, which were summarised under three heads. He wanted, firstly, to remind these arbiters of the fate of nations of the efforts Iran had made to facilitate their approaching victory and of the hardships which her people had suffered as a result of the war and their collaboration with the Allies. The second point referred to the numerous verbal and written assurances of the Allies that not only the independence and territorial integrity of Iran were to be respected but also strengthened. Finally, in the third point, the visiting leaders were politely but unmistakably reminded of their principal undertaking, in accordance with the terms of

[5] *Mission*, p. 80.

the Tripartite Treaty, to hand over the management of the country to its rightful government. The Shah instructed the Foreign Minister to conclude this memorandum by expressing a hope that the three leaders would confirm these agreed points in a public declaration. The memorandum was submitted on November 29, the second day of the Conference.[6]

The Shah had instructed the Prime Minister, Ali Soheili, and the Foreign Minister to remain in close contact with the senior staff members of the three Great Powers throughout the conference. Soheili and Sa'ed had several meetings and discussions with Molotov, Eden and General Horley, Roosevelt's Special Envoy in Tehran. These deliberations centred around the main theme which the Shah discussed with Roosevelt, Stalin and Churchill, and which was clearly set out in the Foreign Minister's memorandum. The cumulative effect of the Shah's efforts was a decision on the part of his guests to make the desired declaration on their attitude to Iran. This declaration became the sheet-anchor of Iran's policy in the immediate post-war period, and especially during the bitter dispute with Stalin over Azerbaijan.

'The governments of the United States of America, the U.S.S.R. and the United Kingdom', it read, 'recognise the assistance which Iran has given in the prosecution of the War against the common enemy, particularly by facilitating the transportation of supplies from overseas to the Soviet Union.' It then went on to recognise the special economic difficulties which the war effort had caused in Iran and to pledge economic assistance. Finally, it outlined the future in these words : 'The governments of the United States, the U.S.S.R. and the United Kingdom are at one with the government of Iran in their desire for the maintenance of the independence, sovereignty and territorial integrity of Iran. They count upon the participation

[6] Shamim, pp. 38–9.

of Iran, together with all peace-loving nations, in the establishment of international peace, security and prosperity after the war, in accordance with the principles of the Atlantic Charter, to which all the four Governments have subscribed.'[7]

The Declaration of December 1 was received with great relief by the people of Iran who, as the Shah was to remember later, 'were filled with joy'. Their relief stemmed from the fact that they 'had been apprehensively wondering whether their homeland would regain its independence after the war',[8] and the Declaration could not have been more categoric on this particular point. Once again the Allied leaders had pledged their word of honour to evacuate their troops from Iran, and to restore her independence. Of course, the Shah was aware that this was no more than a diplomatic declaration ; but there was no other way in which he could obtain from the Allies a guarantee of the independence of his country. The Tehran Conference, by all accounts, seemed to have achieved considerable success in finding a common approach between the Allies. The record of its secret negotiations was as yet unavailable. Very few persons, outside the small group of Allied diplomats who participated in the plenary and secret sessions, knew of the undercurrents of antagonism which characterised the compromises that were reached. Even its participants could have hardly appreciated at the time that the warm climate of friendship engendered at Tehran would give place to the blizzard of the Cold War once Germany surrendered.

The Shah, through a combination of circumstances, had been a close spectator of this great contest of wills between the representatives of 'the Big Three'. It was a great experience for a young intellectual who had celebrated his twenty-fifth birthday only five weeks earlier. It was also a rewarding experience : he had set for himself certain basic objectives once he knew that

[7] For the full text see Shamim, pp. 39–41.   [8] *Mission*, p. 80.

the conference would be held at Tehran, and had achieved all of them by the time it ended. His country at least would not be a loser in the game of power politics of which this conference was the first round, however adversely it affected the Poles and the Balkan nations.

The Shah was the principal architect of Iranian strategy at Tehran. As later events proved, at least one of the three Allied leaders had other plans for Iran than those he had publicly supported. If the Shah had either taken a back seat or made diplomatic errors, the Declaration could easily have been shelved on Stalin's insistence. Had this happened, the Shah would have been in a weak position less than three years later when he had to confront Stalinist expansionism. His shrewd political understanding led him to believe that, in the winter of 1943, Stalin could neither advance his claims against Iran nor withdraw from his commitments under the Tripartite Treaty. It was this conviction which formed the basis of his proposal that the three Allied leaders must reiterate their pledge to Iran by the Declaration of December 1.

The Shah had good reason to believe that his 'country's travail was nearing its end'. The war appeared to be exhausting Nazi power. The main strength of the Nazi armies had been broken. Mussolini had fallen and by the time Hitler lost the Battle of the Kursk Bulge, Italy had been knocked out of the war. The three Allied leaders were optimistic : 'We came to Tehran full of hope and determination, and leave this place in truly perfect friendship in spirit and intention.' Little did the Shah know that his country was far from the end of its troubles, and that a new struggle was about to unfold. 'What had gone before was as nothing compared with what was soon to come.' 9

9 *Mission*, p. 81.

CHAPTER ELEVEN

The Conflict with Russia

THE Thirteenth *majlis* had been prorogued on November 13, before the Tehran Conference met. The Shah had already ordered elections for the Fourteenth *majlis* when the decision to hold the summit conference in Tehran was announced. The election campaign was thus in full swing at the time of the conference, but was halted for a week to permit Churchill, Stalin and Roosevelt some peace. Once they had left, the campaign was resumed, and immediately the first clear signs of the incipient conflict with Russia became visible. The Russian authorities in the northern provinces had already taken an undue interest in the choice of candidates. Now they directly intervened in two constituencies during polling and their efforts, not surprisingly, led to the election of one of their nominees as deputy for Bandar Pahlavi.[1] The Prime Minister could do little to prevent Soviet intervention on behalf of Tudeh candidates in several other areas, but despite this, the Tudeh secured only nine seats in the *majlis*. Six of its deputies were elected from the northern areas of Azerbaijan, Gilan and Mazanderan and two from Khorassan. The ninth candidate was elected from the industrial city of Isfahan.[2]

The Shah opened the *majlis* on February 26, 1944. Its first task was to examine the credentials of its newly elected deputies.

[1] Arfa, p. 323.   [2] Shamim, p. 43.

It found those of Jaffar Pishevari, the Tudeh deputy from Tabriz, defective. The matter was voted upon and by a majority Pishevari was debarred from taking his seat. From this moment began the Tudeh revolt against the constitutional government and monarchy. The remaining eight Tudeh deputies immediately launched a well organised plan to disrupt legislation, as a result of which the Fourteenth *majlis* was to become the most tumultuous and troublesome session in the parliamentary history of Iran.

The Shah had appointed Mohammad Sa'ed, the former Foreign Minister, to replace Ali Soheili as Prime Minister when the latter resigned on March 16. Ten days later, Sa'ed's cabinet was sworn in, with Sa'ed himself keeping the portfolio of Foreign Affairs. His cabinet, which remained in power for only seven months, faced constant opposition from the Tudeh, which by this time had shed any pretence of being a united front movement and now openly revealed its communist principles. One of its aims was to oppose existing governments by violence, and from this period it never concealed its policy of overthrowing any cabinet which did not prove subservient to its purposes. It instructed its deputies to wreck the *majlis* 'from within', and this obstructionist attitude destroyed all prospects of parliament's smooth functioning, as well as shortening the lives of several cabinets.

The Shah saw that the violent policies of the Tudeh were linked with the change in favour of the Soviet Union in the fortunes of the War. The Soviet offensive had opened on February 14 and had, within the first few days, breached powerful German fortifications and advanced rapidly. The three-year-old siege of Leningrad was lifted; troops on the Volkhov front defeated Nazi forces in the Novgorod area; and by June 21, the Soviet offensive was in full swing throughout the front.

Now that his troops were penetrating beyond their frontiers, Stalin decided to turn his military advantages to political ends. The first sign of his new expansionism was, significantly enough, a demand on Iran. He sent Sergei Kaftaradze, then assistant foreign commissar, to Tehran with a proposal for a Soviet oil concession over the entire northern regions. Moscow was willing to offer 49 per cent of the revenues from these new oil-fields to Tehran, keeping 51 per cent for itself. Iran was not unfamiliar with the Russian plan to create for themselves a rival oil empire in the north to counterbalance the British complex in the south. This Russian plan had been frustrated during the Czarist period : now, once again, the same proposal was revived by Stalin ; but Kaftaradze was too blunt. He made it clear that the Soviet Union would back its demand for the northern oil concession with all the political and military power at its disposal.[3]

The Shah resented the method by which Stalin had made this demand, and was also aghast at its arbitrary commercial terms. Iran was being treated like a colony, and Stalin must be shown that he had made a grave mistake. Once the resistance of the Shah's government to the Russian proposal became known, the Tudeh took the matter into the streets. The first demonstration in support of granting oil concessions to Russia was staged in Tehran on October 27, when few people were surprised to see that the demonstrators were accompanied by Soviet soldiers in trucks.[4] Stalin had never been the man to take no for an answer. The Tudeh, on the other hand, needed to convince Iranian nationalists : it therefore based its case on the idea that the Soviets and Britain should maintain a parity of influence in Iran. Since there was a British oil empire in the south, a similar Soviet complex in the north was not only justified but essential. This proved to be the greatest political

[3] Arfa, p. 329.   [4] Shamim, pp. 45-6.

mistake which the Tudeh committed. Its leadership had failed
to take into account the basic changes which the war in general
and the Shah's firm policies in particular had brought about in
the political life of the country. The concept of maintaining
a parity of influence between Britain and Russia might have
appealed to influential Iranians in earlier days. It was an anachronism in 1944. The minds of the people at that time were
preoccupied with a more pleasant concept — of an Iran where
no foreign influence would be tolerated.

The Tudeh tried to fight the matter out in the *majlis*, but most
of the deputies supported the Shah, and even those who drew
their inspiration from the Anglo-Iranian Oil Company were
bound to oppose the grant of the northern concession to the
Russians. The *majlis* was not content with an expression of
opinion. It passed a resolution which deprived the government
of the right to negotiate any grants of oil concessions with any
foreign power. It declared that if the Soviet Union was in
need of oil, the government of Iran would happily supply it by
undertaking its own exploration projects in the northern provinces.[5]

While the Soviet authorities and the Tudeh increased pressure
on Iran, the war ended with the defeat of Germany and surrender of Japan on August 15, 1945. The Shah immediately
reminded his Allies of the provisions of the Tripartite Treaty
dealing with the speedy withdrawal of their troops. The latest
date by which British and Russian troops would have to be
evacuated was February 15, 1946. Some other issues also
were still outstanding. In accordance with the agreements
between Iran and the Allies, Iran had to be compensated in
monetary and economic matters — large sums of Iranian currency had been advanced to the Allies to defray their expenses

[5] Shamim, p. 46. This resolution was mainly inspired by Dr Mohammad Mossadeq.

in Iran. They had also to compensate Iran for damage done to the railways, roads and other transport installations, and agreed to render this compensation in gold. Iran having fulfilled her wartime commitments, the time had now arrived for her Allies to honour their own.

The Shah announced the end of the war in a radio broadcast to his people on August 16, 1945. At the same time he issued instructions for the preparation of plans to secure the independence of the country and the fulfilment of Allied commitments. His broadcast made several issues clear both to his people and to his Allies : 'We all know what wounds and injuries have been inflicted on the world by the war and what efforts are needed to make up for them. Now that this great fire has been extinguished, and we have obtained our objective in establishing peace and tranquillity, I participate happily in this celebration and express my felicitation to all nations, particularly the Five Great Powers, and bring tidings of joy and happiness to the Iranian nation which has emerged proudly and victoriously.'[6] Iran had contributed towards this victory to her utmost. The Western Allies had sent to the Soviet Union through Iran more than five million tons of supplies — nearly half America's and Canada's aggregate overseas war shipments. The Trans-Iranian Railway had carried more than half of this total, and the rest had been sent by road. The Iranians had operated their own fleet of more than four thousand lorries. They had also supplied labour for the numerous transport operations of the Allied powers.[7]

The Shah, though primarily concerned with Iran, was already thinking of broader questions. On August 22, 1945, six days after the termination of the war, he said, in the course of a speech : 'Iran is proud to have co-operated for the success of her Allies and all the Allied nations within the limits of the

[6] Shamim, p. 47.   [7] *Mission*, p. 78.

means at its disposal. We feel certain that the life and wealth which have been sacrificed unsparingly in this way will lead to the establishment of a lasting peace under the auspices of the United Nations Organisation, and will safeguard the respect for the rights of all nations, great or small, strong or weak.'[8]

The Shah welcomed the establishment of the United Nations Organisation. He believed that if the United Nations proved effective smaller nations could now be spared the sort of experiences Iran had undergone : but at the same time he was no mere visionary. He accepted that the character of the United Nations would be shaped largely by the Great Powers. A month later he expressed this belief in a Press interview : 'The existence of the United Nations Organisation is a source of confidence for the future, and now the preservation of world peace and everything in general depends on whether the Great Allied nations can live together in a friendly manner and believe in preventing further bloodshed.'[9] Thus the Shah, then twenty-six, had warned, even if indirectly, against the possibility and the dangers of a division among the Allies. His warning was to come true and, tragically enough, it was his country and Asia as a whole which were to be involved in this new division. By February 15, 1946, British and American troops had been evacuated, but the Soviet Union refused to follow the example of its wartime Allies. It produced the lame pretext that it had met with 'hostile treatment' from the government of Iran and the Shah, who had rejected the proposals for oil concessions in the north. This was the first public indication of the coming dissolution of the anti-fascist coalition.

The Stalinist attempt to continue the occupation of the northern areas had been fully backed by the Tudeh. In the latter part of the war, the Soviet authorities had treated the northern areas under their military control as if they were a

[8] Shamim, p. 47. [9] Ibid. p. 45.

separate state. They had taken every possible measure to destroy the authority and influence of the central government in Azerbaijan, Gilan and Mazanderan. The weakening of the authority of Tehran had given unprecedented power to the Tudeh, now working under Soviet military and political patronage. It had succeeded in disrupting the administrative machinery and corrupting several members of the armed forces. In August 1945, the Tudeh forcibly took over several government buildings in Tabriz. In support of the Tudeh operation, the Russian army confined Iranian troops to their barracks. A separate state of Azerbaijan was about to be established.[10]

The Shah could not tolerate this situation. He decided to send troops to re-establish law and order in the northern provinces in general and Azerbaijan in particular. In November 1945, he ordered troops of the Imperial Army to set out from Tehran, but when these troops reached Qazvin the Soviet forces, stationed at Sharifabad, halted them. This Soviet move was a challenge to the authority of the Shah and the government of Iran, besides constituting an attack on the sovereign rights of the country. That this was no isolated act, but part of a carefully planned scheme, became clear with the quick political reaction of the Tudeh in Azerbaijan. They changed their name to the 'Democratic Party', and were speedily placed in control of the province by the Soviet authorities. By mid-November, their armed partisans had set out to crush the resistance of the few vocal adversaries to their separatist policy. They attacked police posts, and completely cut off Tabriz and Azerbaijan from the rest of Iran.

The Democrats proclaimed their real separatist purpose on December 11. A provincial 'National Assembly', composed of 101 deputies, was announced. All its members were chosen by the Democrats, but they still found it essential to maintain a

[10] *Mission*, p. 115.

façade. They argued that technically the establishment of the separatist 'National Assembly of Azerbaijan' was legal because the Assembly did not constitute any expression or declaration of independence on the part of Azerbaijan. It merely represented a desire for autonomy within the Iranian state, and thus fell within the provisions of the Iranian constitution concerning provincial councils. This façade collapsed when the Assembly nationalised the banks. It also took other measures which further emphasised its secessionist tendencies : it stipulated that only the local Turki language should be used in schools and for official business ; and selected Jaffar Pishevari, the communist leader who had spent most of his life in the Soviet Union, to act as 'Prime Minister' of the province of Azerbaijan.[11]

The Shah protested to the Soviet Embassy in Tehran and to Moscow, but the Russian response was totally negative. An open clash could no longer be avoided. In place of the hoped for era of peace and tranquillity, a period of what he later described as the 'tumultuous years' had set in.

[11] For a short summary of the events in Azerbaijan and details of the Kurdish Secessionist movement, see Eagleton, William, *The Kurdish Republic of 1946* (London, 1963). For the events described here see pp. 59–60.

CHAPTER TWELVE

Northern Revolt

IN the December of 1945 it was not easy for any small nation
to challenge the will of Stalin. He was at the height of his
power and prestige both at home and in Asia. Even the political climate was dominated by a sense of genuine admiration
for the heroism displayed by the Soviet forces under his command. Few Western statesman were willing to dispute his
claim to political compensation for the enormous sacrifices
of the Soviet people. The leaders of the Western alliance
had reluctantly come to recognise as legitimate the demands
which Stalin made for the re-organisation of the frontiers of
various central and eastern European states. After Tehran, the
process of adjustment to what Stalin considered the national
interests of the Soviet Union had continued at Yalta and
Potsdam.

The insurrection in Azerbaijan had been plausibly contrived.
The Pishevari regime had not claimed the *de jure* status of
an independent government. Indeed, it had falsely insisted
that the new political structure in Azerbaijan had been created
in accordance with the Iranian Constitution. It had also
sought an alliance with a group of separatist Kurds known
as the Komala faction. The Kurdish problem as such had
never existed for Iran. The Kurds in Turkey and Iraq,
on the other hand, periodically rose in revolt, demanding

118

The Tehran Conference: with Stalin

Planning the New Iran

the creation of a Kurdish state. The Iranian Kurds had only once before tried to follow suit, when Reza Shah had quickly suppressed their revolt. Now, under the undisguised patronage and active guidance of loyal Stalinists, and in alliance with the Democrats in Azerbaijan, the Kurds were encouraged by the Komala faction to defy the authority of the central government.[1]

The Shah had to try to assess the basic ambitions of the Stalinist regime in relation to Iran. It was clear to him that the so-called autonomous government of Azerbaijan was no more than an expanded and more ominous repetition of the Soviet Republic of Gilan. The Gilan Republic had been an experiment which the Comintern wanted to try out before it extended its activities to the whole of Iran. It had failed. Now a similar experiment was being made not only in Azerbaijan, but also in Kurdistan. Clearly, the Soviet policy was gradually to create two new 'Soviet Republics' which would ultimately be absorbed within the Soviet federation. Once the process of Iranian territorial disintegration had begun, Pishevari and his colleagues were expected to be able to stage a national revolt throughout the country. The Tudeh had already secured mass support for itself among the working people. Thus the stakes were much higher than just the secession of Azerbaijan and Kurdistan.[2]

Having realised how dangerous it would be to let events in the north drift, the Shah turned to the Western Allies for support. The United States responded immediately. James Byrnes, then Secretary of State, publicly expressed the opinion of the Truman Administration that the protests lodged by the

---

[1] The term 'Komala faction' really signifies *Komala i Zhian i Kurdistan*, meaning the Committee of the Resurrection of Kurdistan, which was set up on September 16, 1942, near Mahabad in Kurdistan by a group of Kurdish secessionists led by Haji Daud.   [2] *Mission*, p. 114.

government of Iran against Soviet support for the separatists in Azerbaijan and Kurdistan were justified, and tried to persuade Molotov of the justice of the Iranian case. Molotov was unwilling to budge from the position which Stalin had taken. Ernest Bevin, then British Foreign Secretary, sought to break the developing deadlock by proposing a committee of representatives of the three Allied governments to consider the general position of Iran and settle privately the questions of Azerbaijan and Kurdistan.[3]

The British and American Ambassadors brought this information to the Shah, who told them that it was essential his people should know of the British proposals. Accordingly, he instructed the Prime Minister to announce this new development in the *majlis*. As expected, the *majlis* reacted adversely, rejecting the Bevin proposal and refusing to permit the future of Iran to be the subject of a committee decision by the three Allied powers. Its message to London, Washington and Moscow was candid. The war was over, and Iran had done what she could for its success : the Allied governments must now honour their commitments. There was no scope for any 'negotiations', for the issues involved were beyond the pale of any doubt. The Soviet position was plainly indefensible.

The Shah had brought the issue into the open because he wanted the Western Allies to realise the depth of Iranian national resentment at the prospect of becoming once again a pawn in international power politics. The popular reaction having been established, the Shah then instructed the government to raise the issue before the newly-founded Security Council of the United Nations. In fact, the complaint of Iran against Soviet interference in her internal affairs was the first appeal by a small nation submitted to this highest forum of the new international organisation. It also proved to be its first

[3] Shamim, p. 56.

test. The head of the Iranian delegation at the United Nations invoked Article 35 of the Charter on January 11, 1946. Eleven days later, the Council, after listening to Iranian and Soviet representatives, recommended that the two governments concerned should solve their differences by direct negotiations.

Meanwhile, the Tudeh had marshalled all its resources for a campaign against the government. Large rallies were addressed by its leaders seeking support for the Soviet-inspired separatists in Azerbaijan and Kurdistan. The Fourteenth *majlis* became a platform for Tudeh attacks on any deputy who stood by the territorial integrity of the country. The government of the day, headed by Ebrahim Hakimi, eked out a precarious existence in the face of this furious onslaught for some days, but on January 20, as Soviet interference became an international issue, Hakimi resigned. His place was taken by Ahmad Qavam, who lost no time in submitting to Soviet pressure. On January 28 he sent a telegram to Stalin indicating his willingness to go to Moscow for direct negotiations, and left immediately in the expectation of solving the problem before any further discussion could take place in the Security Council. He was received by Stalin and Molotov with whom his negotiations lasted until March 8. Qavam made three main concessions to the Russians. He agreed to Soviet troops remaining in some districts of Iran for an indefinite period. He showed his readiness to recognise the 'internal independence' of Azerbaijan, and this constituted the heart of his main compromise proposal. The 'Prime Minister' of Azerbaijan was to act as 'Governor-General of the province'. The Pishevari regime was to forgo the pleasure of having its own ministers of education and foreign affairs, and had also to agree to a commander-in-chief appointed by the central government. Qavam further agreed that the separatist regime should keep 70 per cent of the tax revenue of the province and continue to use Turki as its official language, except for communications with the central government, which were to be conducted solely in Farsi. As a *quid pro quo* for this compromise, Qavam had wanted the Soviet government to waive its demand for a northern oil concession. Instead, he suggested that a joint Russo-Iranian company be formed to explore and produce oil in the north. The Soviet Union was to hold 51 per cent of the shares and Iran 49 per cent for the first twenty-five years, both parties to hold equal shares for the subsequent quarter century.[4]

While Qavam was engaged in these negotiations at Moscow, the day for the withdrawal of Soviet forces dawned on March 2, 1946. Stalin summoned Qavam to a meeting at which he announced that Soviet armies would withdraw only from the Khorassan and Semnan areas. On the evening of March 3, the Soviet forces, in a dramatic manœuvre, began to withdraw from Tabriz, but not in the direction of Russia. They moved instead towards Tehran and the Irano-Turkish frontiers. This was the first post-war Russian military move beyond their Asian frontiers. Within weeks, Stalin had sent tank and infantry units to reinforce the columns which had moved out of Tabriz. As part of this plan, he also deployed additional troops along the Soviet frontier with Turkey : simultaneously a sudden and virulent blast of propaganda was unleashed against Turkey.[5]

As part of his diplomatic surrender — which some western observers later evaluated as a cunning move in 'oriental' diplomacy — Qavam had agreed to withdraw the Iranian case from the agenda of the Security Council. This had pleased Stalin as much as it had irritated the Shah and the nation. It had been decided earlier, when Qavam left for Moscow, that if Iran could remove the Soviet presence from her northern provinces by making minor concessions, these should be offered. But

[4] Shamim, pp. 59–60.   [5] *Mission*, p. 116.

Qavam had far exceeded his brief. He had not been authorised to offer a withdrawal of the Iranian case from the Security Council. Such a capitulation would have completely destroyed the basis of Iran's argument that the Soviet Union had no right to interfere in the internal affairs of the country. Qavam probably took this step in order to appease both Stalin and his own fanatical followers at home, who had already created conditions of near chaos.[6]

Hossein Ala, one of the Shah's most trusted diplomats, was at this time Iran's Ambassador in Washington, and representative at the United Nations. Ala knew that the Shah would not agree to Qavam's proposals in general, and particularly the withdrawal of Iran's plea from the Council. Accordingly, he resolved to follow the Shah's instructions and defy Qavam's authority, believing it his duty to follow the policy of the Shah and the *majlis* rather than that of the Prime Minister, who seemed to have lost all sense of proportion in Moscow. Ala reported to the Security Council that direct negotiations between his country and the Soviet Union had failed, and the Shah immediately and publicly endorsed his action. With this announcement, the conflict intensified. The United States emerged on Iran's side. Harry S. Truman, the new President, believed in what at that time was called 'the strong line against Russia'. Truman sent a message to Stalin, couched in terms comparable with those of an ultimatum, demanding that Stalin honour his commitments under the Tripartite Treaty.

The conflict had shown on a worldwide stage that the Shah was no man of cardboard. He could not be bullied into surrender, even when Stalin had succeeded in bending the will of his Prime Minister. Pragmatist as he was, Stalin realised that insistence on the continued presence of Soviet troops in Iran gained him little but political dishonour. The Soviet reluctance

[6] *Mission*, p. 116; Shamim, p. 58.

to withdraw its forces from Iran, as agreed, had provoked a reaction of shocked disgust among Asian countries. Protests against Soviet policy and messages of support for the Shah were growing, and the Indian nationalists, despite their traditional admiration for the Soviet Union, were among the first to give vent to this feeling. Five days after Ala had carried out the Shah's instructions and defied Qavam, Andrei Gromyko, the Soviet representative at the Security Council, dramatically announced that all Soviet forces would be withdrawn from Iran in five or six weeks 'if no unforeseen circumstances occur'.

This was a victory for the Shah, but its extent was limited. Qavam clearly believed that the security of Iran lay in establishing friendly relations with Stalin. 'He seemed to be under the influence of the Russians.'[7] Meanwhile the term of the Fourteenth *majlis* had ended on March 12, so that Qavam was now free to pursue his peculiar policy of appeasement toward the Tudeh and the Azerbaijan separatists at home, and of surrender to Stalinist expansionist policies abroad. The Shah had made no secret of his strong disagreement with this policy, and the differences between him and his Prime Minister increased daily. Qavam decided to force the issue : he sought an audience at which he declared that either the Shah should take all the decisions, or they should be left to him.

The Shah, above all, did not want to precipitate the collapse of constitutional democracy in Iran. There were enough indications to show that if Qavam was refused the powers he had requested the Tudeh would have taken to the streets and thrown the country into anarchy. The risks involved in any refusal to Qavam of the powers he had requested were therefore considerable. On the other hand, Stalin had already threatened to invoke the Soviet-Iranian Treaty of 1921 and to

[7] *Mission*, p. 116.

claim the right to send Soviet troops into the country. If he had done so, the Western Allies might or might not have rushed to Iran's aid. Even if they had, a new war on Iranian soil would have certainly ruined the country. The Shah needed to gather all his political wisdom in dealing with the situation. It was difficult to assess what Qavam might do in furtherance of his policies if he were given complete authority. On the other hand, the people of the country would certainly not tolerate any further surrender of Iran's national honour. With all these factors in mind, the Shah decided to grant Qavam's request for complete authority during the interim period until the Fifteenth *majlis* was convened.

Having secured these powers, Qavam signed an agreement with the Soviet Union on April 4. The Russians undertook to withdraw their troops and in return Qavam was to place the proposal for a joint Russo-Iranian oil company before the Fifteenth *majlis* for approval within seven months. Both sides agreed that the question of Azerbaijan was an internal matter and that the issue could be settled through negotiations between the 'government' of Azerbaijan and the central government. Qavam clearly considered this to be a great achievement. He appeared to believe that the agreement had solved all the problems, and welcomed the approval he received for it from the Tudeh and its allies. The Azerbaijan separatists celebrated while Pishevari, his confidence restored, made new demands. He required of Qavam that officers who had deserted the Iranian army and joined his forces should be reinstated in the Imperial Army and that officers commissioned by his regime should also be accepted. Qavam readily agreed to this, and approached the Shah for his assent. The Shah was unwilling to give this and the audience was stormy. Indeed the Shah was so angered by the proposed agreement that he told Qavam that he would rather cut off his own arm than affix his signature to

such a document.[8] Qavam, undeterred by the Shah's indigna-
tion, proceeded with the execution of the policy he had adopted
by removing all restraints on the Tudeh. He also invited Pishevari to Tehran and attended the reception organised by the
Tudeh for the Azerbaijan separatist leader. At Pishevari's
invitation, Qavam sent his deputy Prime Minister to Tabriz
and publicly endorsed the policies of the regime.

The Shah was becoming anxious. He could see that the road
Qavam had taken would lead to the eventual dismemberment
of the Iranian state. Though Soviet troops had withdrawn by
May 9, they had left a powerful base for future military activities in Azerbaijan. Tabriz radio had become a fountain of
vicious propaganda against all those who would not support
the pro-Soviet policies of Qavam. It continuously urged the
working people of the rest of the country to rise in revolt so
that the whole of Iran could benefit from the example of Azerbaijan. The Tudeh had transformed itself into the stormy
petrel of what its propagandists called the 'coming revolution
in Iran'. Hardly a day passed without clashes between the
Tudeh and the police in such industrial areas as Mazanderan,
Gilan, Isfahan and Khuzistan. Since there were three Tudeh
ministers in the Qavam government, party followers ignored
the framework of law and violated order at will.

The Shah warned the Prime Minister against the increasing
deterioration in the condition of the country, but Qavam considered himself its saviour, and ignored these warnings even
though he listened to them courteously enough. Qavam considered himself to be in a very strong political position, thanks
to his Tudeh support. Stalin was happy with him, and everything indicated that both Washington and London thought of
him as a 'cunning oriental devil'. As an eyewitness of this
period has written : 'Though not openly saying so, the British

[8] *Mission*, p. 117.

and Americans appeared to be favourable to Qavam, whom they considered able to maintain the balance between their interests and those of the U.S.S.R.'[9]   Mozaffar Firuz, a politician closely associated with the Tudeh, had joined him, and become his deputy.

In September the progressive disintegration of the country and the domination of the Qavam government by Firuz and his Tudeh allies prompted several tribal chiefs to rise against the government.   Earlier rumours had it that circles close to the Anglo-Iranian Oil Company were planning to detach Khuzistan from Iran and annexe it to Iraq.[10]   On September 20, all the tribes of Fars, the Persian Gulf Coast and eastern Khuzistan rose against the government.   The rebels sent an ultimatum to Qavam demanding the dismissal of the Tudeh ministers.   They wanted the government to outlaw the Tudeh, adopt a more nationalist policy and grant autonomy to Fars.   By October, the poison of separatism, brewed in Azerbaijan, had spread to the southern and western parts of the country.

The Shah was no longer willing to remain an inactive witness of the tragic drama now unfolding.   On October 15, he summoned Qavam to an audience, which proved brief.   The Shah categorically instructed Qavam to dissolve his cabinet and form another, in which the Tudeh was not represented.   The next day he issued a *Firman* decreeing new elections.   He was not going to permit the slow death of Iran.

[9] Arfa, p. 361.   [10] Ibid. p. 373.

CHAPTER THIRTEEN

Stalin Steps Down

'WHEN I ordered new elections throughout the country', the Shah later wrote about this first step in the liberation of Azerbaijan, 'that was exactly what I meant — and the country plainly included the province of Azerbaijan.'[1] The royal decree instructing the government to prepare for a general election was meant to end separatism. Nobody could doubt its essential purpose : it was a blow to the pipe-dreams of the tribal chiefs in south and west Iran ; it served as a warning to the patrons of those chiefs ; and above all it conveyed the Shah's decision to demolish the myth of the 'autonomous republics' of Azerbaijan and Kurdistan. The separatists in the north, their backers at home and abroad and the Western Allies were intended to realise that there was only one government in Iran.

The separatists in Azerbaijan were not slow to recognise the mood and motive of the Shah. The Tudeh too realised that the end of the 'autonomous republics' in the north would be the beginning of the end of its power and influence. First reaction came from Tabriz radio, which declared that there could be no elections in Azerbaijan or Kurdistan. The royal decree was totally rejected by the Pishevari regime as soon as it was issued. The regime would not permit the imperial army to enter Azerbaijan and, should they attempt to 'invade' the province, they

[1] *Mission*, p. 117.

would be resisted by force of arms, and defeated. The regime threatened that, after this 'defeat inflicted upon the imperial army', its forces would march south to Tehran. 'Liberation' of Iran would thus be accomplished in one sweep by the 'revolutionaries'. The propaganda of the separatist regime and the Tudeh rose to a crescendo of hysteria, capped by the chant of Tabriz radio: 'There is death, but there is no retreat.' [2]

The Shah at no stage accepted the claim of the separatists that they could carry the people of Azerbaijan or Kurdistan with them, much less the people of the rest of the country. He based this conclusion on his belief that the vitality of Iranian patriotism could not be emasculated by treacherous propagandists. The separatist regime relied upon the strength of the Stalinist armies. Indeed their survival until now had depended on the presence of Soviet troops, and their continued existence also depended on the superior force of foreign arms.

The most important factor to influence the Shah's strategy was his evaluation of Stalinist policy. He had come to the conclusion that Stalin could not intervene directly and still hope to secure both his objectives. Therefore he must choose between them: either he could save the separatist regimes in the north or sacrifice them to gain his oil concession. Any military intervention on his part would inevitably provoke a violent anti-Russian reaction in Iran. At the same time, the oil concession, already granted in principle by Qavam, could not become operative till the *majlis* ratified it. The Shah's decree meant that no truncated *majlis*, without representatives from the two separatist northern areas, could be elected. In these circumstances, if Stalin wanted his oil agreement ratified, he would have to abandon the separatists.

As a means of testing this analysis, the Shah concentrated his troops at Qazvin. The province of Khamseh, which lay between

[2] Shamim, p. 62.

Qazvin and Azerbaijan, had been occupied by the forces of the Pishevari regime, and the Shah ordered his troops to clear it of the separatists. The imperial army entered Zanjan, the provincial capital, unopposed. While the separatists hurriedly retreated to Mianeh, in Azerbaijan, the national troops were welcomed by the people of Khamseh.[3] This success indicated that the separatists' political influence was marginal, and confirmed the accuracy of the Shah's analysis. It also made the Tudeh desperate. Now forced out into the open, it organised riots in Mazanderan. The central government retaliated by arresting several of its leaders. Qavam found that he too was now a target for the Tudeh. The police, in the course of raids on Tudeh offices, seized documents which suggested that the party was planning the final disposal of Qavam. In the light of this discovery, the Prime Minister had to act in sheer self-defence. He came down heavily on his erstwhile Tudeh friends, and the party went 'underground'. Mozaffar Firuz was shunted off to Moscow as Ambassador. Qavam had finally recognised that the Shah had been right in his political analysis all the time.

The Shah had already assumed active field command of the army, which he now ordered to march on Azerbaijan and suppress the rebellion once and for all. These orders formed part of a declaration by the Qavam government, issued on December 3, which stated that in order to implement the royal decree for a general election the imperial army was to occupy all regions where elections would be held, including Azerbaijan. The Pishevari regime branded this declaration as a clear violation of the agreement previously reached with the central government. The Shah's only response was to set up a War Council which met at his palace. The Shah was in favour of advancing into Azerbaijan without any further loss of time,

[3] Arfa, p. 377.

though some of his advisers were hesitant as they still feared that this would provoke Soviet military intervention.

The Shah, although prepared to concede that his analysis might be wrong, preferred to face the consequences of such an intervention should it occur. The alternative, he told his advisers, was even more disastrous — abandoning all hope of preserving the country's unity. It was at this juncture, when the decision to advance into Azerbaijan and Kurdistan had been taken, that the Soviet Ambassador in Tehran urgently requested an audience — an audience which the Shah was always to remember. 'When he appeared', the Shah later narrated, 'he began to speak in threatening tones, protesting that our military moves in Azerbaijan were endangering the peace of the world. In the name of his government he demanded that I, as King and Commander-in-Chief, should withdraw my forces. I told him that on the contrary, the situation until then prevailing in Azerbaijan had been endangering the peace of the world, and that I was refusing his demand.' [4]

The Shah knew that the Soviet Ambassador was not speaking from a position of strength. In the Qavam-Soviet agreement, Stalin had accepted that the dispute over Azerbaijan should be settled internally. The Soviet Union had opted out of the dispute by agreeing that its solution lay in direct negotiations between the people of Azerbaijan and the government in Tehran. The position of the Pishevari regime, despite its boasts, had already been exposed as weak, and the Soviet Ambassador should have been fully aware of this. News of the Shah's decision to move troops into Azerbaijan had already reached the common people of the province, who had begun to defy the Pishevari regime. Even the 'Governor-General' of the province, who had earlier collaborated with Pishevari, had seen the writing on the wall. He had sent a telegram to the Shah

[4] *Mission*, pp. 117–18.

offering 'unconditional surrender' of the rebel forces. The Shah showed this telegram to the Soviet Ambassador. 'The Ambassador was stunned,' the Shah later wrote; 'apparently he had yet not received the news. Unable to think of anything to say, he departed.' This virtually ended all speculation about the possibility of Russian intervention.

Under the Shah's orders, the Iranian army moved to the north in three columns: the principal column marched via Zanjan and Mianeh; the other two via Bijar–Shahin–Dezh–Maragheh, and Saqqez–Mahabad, respectively. On December 8, the Pishevari regime was officially outlawed, and the Shah flew over the rebel positions to ascertain their strength. On December 10, the main column of Iranian troops crossed the Qezel Owzan river, where the rebels had blown up the bridge. A short engagement followed on the Qaflan Kuh, in which the rebels were defeated, and the imperial troops captured Mianeh. On December 11, the Bijar column, after routing the rebels, liberated Shahin Dezh. A popular rising took place in Azerbaijan as the news of the victorious march of the imperial army spread. Armed Tabrizi nationalists had already made surprise attacks on the headquarters of the Democratic Party. The troops of the Pishevari regime were retreating from Mianeh to Tabriz when word reached them of an uprising at their destination. They were now caught between the advancing troops of the imperial army and the armed civilians in Tabriz. Meanwhile, similar uprisings had taken place in Rezaieh and eastern Azerbaijan.

Both the Pishevari regime and the Kurdish regime of Haji Baba Shaikh had been assured by the Russians that their power would not be permitted to collapse in the face of an advance by the imperial army. None of the promised help arrived. Soviet policy had once again shown its pragmatic character. Stalin had abandoned his puppets in Azerbaijan and Kurdistan. The rebel opposition now collapsed. Only five thousand of its troops were able to find refuge in Russia and Iraq : several hundred of them were captured by the armed civilians who were keen to settle their scores with them on the spot. As the Shah later wrote, the 'Iranian army had to intervene to keep the people from exterminating the communist prisoners'.[5] At the same time, the Kurdish rebels were defeated by the column that had advanced via Shahin Dezh and which had joined forces with the Saqqez column. These troops eliminated the relatively disorganised forces of the Komala faction. On December 12, the national army entered Tabriz and Rezaieh. They were greeted by the population of the two cities as long awaited liberators.

Qavam still remained Prime Minister. His continuance in power later led to one of those prejudiced assessments which have been a common failing among many Western historians of Iran. Commenting on this, an Iranian observer has written : ' It has become the fashion, especially in foreign circles, to credit Qavam with the survival of Iran's independence, which they consider due only to his shrewdness and political ability. . . . This survival was directly due to Mohammad Reza Shah's action through his loyal army, which he directed and inspired. In the same way, it was due to his fearless decision that the army had moved forward and reconquered the Azerbaijan province, whose population counts among the most patriotic and loyal in Iran.'[6]

The defeat of the separatists in Azerbaijan and Kurdistan compared in many ways with the defeat of Kuchik Khan and the 'Soviet Republic of Gilan'. In both cases the danger to Iran was averted by a Pahlavi. In both cases the Soviet Union had inspired the separatists. In both cases the unwillingness of the people of the northern provinces to be 'liberated', had

---

[5] *Mission*, p. 117.   [6] Arfa, p. 379.

ultimately led to their rising in support of the central government against their self-styled liberators.[7]

Yet, in December, 1946, the problem created by the separatists in the northern provinces was qualitively different. The struggle which the Shah led was part of a great historical process then developing in Asia. In 1946, after two centuries of stagnation and subordination at home and abroad, Asia was once again emerging. The collapse of the British empire in the Indian subcontinent had paved the way for the rise of India, Burma, Ceylon and the new state of Pakistan as sovereign powers. The last efforts of the French colonial system to reassert itself in west Asia had already failed. In other parts of Asia, too, the final stage in the battle for national independence had been reached. A new sense of Asian destiny had begun to inspire Asian leadership.

The Shah had made a major contribution towards the task of freeing Asia by his successful resistance to Stalinist expansionism. He had, in effect, broken through the earlier psychological and political barriers by which the overlordship of the victorious powers had been accepted without protest. He had effectively shown that Stalin could not ride rough-shod over Iran. True, the Shah was assisted by other international developments such as the Cold War. These, however, did not really emerge until after his single-handed victory in Azerbaijan.

This Russian defeat carried much larger connotations. It exposed Stalinist objectives in their ugly nakedness for the first time not only to the West but also to Stalin's opponents within the Soviet Union, as Nikita Khrushchev was to reveal later. Many an Asian leader, too, learnt a serious lesson. But above all, the victory gave a new sense of confidence to Iranian nationalism. 'The importance of these events', the Shah has explained, 'was so clear that the Iranian nation declared that

[7] *Mission*, p. 117.

day, which coincided with the termination of this rebellion, a national festival, and named it Azerbaijan Day. Since 1946, the anniversary of this day, when Azerbaijan was saved and our sovereignty over that zone was restored, is celebrated by the whole nation.' The Shah had come to the throne in uncertain times nearly five years before. Now he had proved his talents as monarch of his people. He had hoped to meet the people of Azerbaijan immediately after the defeat of the Pishevari regime, but other events delayed the fulfilment of this desire for six months. When he finally arrived at Tabriz, he received a delirious welcome. On his return to the capital the population of Tehran responded with equal enthusiasm.

The Shah did not permit himself to be swept off his feet by this, knowing that he had reached only the first milestone in a long journey. He felt that the occasion called for a renewed pledge on his part to his people. In response to the tremendous reception which he received at Tehran and Tabriz, he said : 'This warm and affectionate sentiment which I observe in the people encourages me more than ever in my desire to serve. However selfish I might be, I realise fully that the power of kingship depends upon the power of the nation. And the pedestals of the throne have their security in the hearts of the people. My wish is that every Iranian will benefit equally from his national and social rights and that the sacred principles of the constitution and real democracy are perfectly established in my country.' [8] He concluded his address with a phrase which was to become the sheet anchor of his future policy, ' There is no honour ', he said, ' to be the King of a poor people.'

[8] Quoted by Shamim as preface.

PART THREE

THE SECOND REVOLUTION

A willow-branch reminds one that a youth
  Can easily be bent towards the Truth ;
Old reprobates a sterner fate require,
  For they will straighten only in the fire.

"Sa'adi" (Musharaf-ud-Din)
1184–1292

CHAPTER FOURTEEN

The Shadow of the Oil Crisis

RELIEVED of the burdens of military occupation, internal subversion, separatism and threats of renewed war for the first time, the Shah turned energetically to the task closest to his heart. He had now the time, so he thought, to devote himself to the firm assertion of the 'social and economic rights of the citizens', which he had come to accept as the 'foundation of the power of the nation'. He had already begun to take positive steps in this direction, despite the limitations imposed by circumstance: for example, in 1944 he had ordered the government to look into the conditions of industrial workers. On his instructions, the Department-General of Labour had been set up to investigate complaints by workers, and to settle their disputes with employers. At the same time, he had ordered the establishment of a High Council of Labour and Economy. In May, 1946, these steps led to the passing of the first labour law in the modern history of Iran. By this, the working day was reduced to eight hours and the week to forty-eight hours. Weekly and annual holidays with pay were instituted. The employment of children under twelve, and night work for women and youths under sixteen in factories, was prohibited. The new law also fixed minimum wages related to the cost of living in different parts of the country.[1]

[1] Pahlavi, His Imperial Majesty Mohammed Reza Shah Aryamehr, Shahanshah of Iran, *The White Revolution* (Tehran, May 1967), p. 78.

The conditions, of occupation and near anarchy, of the previous five years had seriously worsened the economic situation of the country. Every item of necessity was in short supply. Prices, which had risen due to the inflation caused by the peculiar problems of occupation, had remained high. The Tudeh agitation had further disorganised the precarious balance of Iran's underdeveloped economic system. The old equilibrium between the urban and rural sectors of the national economy appeared to have gone forever. Nor could such damage be repaired by piecemeal measures. A co-ordinated and comprehensive economic plan appeared to the Shah to be the only answer.

He had always wanted to organise planned economic development for Iran. Even if the situation had not been as critical as it then was, he would have adopted this course. Before the beginning of the Second War he had convinced Reza Shah that a proper programme of economic and social reconstruction was overdue ; and his father had ordered the setting up of an Economic Council to study this proposal. However, the war and the occupation had meant that this newly formed body never became effective.

The year 1946 was an auspicious moment to launch a concerted project for a planned economy. The end of the war had seen the birth of a new climate of nationalist aspiration. The feeling that Iran must now rise as an economically and politically strong nation was shared by both the urban and rural sections of the population, especially after the victory in Azerbaijan. This new nationalist upsurge could easily be harnessed to policies of social change. Moreover, at the end of the war, the occupying powers had compensated Iran in gold for Iranian currency used during the occupation, Britain and the Soviet Union each paying eleven tons, deposited to the credit of the Bank Melli (National Bank of Iran) in London and Moscow. With other savings, the total value of Iran's reserves was 18.5 times higher than in 1940.

The Shah wanted the government to set its own house in order. The government factories set up by Reza Shah for the manufacture of textiles, sugar and cement were in a deplorable condition. A new bank, the Industrial and Mineral Bank, was created to co-ordinate all such government institutions and industrial units, with the exception of the oil industry, tobacco monopoly, railways and granaries. He also wanted the government to draw up a national plan of economic development so that effective and immediate steps, leading to a balanced and rapid improvement in the standard of living, could be taken. A committee was appointed to draw up a Seven Year Plan. The Shah took a personal interest in the work of both these projects, and had high hopes that these measures would initiate the westernisation of Iran.[2]

The first draft of the Seven Year Plan was prepared by the committee from projects submitted by various ministries, and proved to be extremely ambitious as a result. Even with all the foreign exchange now to hand, the plan was, nonetheless, too expensive for the government's reserves. The government therefore invoked the promises of Allied support contained in the Tripartite Treaty.

There was little point in approaching the Soviet Union after the troubles in Azerbaijan and while the Soviet demand for the oil concession in the north was still pending. On the other hand, the Western Allies had set up an International Bank for Development and Reparations. The government approached the International Bank for assistance in carrying out the plan. The International Bank wanted to examine the feasibility of the Seven Year Plan, and entrusted this task to an American company, whose experts were to investigate it in detail.

[2] Shamim, pp. 62–5.

Meanwhile, elections were held for the Fifteenth *majlis*, as a result of which Qavam remained Prime Minister. He had formed a new party on the eve of the elections, the Democratic Party of Iran, which had won an overwhelming majority. The Tudeh had reaped the bitter harvest of its previous policy and was completely eliminated. However, a small group of right-wing politicians, opposed to Qavam and the Democrats, had also managed to get elected. Among these independent conservatives was Dr Mohammad Mossadeq, who had been a member of the *majlis* for nearly thirty years and, in the course of his parliamentary career, had become a formidable force.

Mohammad Mossadeq was born in 1881, son of a landlord and himself a landlord.[3] His family owned several villages near Tehran. Mossadeq had been educated in Europe, studying law and allied subjects in France and Switzerland. On his return home he had joined the Qajar Civil Service, and became head of the Finance Department of the Qajar administration in Khorassan. He had resigned from the Civil Service after parliamentary democracy was introduced in Iran, and co-operated with the Constitutionalists in the early days of the movement. By 1915 he was a member of the *majlis* and even at this early stage was known as an extremely vocal politician, whose antagonism could make him a dangerous opponent to those in power. On the eve of the Revolution of 1921, he had been appointed Governor-General of the province of Fars. At this stage, he was highly thought of by the British authorities in

[3] No biography of Dr Mohammad Mossadeq has been published in English. I could find none even in Farsi which could be considered authoritative, though several articles have been written about his life. As a result I could only collect material during personal conversations with his former colleagues, and this was seldom documented. However, the *majlis* records outline his political career, and though I have not cited them directly, I have referred to them wherever they have been quoted in works written by his contemporaries.

Iran. To quote the Shah : 'The British engineered his appointment as Governor-General of the province of Fars, and later he held the same post in the province of Azerbaijan'.[4]

Mossadeq's role in the Revolution of 1921 had been dubious. He had at no stage wholeheartedly supported the movement behind the Revolution, and it was believed that he was jealous of Syed Zia. His moves to dethrone his rival had been frustrated, and he held the Cossack Brigade and Reza Khan, its commander, responsible for his failure. The hostility he felt towards Reza Khan became increasingly bitter as the years went by. Both Mossadeq's antagonism to the new leadership of Iran, and his own ambitious temperament, made his actions unpredictable even at this early stage of his political career. When the *majlis* debated the termination of the Qajar dynasty in November 1925, Mossadeq was guided by these personal considerations. Ahmad Shah Qajar had by then refused to return to Iran. The *majlis* therefore decided to end the Qajar dynasty, by a majority of 117 to 5. Among those who would not agree to the termination of the disastrous rule of this discredited dynasty was Mohammad Mossadeq.[5]

In the succeeding years, Mossadeq made various political alliances. He served as a member of several cabinets and held, for short periods, the portfolios for finance, justice and foreign affairs. His activities on the eve of the Second War, and during its first phase before the Soviet Union was invaded, were looked upon with suspicion by Reza Shah. He had been imprisoned and was released only at the intervention of the Shah, then Crown Prince. After the Shah's accession to the throne,

---

[4] *Mission*, p. 83.
[5] Arfa, p. 183. The other four who voted with Dr Mossadeq were : Hossein Ala (later a leading diplomat and Prime Minister), *Mullah* Modarres (who fought with Reza Shah), Hassan Taquizade (later a trusted lieutenant of Reza Shah) and Seyid Yaqub Anvar.

Mossadeq had acquired the reputation of being a firm opponent of all foreign influence, and few could afford to ignore his long career in parliamentary politics and reputation as an elder statesman.

The Shah had met Mossadeq twice during the war. The first occasion had been at a time when he was angry and irritated by the way the British and the Russians had influenced the elections to the *majlis*. 'Officials of those countries', the Shah wrote later, 'would actually prepare the list of candidates for parliament and then would instruct whoever was our Prime Minister to see that only their candidates were nominated and elected.'[6] The Shah therefore consulted several senior politicians including Mossadeq. The reasons for consulting him were later summarised by the Shah : 'Our relations were good at that time, for he was a respected public servant and he symbolised opposition to foreign influence in all its forms.' The Shah had considered the idea of nominating him Prime Minister, such nomination being a Crown prerogative under the Constitution. He wanted Mossadeq, as Prime Minister, to hold a new general election and ensure that foreign influence did not affect its results. When the Shah asked him to accept this responsibility, Mossadeq agreed to do so on two conditions.

Mossadeq, firstly, wanted a personal bodyguard to protect him from attempted assassination, to which the Shah readily agreed. Secondly, he wanted the 'prior approval of the British to the whole plan'. The Shah was astounded and enquired if Mossadeq had thought about Russian approval. Mossadeq replied that the Russians did not count. 'It is the British', he added, 'who decide everything in this country.' The Shah was amazed at this reaction from Mossadeq, because after all he had called in this elder statesman for advice in the belief that he was opposed to all foreign influence. The Shah pointed out to

[6] *Mission*, p. 86.

Mossadeq that there was no need to consult the British authorities on this matter and that Reza Shah had never obtained British approval for his actions, but Mossadeq would not agree. He maintained that the Shah was young, and knew little of politics. He could not waive his second condition, and would co-operate only with British approval.

The Shah then weighed the various factors involved in seeking British approval. To quote him : 'I found this attitude disturbing and dangerous. Yet, I had to take into account the delicate situation in my country, at the mercy of occupying forces able to intervene in any domestic clash. In a crisis Mossadeq's patriotism and popular appeal could be invaluable. For these reasons, I reluctantly told him that I would send a representative to consult the British Ambassador in Tehran. But in order not to comply with Mossadeq's demand that I consult with the British alone, I told him that I would also have to send somebody to check with the other occupying power.'

Next day the British Ambassador declined to endorse the plan. He claimed that it would disturb political life in Iran to hold new elections. The Soviet Ambassador offered no objection on his part. On receipt of these replies, the Shah telephoned Mossadeq and told him that though the Russians had agreed the British answer was negative. Mossadeq was no longer interested in the proposal.[7] The reply from the British Ambassador had abruptly terminated his interest in holding elections as new Prime Minister. The difficulties in parliament continued. The work of the government had been made almost impossible by a rule which required a two-thirds quorum for conducting parliamentary business. The *majlis* also required a three to one majority to pass any legislation. Mossadeq at that time commanded a small group of forty deputies, who regularly absented themselves and thus stalemated proceedings by

[7] *Mission*, pp. 86–7.

making it impossible to find a quorum. This led to the Shah's second meeting with Mossadeq.

The Shah summoned Mossadeq and his group to an audience, and enquired why they were so intent upon frustrating every move of the government. Without hesitation, Mossadeq explained to the Shah the reason for the policy which he and his group pursued : the Russians, he bluntly said, did not approve of the Prime Minister in power. The Shah could not understand Mossadeq's logic. This was the man who only a few months earlier had accepted a British veto and dismissed the Russians contemptuously. Now he appeared to be the parliamentary instrument of Soviet interests. The Shah naturally asked him why. Mossadeq gave no answer, nor would he give up his obstructionist policy.[8]

In the Fourteenth *majlis*, Mossadeq had continued the same policy. He was then rapidly becoming a symbol of emotional, even if irrational, nationalist negativism. In 1944, during the crisis created by new Soviet demands for an oil concession in the north, and American and British requests for additional concessions in southern Iran, Mossadeq had risen sharply in public esteem by moving the bill which forbade the government to negotiate any oil concession without the approval of the *majlis*. This bill was approved by a large majority in the *majlis*.[9] The deputies knew that the nation was no longer willing to add to what it considered to be the burden of the British concession in the south : yet since the government of the day was not considered strong, it could easily have been swayed by any of the three candidates for further oil concessions. 'The bill was a timely one.'[10]

Mossadeq was lionised by the opposition press for his nationalist attitude. He had won, after the passage of the bill, a considerable following among professional and intellectual

[8] *Mission*, pp. 87–8   [9] Shamim, p. 46.   [10] *Mission*, p. 88.

groups in the towns. Ever since then, he had taken an un-compromising stand on the oil question, and his minority po-sition in the *majlis* gave him sufficient opportunity to condemn the policies of the government. He made highly emotional speeches which were fully reported in the press. In December 1944, he walked out of a session of the *majlis*, condemning it as 'a nest of thieves'. This led to popular demonstrations in his support, and the situation became so critical that the army had to move in to protect the deputies from assault and the *majlis* building itself from destruction.[11]

The elections for the Fifteenth *majlis* had been delayed for sixteen months because of the Russian occupation of the northern provinces. However, on July 16, 1947, it was in-augurated by the Shah, and began its work a month later, on August 17. Right from the outset it was confronted by crisis. The question of the Soviet demand for an oil concession had to be resolved. The Soviet Union now based its case on Qavam's agreement in principle. It argued that it was under the terms of this agreement that the Soviet troops had been withdrawn from the northern areas. Thus, the Soviets added, they had fulfilled their part of the bargain. It was now for Qavam to discharge his responsibilities. He must secure the endorsement of the *majlis* for the agreement and begin forthwith the work of forming a joint Russo-Iranian oil company.

The Shah rejected the premise of the Soviet argument, main-taining that the withdrawal of Soviet troops was not related to Qavam's concessions since it had been part of the Tripartite Treaty, by which the Soviet Union was obliged to withdraw its troops within six months of the armistice. The western allies, Britain and the United States, had acted within the terms of this treaty and the Soviet Union, even when it belatedly pulled back its troops from Iranian territory, and had only

11 Arfa, p. 333.

honoured this earlier commitment. The deputies of the *majlis* endorsed the Shah's attitude, and so did the country. Iran refused to accept the Soviet argument and resolved to treat the question of an oil concession in the north solely on its merits. Apart from a small minority, public opinion was strongly against any such grant.

CHAPTER FIFTEEN

The Challenge from the South

THE last stage of the crisis with the Soviet Union was soon reached. The Soviet Ambassador, suspicious of the procrastination of Qavam in securing the *majlis'* approval to the agreement, brought into play the few remaining diplomatic weapons at his disposal. The ambassador, Sadchikov, told Qavam that if the concession were not ratified by the *majlis*, considerable unpleasantness in Soviet-Iranian relations would follow. Stalin ordered a concentration of his forces on Iran's northern frontier and the movement of Soviet warships towards Bandar Pahlavi on the Caspian, but this show of military strength made little impression on Iran. Diplomatic pressure was also maintained on Mozaffar Firuz, then Iranian Ambassador in Moscow. Firuz, for his part, was impressed : he was convinced of adverse developments should the agreement-in-principle not be ratified. He believed that Soviet armies might re-enter Azerbaijan, accepting the Soviet case that their withdrawal had been a consequence of the 'understanding' that the oil concession would in fact be granted to them. These views Firuz expressed to Qavam in a long letter which the latter showed to a meeting of the leaders of the various groups in the *majlis*. However, Firuz's views had no effect on their opposition to the ratification of the agreement.[1]

The Shah maintained close liaison with the leaders of the

[1] Arfa, p. 385.

majlis, and had already informed Qavam of his opposition to the agreement. The knowledge that the Shah was opposed to the concession heartened the attitude of both the public in general and the deputies in particular. Qavam himself was no longer keen on the ratification. Yet he had to go through the motions of presenting the bill for ratification, and this was submitted to the *majlis*. Heated debates followed. Among those who attacked the bill virulently was Mossadeq. On the night of October 22, as was expected, the *majlis* adopted a resolution rejecting ratification. This was to prove the harbinger of a new national crisis.

The *majlis* resolution declared that Qavam had acted in good faith over the agreement he had entered into with the Soviet Union. After this preamble, it pronounced the negotiations and agreement of April 1946 to be null and void. It rejected, in effect, the entire policy which Qavam had followed before the Soviet withdrawal from the northern areas. The remaining four paragraphs of the resolution dealt with the oil question in general and with the Anglo-Iranian Oil Company in particular. In the second paragraph, the *majlis* asked the government to make geological surveys of the country with a view to discovering new oilfields within the next five years. In the third paragraph, the *majlis* reiterated the principle laid down by Mossadeq's bill in 1944 : it 'absolutely forbade' the government 'to grant any concessions of oil or its derivatives in the country to foreigners or to form a new company for this purpose in which foreigners may have a share by some means or the other'. In the fourth paragraph, the *majlis* tried to pacify the Soviet Union. If, after the survey referred to in the second paragraph, it was established that there were oil resources in the northern provinces which could be commercially exploited, the government would negotiate with the Soviet government for the sale of such products.

The final paragraph of the resolution was to become the sheet-anchor of national policy for the next two years. It stated that the 'government is bound in all cases where the rights of the Iranian nation have been damaged in connection with the national resources, whether underground or otherwise, particularly concerning the oilfields of the south, to make necessary negotiations and to take steps for demanding the settlement of these rights and to inform the *majlis* of the results.'[2] The *majlis* clearly aimed at forging an entirely new policy towards the Anglo-Iranian Oil Company, and even the somewhat vague phraseology did not conceal its real purpose. The Shah fully supported the resolution : in a sense, he had been its originator. His firm stand against Stalinist expansionism in the north, his battle against separatism and his refusal to capitulate on the oil concession had given new confidence to Iranian nationalism. He had given a lead to what he later called 'positive' nationalism : he was not opposed to foreigners for the sake of mere opposition ; what he wanted was to extend and expand Iranian independence on a firmer economic basis. He had already decided that the oil revenues must be used to finance the Seven Year Plan. The American company engaged to prepare the details had submitted its report, in which its experts had recommended a much wider scope for the plan. This involved costs which Iran could not possibly afford. The Shah ordered that, taking the report as a basis, Iranian experts should prepare a new plan, less ambitious and requiring one third of the finance. This new plan had been prepared and submitted to the *majlis* for approval shortly before the oil resolution of October 22 was adopted and a new oil policy emerged.

Meanwhile a parliamentary crisis had overtaken the long rule of Qavam. His Democratic Party was split, his attempts to patch up the differences failed and, on December 10, he

[2] Full text quoted in Shamim, pp. 74–5.

resigned. The Shah nominated Ebrahim Hakimi as the new Prime Minister, and this appointment was approved by the *majlis* on December 27. It was Hakimi who piloted the amended Seven Year Plan through the *majlis*. It was passed on January 21, 1948. Under its terms, the newly formed Plan Organisation was entrusted with the duties formally discharged by the Industrial and Mineral Bank.

It was about this time that the United States began to develop an active policy towards the Middle East in general and Iran in particular. American political experts had always treated Iran as an appendage to the Middle East, and had been content to watch Anglo-Russian rivalry from a distance. The first American advisers to Iran in 1911 had not come because of official American interest, but at the invitation of the Iranian government. The second American financial mission, led by Arthur L. Millspaugh, had also come at the invitation of Reza Shah. Millspaugh had returned to Iran during the Second War as head of an American economic and financial mission, once again on Iranian initiative, and the Shah had appointed him Administrator-General of Finance.

During the war a more active policy began to emerge. The American army had created a good impression and as a result the government had developed good relations with the American military mission, headed by Major-General Clarence S. Ridley. The Shah had also engaged the services of an American police expert, Colonel H. Norman Schwartzkopf, as Chief of Police. However, all these appointments were made, as before, on Iranian initiative. Iran wanted American citizens in these key positions because she was chary of increasing the influence of the other two Great Powers.[3]

After the Shah's victory over the Azerbaijan separatists, a

[3] Roosevelt, Kermit, *Arabs, Oil and History*; *the Story of the Middle East* (London, 1949), p. 197.

new interest in Iran had begun to develop in the United States. In April 1947, President Truman had announced the new American policy of an international 'containment of Communism'.[4] This containment policy, or 'Truman Doctrine', directly assured the Greek and Turkish governments of American support. The Truman Administration had promised specific economic and military aid to assist them in the problems connected with the growth of Communism.[4] The new American Ambassador, George S. Allen, had, as part of this policy, promised American support to Iran in her opposition to the Soviet demand for the northern oil concession. Allen had stated: 'We, and every other nation in the world, however, do become concerned when such proposals are accompanied by threats of bitter enmity or by a statement that it will be dangerous for Iran to refuse. . . . Patriotic Iranians, when considering matters affecting their national interest, may, therefore, rest assured that the American people will support fully their freedom to make their own choice. . . .' This statement was a part of a speech made by Allen to the Iranian-American Cultural Relations Society. Its impact cannot be over-emphasised, even though the promised support was but vague. A new power had entered the Iranian political scene.

The Soviet Union at this point bowed out. The Cold War had already commenced, and Stalin now needed to confront the power of the United States. He had mobilised Communist Parties in Europe by late 1947 and his position was further strengthened by the support of the Chinese Communist Party, which was engaged in the final stages of the liquidation of the Chiang Kai-shek regime. The problems arising out of the division of Germany and Berlin required all his attention. The oil

---

[4] For a historical survey of post-Second War American interest see Campbell, John C., *Defense of the Middle East* ; *Problems of American Policy* (New York, 1958), pp. 29–38.

concession in the northern provinces of Iran had suddenly become a matter of negligible importance. For the next twelve years the Soviet Union was to adopt a policy of distant friendship towards Iran.

This removal of the Soviet threat intensified the old Iranian antagonism towards Britain. The *majlis* resolution of October 22 had been adopted to prevent the grant of an oil concession to the Soviet Union. The last paragraph of this resolution had originally been introduced to buttress Iran's case against Stalin's demand. Now that this demand had been successfully rejected, this paragraph became the focus of attention for the nationalist movement in another context. The long list of the real and imaginary sins of the Anglo-Iranian Oil Company began to be catalogued in the Press.

However, the Company did not appear to be in the least concerned with this agitation, and continued to behave as if nothing had changed in Iran or indeed elsewhere. Its representatives in Tehran, as well as in the south, ignored any suggestion that the Company might take notice of the changed temper of the people. This proved to be a fundamental mistake. Had the Company been less insensitive at this early stage to what it itself later accepted as the legitimate aspiration of the government and people of Iran, its own future, as well as the future of Iran, might have been very different.[5] The Company's complacence further provoked the deputies. They began to champion in the *majlis* the growing national demand for a larger share in the oil revenues, and Hakimi was all too aware of their resentful mood.

Hakimi had informed the Company of the advisability of talks in the light of the last paragraph of the *majlis* resolution, but the Company continued to show its indifference by ignoring the new Prime Minister's advice. This still further irritated the

[5] *Mission*, pp. 89–90.

deputies, who from now on never allowed the pressure on Hakimi to relax. Ultimately, the Company was compelled to send one of its directors, N. A. Gass, to Tehran. Gass was abrupt in dealing with the basic demand implicit in the *majlis* resolution. He told Hakimi that the Company was unwilling to consider any revision of its 1933 agreement with Iran. If the government of Iran believed that the Company had violated this agreement in any way, he was authorised by his Board of Directors to deal with it. He had caught Hakimi unawares. The Prime Minister had not prepared his case. He could only refer to Article 16 of the 1933 Agreement which required that the Company promote Iranian nationals to higher technical and skilled jobs within eight years of the date of the agreement. That this had not happened was known to everybody. Two former Prime Ministers, Bayat and Sa'ed, had reminded the Company of this breach of the agreement. Gass did not accept Hakimi's complaint, and deadlock followed when he pleaded that he had no authority to negotiate any basic questions with Hakimi. After long and unfriendly talks, Gass returned to London.[6]

The Shah had followed every stage of the Hakimi–Gass talks. He was surprised at the attitude of the Company, as he had hoped that the British government would have learnt its lesson from its duel with nationalism on the Indian sub-continent and would have begun to respect Asian nationalism as a whole. He had recognised the British abdication of power from the Indian sub-continent as an act of great statesmanship, and had therefore expected the British government — particularly as a major shareholder in the Company — to persuade it to formulate a reasonable attitude towards Iran's general demands. These demands were not even clearly formulated during the first talks. Hakimi merely suggested to Gass the

[6] Shamim, p. 76.

need for a reorientation of the Company's relations with the government. The Shah's attitude hardened as he realised that the Company, through Gass, had made it plain that there was no intention on its part of accepting any compromise with Iran. It now seemed to him that the British government was backing what he thought was a deliberate attitude on the part of the Company to pay no heed to Iran's needs.[7] Like his father, he had been dissatisfied with the Company's conduct for some time, and now a Labour government in Britain seemed to be supporting conduct more appropriate to the era of gunboat diplomacy. The Shah found this strange, since Britain and its socialist leaders knew that Iran and her oil had helped to win not one, but two world wars. Even Curzon, imperialist dreamer as he was, had conceded : 'Truly posterity will say that the Allies floated to victory on a wave of oil'.[8]

The Shah expected some return from Britain for the help given in terms of Iranian oil to the Allies in the Second War, the extent of which he described thus : 'During the Second World War output fell for a time because of shipping and other difficulties. But even in 1941, when production reached its lowest level of 6.6 million tons, it was over seven times as high as in the peak year of the First World War.'[9] By 1944 the Company had reached a production of 13.2 million tons and, in 1945, 16.8 million. Thereafter, it had been able to implement a modernisation and expansion programme. By 1947 the Abadan refinery had become the largest in the world and production had reached 19.2 million tons. In fact, in the years of the crisis, production rose from this figure to 31.8 million in 1950.

The failure of the Hakimi–Gass talks was not taken lightly either by the Shah or by the *majlis*, where the attack was led by Mossadeq. He condemned Hakimi for his alleged inefficiency

[7] Shamim, p. 90.   [8] Quoted in *Mission*, p. 271.   [9] Ibid. p. 275.

in handling the negotiations, and his followers charged the Prime Minister with being an agent of the Company and a traitor to national interests. The Press was no less harsh on him, and it was clear from the moment the Hakimi–Gass talks failed that this would cost Hakimi dear. After a stormy session in the *majlis*, Hakimi resigned on June 8, 1948.

The Shah nominated Abdul Hossein Hajir to take the fallen Prime Minister's place. Hajir incorporated the final paragraph of the resolution of October 22 into the government programme which he presented to the *majlis* when his nomination was put forward for approval. Hajir was an energetic and fearless young politician who enjoyed the Shah's confidence. He realised that the question of oil in the south could not be divorced from the question of Iran's economic development, but was concerned more with the substance of the dispute than the form. Several deputies knew Hajir's views and some of them attacked him even before he resumed negotiations with the Company.

Hajir realised that he was dealing with an opponent whose experience in oil was second to none. He was modest enough to accept that Iran did not possess the technical knowledge required to argue its case against the Company effectively, nor did he forget that Hakimi had been out-manœuvred by Gass. He therefore won the approval of the Shah and the *majlis* for the employment of three oil experts who were citizens of neutral European countries. They were to study the dispute and assist the government in the difficult negotiations with the Company which lay ahead.[10] Hajir came under attack yet again for seeking the assistance of these 'foreign' specialists. He retaliated sharply and staked the existence of his government on this question. With the Shah's support and encouragement he won a second vote of confidence from the *majlis*. It was only after

[10] Shamim, p. 77.

this skirmish with Mossadeq that he could settle down to the serious business of preparing Iran's case against the Company. Once again he consulted the Shah, under whose guidance a twenty-five point memorandum was drafted listing the objections to the southern oil concessions and the infringements by the Company of the 1933 agreement.

By this time, the Company's attitude had begun to change, and it had started to react to the government demands. It even appeared keen to talk with government representatives, but it soon transpired that the Company had only changed its tactics. These appeared to be based on the assumption that with proper and effective manipulation the national movement could be divided ; and that when such a division had been organised the extremists like Mossadeq could be isolated. The Company seemed to believe that the storm would then pass enabling it to offer some concessions and save the basic structure of its privileges. That at least was how its policy was interpreted both by the Shah and the nationalist movement.[11] While the Company continued to live in its own dream world, Hajir's government came under still greater pressure in the *majlis*, and fell on November 7, 1948.

The Shah treated the fall of the Hajir government as a portent. The temper of the *majlis*, preoccupied with settling its scores with the Company, was turning sour. It refused to tolerate any government which could not bring the Company to its knees. Within less than a year, two cabinets had fallen. In order to achieve some sort of stability in the *majlis*, the Shah nominated Sa'ed to take Hajir's place. Sa'ed pledged his adherence to the measures taken by the preceding governments to settle Iran's dispute with the Company. Yet he failed to stem the tide of

[11] For example, Shamim remarks that the Company's policy was aimed at gaining 'benefits from the incidents which might occur in the convulsive political atmosphere in Iran', p. 77.

angry public opinion, of which Mossadeq was increasingly becoming the spear-head, both in the *majlis* and in the country at large.

The Board of Directors of the Company now sent Gass once again to Tehran, and talks were resumed. They did not begin well. Gass again reiterated that the purpose of his visit was not to revise the old concession. He had not returned to Tehran to negotiate an agreement contrary to the interests of the Company. He was willing to discuss only the question of royalties, and certain minor articles of the 1933 agreement. The knowledge of the Company's unchanged attitude added fuel to the fire. New forces had already made their entry into Iranian political life by this time. They were sharply distinguished from the constitutionalists by their ideology and tactics, believing in terror as a means and accepting assassination as a method. Their appearance ushered in an era where the assassin's gun was used more often than the ballot box.

CHAPTER SIXTEEN

Attempted Assassination

B Y the start of 1949 the Tudeh had begun to win new recruits. Three years had passed since the defeat of the separatists in Azerbaijan, when the Tudeh had gone underground. Despite Qavam's attempts to suppress it in the last stages of his own career, the Tudeh inner circle had remained relatively intact. Its cadres still operated among professional and industrial workers in the towns. The refusal of the Company to give serious consideration to national grievances provided the Tudeh with the platform it required. Earlier, the Tudeh only thrived when it clothed its programme in a nationalist costume. The separatist movement in the north had unmasked it. The new and intense agitation on the oil question now offered the opportunity which it had been awaiting. It lost no time in adopting a programme demanding the outright nationalisation of the Company, although loyalty to Moscow required continued support for a Soviet oil concession in the north and weakened its position to some extent. However, it soon built up close contacts with the main nationalist group and began to gather strength in the cities.

At the other extreme, new parties and groups had appeared on the far right. Though none of these had large mass followings, at least two of them appeared to have a special character in that they were organised and led by the Muslim clergy.

Fadayan-Islam was a small political group which was led by a half-educated fanatic, Sa'ed Nawab Safavi. This man was in his early thirties and known as an eccentric. *Mujahidin-Islam* was the second group, controlled by Shams Qanatabadi : the *ayatollah* Kashani later became its leader. Qanatabadi was an opportunist politician, whose career had survived several political somersaults. Both these were small groups, thriving on the support of the *mullahs* and religious students, though they had some following among the more superstitious sections of the urban working people. They favoured a religious approach to politics, and were opposed to all professional politicians. They felt that all the ills of Iranian society could be eliminated if the state were run by the *mullahs*.

The *Fadayan* was closer in its approach and methods to the Muslim Brotherhood, a religious totalitarian movement originally founded in Egypt. It not only opposed the professional politicians, but also the traditional *ulama*, whom it charged with being compromised by an un-Islamic approach. It was also opposed to the Pahlavi dynasty. However, its most distinctive character lay in its belief in assassination. The *Mujahidin* disagreed with the *Fadayan*, chiefly on the question of assassination. At the outset this difference with the *Fadayan* was not clear : both of them worked together, agitating for a return to the medieval era, when life was dominated by the *mullahs* as interpreters of the Holy Qoran and therefore sole arbiters of people's lives.[1]

The Shah, as the increasingly recognised and accepted leader of his people, had been attacked by all these extremist groups.

[1] There is a surprising paucity of documented studies on these movements, and one is forced to rely on oral testimony in dealing with them. However, for a broad analysis see Halpern, Manfred, *The Politics of Social Change in the Middle East and North Africa* (Princeton, New Jersey, 1963), p. 134 ff. ; see also Binder, Leonard, *Iran : Political Development in a Changing Society* (Berkeley and Los Angeles, 1962), pp. 220–1.

His active intervention in the affairs of his country at decisive moments had aroused their hatred. The extreme left had found in him the focal point of their frustrations. It was he who had decided that the separatists in Azerbaijan and Kurdistan should be crushed, if necessary, by force of arms. The extremists on the right could neither understand nor accept his zeal for the modernisation of the country. They had resented Reza Shah's earlier policy of secularisation of Iran's political life, and the Shah had not only continued with this policy but had given it new impetus. Time and again, he had spoken of the need for improving education and technology. It was almost a foregone conclusion that the extremists should attempt to eliminate him physically.

February 4 was the day of annual celebrations at Tehran University, founded by Reza Shah. The Shah had gone to address the students. He had put on, as was his custom on formal occasions, his military uniform. His car was driven to the entrance of the Faculty of Law, where the celebrations were to be held. The Shah got out of his car and was about to enter the building when several shots rang out. The first three bullets struck his military cap without injuring him. The fourth shot, however, entered his right cheek and upper lip and emerged under his nose. The would-be assassin, who had entered the Faculty gate in the guise of a photographer, was now within two yards of the Shah and levelled his revolver at his heart. The Shah, despite his wound, was in full possession of his senses and remained cool. He later described the event thus : 'We were face to face and there was no-one near to form a screen, so I realised that nothing could prevent his shot from reaching the target. I still remember the reaction which I showed at that unforgettable moment. I thought of throwing myself at him, but reasoned at once that such a leap would make his aim easier, and if I ran away, he would shoot from behind. So I had no alternative but to make certain spiral movements so that in accordance with military tactics, I could mislead him. The man fired another shot which wounded my shoulder. The last shot was jammed in his revolver, so I felt that there was no more danger and I was alive.' [2]

The would-be assassin threw down his useless weapon in rage and tried to make good his escape, but the Shah's attendants surrounded him. He was killed on the spot, which was unfortunate since his real instigators were never discovered. Some evidence during a later investigation pointed to his connection with the *Fayadan*, but this was not conclusive ; other evidence suggested that he was connected with the Tudeh ; and a further source of confusion was evidence of his frequent visits to a foreign embassy.

Although the Shah was seriously wounded, and bleeding profusely, he remained resolute, and insisted that he should continue with his official programme. His advisers would not hear of this. They rushed him to a nearby hospital where his wounds were treated. As soon as this had been done, the Shah broadcast to the nation reassuring his people that, by the grace of God, the assassination attempt had failed.

This unforgettable incident strengthened the Shah's religious beliefs as never before. Though he had had no further visions or visitations since his early childhood, there had been at least two previous occasions when he felt that some superhuman power had helped him. In 1948 he had gone to visit Kuhrang, near Isfahan, to inspect the site of an irrigation dam, using his personal plane which, as a trained pilot, he flew himself. On the return journey he took off with the military commander of the area as his companion in this single-engined plane. Within ten minutes, the engine went dead, and there was no alternative but to make a forced landing somewhere in the mountainous

[2] *Mission*, p. 57.

region below. Such an exercise seemed to mean certain death and yet the plane landed safely. He has recorded this incident in his autobiography : 'As every pilot knows, a plane has a stalling speed below which it will go into a spin. With the engine gone, I had no throttle, nor could I manœuvre within the narrow confines of the ravine ; the only thing was to maintain my speed by going down then and there. Just before we struck, I pulled on the stick to raise the plane's nose to avert a head-on collision with the barrier of rock lying directly in front of us. The plane had barely enough speed left to clear the barrier and could not surmount a boulder lying just beyond. When we collided with it, the undercarriage was completely torn off, but at least that helped to reduce our speed. The plane started to slide on its belly over the rock-strewn ground. A moment later, the propeller hit a large boulder and the plane turned a slow and deliberate somersault, coming to a halt with the fuselage upside down. Neither of us had suffered so much as a scratch. . . . Was that narrow escape good luck, or was it good luck bolstered by something else ?' [3]

This air crash had been preceded by the Azerbaijan crisis, during which the Shah had felt strongly that he had been guided by some divine force while taking his difficult decisions. He had nursed his childhood faith over the years, and these two incidents had already given it a mature base. Now, he had been saved from assassination. The killer could so easily have succeeded — and yet he had failed. Surely this inexplicable failure could not be unconnected with that divine power which had been manifested to the Shah ever since his early childhood. This feeling made a positive contribution to his religious life, strengthening his sense of humility and his devotion to his duty towards his people.

The attempt on the Shah's life led to tremendous reper-

[3] *Mission*, p. 56.

cussions among all sections of the people. Suddenly it was realised that the disappearance of the Shah would have thrown the country into anarchy. Whoever the would-be assassin might have been, and whatever his motives, large sections of the people believed that the attempt was activated by a desire to remove the only unchallengeable political leader in the country. Such a step, if successful, would have opened the floodgates for the various internal and external forces which would have bene- fited from political instability in Iran. No wonder then that it 'provoked extraordinary demonstrations of loyalty throughout the country'.[4]

Immediately after the attempted assassination the Sa'ed government adopted several measures to suppress the extremist movements. The Tudeh was officially outlawed and a large number of people were arrested, including leaders of the right-wing religious fanatics, among them the *ayatollah* Kashani. Even Qavam came under suspicion and orders were issued for his arrest. However, the Shah intervened to save him and, on his advice, Qavam hastily left the country. At this stage the *majlis* realised that it was essential to strengthen the Shah's con-stitutional position. It therefore agreed to make certain pro-visions already contained within the Constitution fully effective. According to Articles 43, 44 and 45, the legislature was to comprise a Senate as well as the *majlis*. The articles con-cerning the Senate had been lying dormant, but were now activated. The *majlis* decided to bring into existence this second House, of which, under the Constitution, half the members were to be elected and the other half nominated by the Shah.

The *majlis* also decided that some basic amendments to the Constitution were required. A royal proclamation was there-fore issued to convene a Constituent Assembly. On May 8,

4 Arfa, p. 388.

1949, this Assembly abrogated Article 48 and added a Supplementary Article to the Supplement to the Constitution. The new Article, which replaced Article 48, gave the Shah power to dissolve either House of the Legislature separately or together. The Shah was to give the reason for any such dissolution in the decree proclaiming it. Re-election to the Legislature was to begin within one month and to be completed within three months. The constitutional amendments also made provisions for methods of amending the Constitution in the future, while laying down that those Articles of the Constitution concerning Islam and constitutional monarchy could not be amended since they were 'eternally unalterable'.[5]

These steps strengthened the constitutional position of the Shah, who now sought to turn national attention to the economic development of the country. The Seven Year Plan had remained a paper project. The attitude of the Anglo-Iranian Oil Company had made it abundantly clear that Iran could not expect any sizeable additional revenue from her own oil in the immediate future. A series of short-lived cabinets complicated other causes of the failure of the Plan, including administrative bottlenecks. Therefore, in the autumn of 1949, the Shah decided to test the quality of American goodwill, which seemed to be abundant, and went to Washington on a State Visit. He had prepared his brief in detail, since he knew that both the Press and the public in the United States would want to know what he intended to do with any aid he might receive. On November 19 he explained at a Press conference in New York the salient features of his programme. 'The programme I intend to carry out', he said, 'involves the sale of extensive lands to the government by landowners and landlords, who do not show any particular interest in their property, so that the government may apportion them, and sell

[5] Shamim, pp. 71 to 73.

them at the same price by small instalments to farmers. Thus, Iranian farmers will be able to cultivate their own lands according to this programme and each farmer will be able to pay his debt in about twenty to twenty-five years.'[6]

The Shah received a friendly reception, and nothing more. As he himself related later, he returned home 'completely empty-handed'.[7] He was disappointed but not bitter. He knew that, despite President Truman's doctrine of 'containment of communism', the United States had not yet developed a real policy in West Asia. It had yet to recover from the shock of the collapse of the Kuomintang regime in China. Iran did not yet present to American eyes a picture of political stability and firm leadership. It was essential, the Shah felt, to convince Washington in this respect. On his return home, he launched a major campaign for administrative reform and efficiency, dismissing a number of officials against whom charges of corruption were proved, and creating an imperial anti-corruption commission. Simultaneously, he announced his determination to carry through the programme of basic land reform.

As a first step towards the radical change in the agrarian structure of Iranian society which he had planned for so long, the Shah announced that his own Crown lands would be distributed among the peasants. The royal decree on this subject was issued early in 1950. It proclaimed the distribution of more than two thousand hamlets and villages which, as Crown Estates, belonged personally to the Shah. He issued orders that immediate surveys be undertaken of these villages so that they could be distributed without delay among the peasants.[8] These reform measures were greeted enthusiastically by the poor both in the towns and villages. However, the landlords,

[6] Shamim, p. 137.   [7] *Mission*, p. 88.
[8] *The White Revolution*, pp. 32–3.

who dominated most of the political parties, were alarmed. They had always viewed the Shah's political philosophy with suspicion, and many of them had hoped that his radical ideas would abate once his youthful enthusiasm subsided. Now they were faced by a new phase in the Shah's policies. The right-wing Opposition formed a new political platform, the National Front, organised by several right-wing parties led by the landlords. Its leadership fell to Mossadeq, whose personal economic interests were now directly threatened.

The Shah continued with his work on the basis that if he showed 'America and the world that Iran would make good use of any additional aid that could be granted', there would be a change of heart in Washington. Once again he was disappointed: 'Our requests for large scale help were again refused. Instead of granting adequate funds, the American Government allocated a token amount of Point Four money and the Export Import Bank of Washington tentatively offered us a loan of $25 million — a small fraction of the minimum necessary to rehabilitate our occupation-devastated economy. Such a serious setback to our hopes convinced many of my people that the United States had deserted them and anti-American sentiment developed with a corresponding strengthening of the National Front Party.'[9] The Seven Year Plan had to be ruthlessly pruned. The experts and advisers who had come from the United States to help in this plan left for home. To reduce the growing feeling of desperation, the Shah then accepted a Soviet offer of a $20 million trade agreement.

Meanwhile, Gass had returned from London almost at the time of the attempt on the Shah's life. He had brought the sad news that the Company was still unwilling to change its policies.

---

9 *Mission*, p. 89. (The American grant was in fact used to good effect in the eradication of malaria.)

At his very first meeting with the Finance Minister, Gass had sung the same old tune : the purpose of his visit had nothing to do with any revision of the oil concession. For the next six months, discussions between the government and the Company had continued. In July, after the Sa'ed government had rejected a proposal for third party arbitration, the Company had for the first time made concrete proposals for settlement. Gass had worked out a formula with the Finance Minister, Golshayan. Sa'ed, apparently tired of the deadlock, had endorsed this formula.

By this formula the Company agreed to increase the royalty from four shillings to six shillings per ton ; to pay one shilling instead of ninepence per ton in lieu of national taxation ; and to guarantee a minimum sum of £4 million in respect of the dividend payments and transfers to the General Reserve. Further pressure from the Sa'ed government produced more concessions. The Company now agreed to an immediate payment of £5 million in respect of amounts standing to the credit of the General Reserve at the end of 1947, and to additional royalties amounting to some £9 million per annum for 1948 and 1949, representing the difference between royalties as calculated under the 1933 agreement and the new formula. This arrangement was to be incorporated as a supplement to the 1933 agreement. It came to be known, in the course of time, as the Golshayan–Gass agreement as the two of them had appended their signatures to it on July 19, 1949.[10]

The news of the formula had leaked to the Press and public even before it was finalised. Mossadeq and the Tudeh Press had condemned it as a 'sellout' on Sa'ed's part. When the agreement was placed before the *majlis* for ratification, it aroused solid opposition. Mossadeq ridiculed its terms : Iran, he argued, was to receive less under this agreement than the

[10] Marlowe, *Iran*, p. 89.

British were paying to Kuwait. This argument sealed the fate of the agreement. Though Sa'ed had a comfortable majority on paper, he could not persuade the *majlis* to ratify it. The bill was debated for four weeks since the deputies, fully conscious of the fact that it was an unpopular measure, were playing for time. They were more concerned with the trends in public opinion at this stage than in the fate of the bill because the term of the Fifteenth *majlis* was about to end and they had soon to face the delicate task of seeking re-election. They had still taken no decisive action by August 7, when the term of the *majlis* expired. New turmoil set in as the nation began to prepare for elections to the Sixteenth *majlis*.

CHAPTER SEVENTEEN

The Rise of Mossadeq

THE end of the Fifteenth *majlis* marked the beginning of the great battle over oil which was to be fought out over the succeeding three years. The four-month election campaign for the Sixteenth *majlis* was violently contested. Tehran was caught in the grip of this election fever even before the old *majlis* was formally dissolved, for the Golshayan–Gass agreement had helped to focus clearly the issues to be decided by the next *majlis*. The heat of controversy spread to other towns and finally reached the rural hinterland while Soviet, British and American interests began to play their part, intensifying old and precipitating new antagonisms.

At the centre of this arena of increasingly bitter conflict stood the Shah and Mossadeq. Both shared one common objective : they were equally determined to assert the right of Iran to exact just returns from the enormous profits till then almost exclusively enjoyed by the Company ; but this was their only common objective. In all other matters their personalities clashed. Since 1941 the Shah, now a mature intellectual, had studied in the hard school of reality and had emerged as a strong leader of his people, capable of planning in perspective. Mossadeq, on the other hand, had remained on the fringe of serious political responsibility throughout the four decades of his political career, and this had kept him away from the ruthless world of realities. He therefore continued to evaluate all problems from his own emotional standpoint.

The Shah opposed the policies of the Company because he believed them to be detrimental to the interests of his people. He wanted to establish a proper balance between the revenues which were morally due to the Company, and those which Iran should receive from its exploitation of her own national wealth. His opposition to the conduct of the Company did not arise from a negative emotional approach. His mind was set on the planned economic development of the country. Because he required finance for the Seven Year Plan, the question of oil became part of the problem of the poverty of his people. The revision of the 1933 agreement was not an end in itself but a means towards this end.

Mossadeq knew what the Shah's position was but neither comprehended it nor made any effort to do so. He was supported by landlord politicians, by the conservative *mullahs* who controlled the huge landed estates donated to religious foundations, and by all those who derived profit from the feudal system. This united front of the conservative, obscurantist and feudal forces became the spearhead of the attack against all efforts to solve the oil crisis by negotiation. Its fanatical attitude toward British interests attracted considerable support from the common people, whose own economic interests were, ironically, opposed to those of its leaders. The Front succeeded in its efforts to divert public concern from pressing agrarian and other economic reforms into emotional anger against the Company.

The Tudeh, which had earlier reorganised its ranks, now sought to regain its influence through the National Front. It conducted secret negotiations with the Front leaders, but these did not achieve the desired results as Mossadeq, although prepared to use the Tudeh, remained an arch anti-communist. It therefore boycotted the elections and, through its clandestine journals, began an attack on the Front's policy.[1] The right wing extremist groups, especially the *Fadayan*, increased their activities during the election campaign. This was to produce a spate of assassinations and attempted assassinations. In November, the *Fadayan* succeeded in murdering Hajir, then Minister of Court, at a mosque. The Front, which needed the support of the religious fanatics, did not condemn their activities.

Pro-British elements tried to take advantage of the political situation, hoping once more to benefit by playing for time and supporting those who could pave the way for the ratification of the Supplementary Agreement. The election results, however, were disappointing both for the Front and the pro-British elements. The Front secured the election of only eight deputies, including Mossadeq himself, while the strategy of the pro-British elements also failed since the Sixteenth *majlis* proved no less determined to oppose the Golshayan–Gass agreement than its predecessor. The new *majlis* was formally inaugurated by the Shah in a joint session on February 9, 1950, and began work nine days later.

The oil problems now dominated all political debate in the *majlis*, the Senate and the country. The Shah's deep study of the situation had by this time led him to the conclusion that the policy adopted by Sa'ed was entirely wrong. It was a capitulatory policy and must be rejected, since the Company's position, backed by the British government, was both morally and legally indefensible. He let it be known that he was opposed to the Golshayan–Gass agreement and Sa'ed, aware of this, did not

[1] For Dr Mossadeq's political views and the class composition of his National Front see Marlowe, *Iran*, pp. 87–8 ; for a detailed analysis of Dr Mossadeq's political philosophy, see below, Chapter 21.

defend it seriously when it was placed before the *majlis* and the Senate for ratification. His policy having failed, Sa'ed resigned on March 22. The Shah nominated Ali Mansur, who had been Reza Shah's Prime Minister at the time of the 1941 invasion, to replace Sa'ed. On April 13 Mansur secured a vote of confidence from both Houses.

Despite his opposition to the Golshayan–Gass agreement, the Shah had not yet given up hope for a constructive solution to the oil dispute. He could not understand the uncompromising position adopted by the Company during the negotiations, which showed 'an amazing indifference to the trend of Iranian public opinion'. Of this approach he later wrote : 'The Company knew very well that Saudi Arabia and various Latin American countries had received more favourable returns from major Western oil concerns than those afforded by our agreements. The Company knew of our irritation due to the high percentage paid in corporation taxes to the British government ; these taxes in fact greatly exceeded the royalties to Iran. The Company knew we were galled by its practice of using much of the lush profits it earned here to expand oil output in other parts of the world.' [2] The Shah had spent long hours in assembling the facts on which he wanted to build Iran's case. His final brief was a telling indictment of the Company and of the British Labour government, which had backed the Company to the hilt.

The Company had at no stage paid royalties to the government amounting to more than 15 per cent of government revenues. In 1950, royalties were a mere 12 per cent, and this constituted a fractional 4 per cent of the national income of Iran. From 1911 to 1920, the Company had paid no royalties at all. From 1921 to 1930, it had paid about $60 million. From 1931 to 1941, about $125 million was received by

[2] *Mission*, p. 90.

Iran. This money had been spent by Reza Shah on military equipment which was subsequently used by the British and Soviet forces during the Second War, without any compensation being paid. Between 1941 and 1950, the Company had paid, in all, $250 million.[3] At the same time, the contrast between what the Company paid Iran and its own profits was staggering. It had recovered its initial investment of $100 million some twenty-five to thirty years earlier, and its gross profits since then had been twenty-five times its original capital.[4]

The enormous profits of the Company went not to Iran but to Britain. In 1950, the Company paid $142 million in taxes to the British government, while total royalties to Iran amounted to only $45 million. The total dividends received by the British Government since 1913 would have been sufficient to finance three Seven Year Plans in Iran. Since 1914 the Company had enjoyed a gross operating income of $5 billion. The British Navy had saved $500 million in cheaper bunkering fuel: the British Exchequer had received $1.5 billion in taxes; the shareholders $350 million in dividends; and the Company itself $2.7 billion for depreciation and expansion.

The sheer contrast between what the Company paid in royalties to Iran, and what other oil companies paid other producing countries amounted to insult and humiliation. Bahrein

---

[3] Of the various studies made on the subject of the financial relations between the Company and the Iranian government, perhaps the most informative is *Report of Oil Mission to Middle East*, prepared for the American Oil Workers' International Union by Lloyd A. Haskins in January, 1953, and reported in *International Oil Worker* (April 6, 1953).

[4] This fact was later repeatedly quoted in comments on the oil dispute during debates in the Security Council as well as in newspapers, see *Oil Forum* (March 1952); *New Republic*, Washington (December 8, 1952); O'Connor, Harvey, *The Empire of Oil* (New York, 1962), p. 326.

received 35 cents per barrel, Saudi Arabia 56, and Iraq 60. In 1950 the Company was paying less than 18 cents per barrel to Iran. This was not all. The Company allowed all the gas from Iranian wells to burn off although Iran was much in need of it. It paid its Iranian workers only a quarter of the wages paid to comparable Venezuelan workers. It had committed flagrant breaches of its 1933 agreement, and neglected the training of Iranians to take over operating posts both at Abadan and in the oilfields. The housing provided for its workers at Abadan, even after forty years, had been condemned by independent authorities as 'abominable'.[5]

It was this state of affairs which the Shah could no longer tolerate and was determined to challenge. He wanted an arrangement with the Company which took all these facts into account, and felt that such an agreement would be in the Company's own interests. The Company was not only systematically imperilling its huge investment in Iran by remaining indifferent to these realities, but was also fanning the fire of Iranian nationalism. The inevitable result of such a policy was the strengthening of the demagogic hold of Mossadeq and the National Front over the people.[6] But the Shah himself was in no position to put across his rational policy to the urban population, which was now being fed hatred for Britain by the National Front and the parties of the extreme right and left. The agitators in the streets of Tehran were no longer merely asking for economic benefits from a new agreement with the Company. The slogan 'nationalisation now' was already abroad.

Soon after Ali Mansur came to power, the *majlis* appointed a committee of eighteen deputies to examine the Golshayan—

[5] International Labour Office, *Labour Conditions in the Oil Industry in Iran* (Geneva, 1958).

[6] *Mission*, p. 90.

Gass agreement presented to it for ratification by the Sa'ed government. It was a foregone conclusion that the new committee, under Mossadeq's inspiration, would not only reject the agreement, but would also recommend nationalisation of the oil industry. It began its work in July 1950. Meanwhile, Ali Mansur, who did not agree with the call for nationalisation, had been voted out of power on June 26, and his place had been taken by General Haj Ali Razmara.

Razmara was known to be opposed to the proposal for nationalisation now being advocated openly and persistently by Mossadeq and his National Front. When he submitted the programme of his new government to the *majlis*, Razmara made no reference to the oil question. It was believed that, since the Shah was opposed to the Golshayan–Gass agreement, Razmara wanted it revised and adjusted in the interests of Iran and then ratified by the *majlis* and the Senate. Razmara attempted to divert the attention of the *majlis* away from the oil question by introducing proposals for large-scale local self-government. He wanted the *majlis* to approve the formation of local councils in towns and villages to make rural and tribal life more self-reliant. The *majlis* agreed to appoint a committee to consider this idea, but refused to relent on the oil question.

As time went by, Razmara faced increasing opposition in the *majlis*. Twice in October, the National Front tried to bring his government down. In November, it once again raised the oil question. The government challenged the position of the Front on nationalisation. In order to weaken Razmara's hand in negotiations with the Company, the *majlis* adopted a resolution which declared : 'The statements of the Minister of Finance in the session of November 25, 1950, concerning oil are by no means confirmed by parliament and are hereby rejected'. This frustrated any hopes that Razmara might have had of securing a revision of the Golshayan–Gass agreement in favour of Iran, though he continued with his efforts to persuade the Company to grant still greater concessions.[7]

The *majlis* resolution brought about a fresh wave of agitation against foreigners. Razmara was condemned in the opposition press as a foreign agent. The time had passed, said Mossadeq, for any revision of the Golshayan–Gass agreement. It was now for the people of Iran to take under their own control what rightfully belonged to them. Mossadeq asked for nothing less than the wholesale nationalisation of the entire oil industry in Iran. Razmara then made a fatal mistake. He appeared before the *majlis* on March 3 to report that the project of nationalisation of the Company would be impracticable as well as illegal.[8]

Defiance of the Razmara government became widespread within hours of this report. The Tudeh was not slow to take advantage of this, and began to work energetically among the army officers. It succeeded to a considerable extent, and ten of its leaders, then in prison at Ghassr, escaped with the help of some of these officers.[9] The *Fadayan* pronounced Razmara a heathen. On March 7, 1951, when the Prime Minister went to attend the funeral of a *mullah* at the Shah Mosque, he was killed by a *Fadayan* fanatic. Twelve days later, Azam Zangeneh, who was Minister of Education in the Razmara government, was shot at Tehran University, and died a few days later.

Hossein Ala, who stepped into the breach created by Razmara's murder, formed a new cabinet on March 12. But before

---

[7] Razmara had actually received a concession proposal from the Company, offering Iran a fifty-fifty split of profits. Razmara did not announce this offer since he wanted to wait till a better climate for its acceptance could be created. Razmara was proved wrong by the succeeding events. There was no chance of its being accepted at this stage. As the Shah wrote: 'But the British proposal was in any event too late, for Persian nationalism had become thoroughly aroused and public sentiment overwhelmingly favoured nationalisation.' *Mission*, p. 276; also Shamim, pp. 84–5.

[8] Arfa, pp. 392–3.   [9] Shamim, p. 82.

he secured his vote of confidence, the die had already been cast on the oil question. The day after the assassination, the *majlis* Oil Committee decided to approve the proposals for the nationalisation of the oil industry. It also asked for an extension of two months to consider methods for the effective execution of the project. Seven days later, on March 15, the *majlis* approved the decision to nationalise, and agreed to prolong the life of the Committee for the period it had requested. It also invited the deputies to submit their views and proposals on this problem within fifteen days.

The Shah had already come to the conclusion that, in the light of the continued indifference of the Company, there was no alternative but to sanction the demand for nationalisation. He had taken a long time to agree to such a radical project, although he had never been opposed to it in principle. His earlier hesitation had sprung from his knowledge that nationalisation would bring with it many technical and financial problems. Iran was not in a position to operate the vast oil empire in the south. It simply did not possess the necessary expertise. And yet the national humiliation inflicted upon the country by the Company could no longer be tolerated. He therefore endorsed the project submitted to the *majlis* for the enforcement of the Nationalisation Law and expropriation of the Company.[10] It was readily approved by the *majlis* on April 29.

The Shah had examined the provisions of the Nationalisation Law carefully. A joint committee of five senators, five deputies and the Minister of Finance was entrusted with the duty of dispossessing the Company at once. It also provided for a deposit of up to a quarter of the current revenue of the Company with the Bank Melli, or any other bank mutually agreed upon by the Company and government, as security, should the Company resort to claims against the government with a view to

[10] *Mission*, p. 90.

delaying the process of its dispossession. The government was charged with the duty of investigating, under the supervision of the joint committee, the rightful claims of Iran and the Company and of reporting on them to the *majlis*.

The Shah had instructed Ala to inform the British Ambassador of the Nationalisation Bill. The Prime Minister had had an unpleasant meeting with the Ambassador, who had categorically refused to acknowledge the measure.[11] Ala had called a cabinet meeting on April 27, and announced his inability to continue. He submitted his resignation to the Shah on the same morning. Even at this late stage, Ala was in favour of a compromise proposal. He wanted to ensure a continued flow of oil. Under this compromise the oil industry, although nationalised, would be kept going with the help of foreign technicians. Mossadeq opposed this compromise. A series of riots inspired by the Tudeh followed. Several people, including three Britons, were killed. The Company reiterated its rejection of all proposals by closing down its operations.

The Shah had now to decide upon a new course of action. Between 1946 and 1951 seven governments had fallen. The departures of Hakimi, Hajir, Sa'ed, Ali Mansur, Razmara and Ala, were directly connected with the agitation on the oil question. Mossadeq and his National Front were principally responsible for bringing down these six cabinets because they had adhered to the principle of compromise. The Front's agitation had led to the rise of several fanatical groups, of which

11 Sir Francis Shepherd, then British Ambassador, was in a difficult position. He was aware of the nationalist sentiment and yet was expected to carry out a policy which completely ignored it. He did, however, try to meet the nationalists halfway in arguments, if not in action. For example, in a letter to Razmara, he said, *inter alia*, 'In my opinion it is extremely unfortunate that public opinion in Iran should, as it is evident, still abide by this old-fashioned opinion that Britain . . . intends to impose imperialism and colonialism. . . .' For extracts of this letter see Shamim, p. 86.

the *Fadayan* presented the greatest danger. Two former Prime Ministers, Hajir and Razmara, had been assassinated by *Fadayan* fanatics, and an attempt had been made on the life of the Shah himself.

The Shah knew 'Mossadeq had already promised the people a new era of prosperity and plenty, to be financed by the oil revenues to which Iran was legitimately entitled'. The liberality of his promises was characteristic of Mossadeq's own emotional attitude to the question. He had told the *majlis*, and repeated from several platforms in Tehran and the country, that he would wring a million dollars a day from the Company. His promises had won him tremendous national support. He had also secured an overwhelming majority in the *majlis*. As the Shah wrote later : 'In fact, how could anyone be against Mossadeq ? He would enrich everybody, he would fight the foreigner, he would secure our rights. No wonder students, intellectuals, people from all walks of life flocked to his banner.' [12]

Mossadeq had carried everything before him. The Shah thought this was the opportune moment to engage Mossadeq's talents and use his popularity as a means of putting the country on the road to stability and prosperity. In fact, the passage of the Nationalisation Bill left no alternative but to harness Mossadeq's energies to make the measure fruitful. The Shah summoned Mossadeq to an audience. He explained to the leader of the National Front his own belief that nationalisation was an inevitable measure. He promised him support if, as Prime Minister, Mossadeq would carry out nationalisation and raise the standard of living of the people. Mossadeq accepted the offer and the Shah nominated him to take the place of Ala.

On April 29, 1951, Mohammad Mossadeq became Prime Minister of Iran. Nine days later, the *majlis* passed a vote of

[12] *Mission*, pp. 90–1.

confidence in his government by the overwhelming majority of 99 to 3. He submitted a very brief programme to both Houses, asking for two months to enforce the Nationalisation Law. He pledged his government to spend the revenues accruing from nationalisation in improving the economic conditions of the country. The Shah watched with restrained hope the rejoicings organised by the National Front at Mossadeq's rise to power. As he wrote later, he was hoping for a new turn in the depressing trend of national life, and waiting to see what measures Mossadeq would take : 'Now was Mossadeq's great opportunity. His success had exceeded his own fondest dreams, as well as those of his followers. Two wonderful years of opportunity lay ahead for him. He was to enjoy my full support for a year and my toleration — agonising though it was for me — during many months thereafter. What would he do ?' [13]

[13] *Mission*, p. 91.

CHAPTER EIGHTEEN

Symbolic Triumph

WHEN the Shah nominated Mossadeq Prime Minister, he was prepared to face a new period of stress and strain. The oil dispute had already developed into a serious trial of strength between Iran and the Company. He had therefore weighed up the various internal and external factors likely to affect the character of the oil crisis before deciding to support Mossadeq, with whose policies he was neither unfamiliar nor particularly impressed. He had taken full account of the prejudices of both the National Front, with which the rightist religious extremists had now made common cause, and the Tudeh. He was aware that the Company could rely on the intervention of the British government. Once that happened, he knew that Britain would immediately use its enormous political, military and economic power against Iran. A determined effort would be made to break Iranian resistance. Such a development would bring in its train Soviet and American involvement in the dispute. The oil crisis would then necessarily become an issue of the Cold War.

On May 8, the Company invoked the arbitration clause of the agreement of 1933 and named Lord Radcliffe as its representative on the proposed arbitration tribunal. The first official reaction from the British government came within ten days of Mossadeq's appointment. The Foreign Secretary,

o

Herbert Morrison, lodged a mild protest at the manner in which the nationalisation of the oil industry had been undertaken in southern Iran. Morrison could hardly have picked an open quarrel on the principle of nationalisation. The Labour government, having propagated the doctrine at home, was in no position to denounce Iran for having taken a leaf out of its own book.

However, the very act of protest on the part of Britain came as a shock to Mossadeq and his Front. They had mistakenly believed that the Company would not receive endorsement for its policy from the Labour government. The latter, as lifelong agitators for socialism, would surely never identify themselves with the monopolistic interests of a capitalist company. Surely they could not permit themselves to become the spearhead of an attack on the interests of a small and poor country, which had been at pains to offer compensation to which it did not consider the Company entitled. Morrison's statement left no scope for Mossadeq's strategy of driving a wedge between the British socialists and the capitalist Company.[1]

However, the Labour government, despite the official support it gave to the Company and its reference to British paratroops standing by, appeared to be in a conciliatory mood. Undoubtedly on the instructions of the British government, as its majority shareholder, the Company sent a delegation to Tehran. On March 29, Basil Jackson, its leader, opened negotia-

---

[1] Dr Mossadeq, like most statesmen, seldom took the public into his confidence on his real reactions to events ; only those who belonged to his inner circle were permitted to know what he felt. The author is greatly indebted to Dr Ali Obeidi, deputy to the Prime Minister in the Mossadeq government, for valuable information on and help in interpreting in a rational manner, as far as possible, various steps which Dr Mossadeq took during this period. In view of the fact that no proper documented history of this period is as yet available, the author had no alternative but to rely on oral testimony of the participants in the events.

tions with government representatives in the cool and pleasant climate of Shimran, not far from the Shah's palace. Mossadeq, of course, was in no mood for compromise. While these talks were in progress, he issued orders that the captains of oil tankers loading cargo at Abadan must tender receipts in favour of the government of Iran now that the Company had been nationalised.

On June 19, Jackson offered certain temporary payments of royalty. He also repeated the private offer made to Razmara of an equal share in the profits for Iran. The government disputed the amount, and rejected the offer, the acceptance of which had cost Razmara his life. The talks broke down on the same day. Mossadeq thereupon announced the formation of the National Iranian Oil Company (NIOC), to replace the nationalised British company and take over all its functions. This step, although expected, led to a certain amount of panic among Company officials. On June 25, Mossadeq warned the *majlis* against the possibility of economic sabotage by the Company and British officials. He cited the example of the Director-General of the Company's operations in Iran, whom he accused of instigating the tanker captains to refuse receipts in favour of NIOC. On June 27, the British personnel of the Company turned down the government's offer of continued employment with NIOC on the same conditions.

About the same time the British cruiser *Mauritius* anchored off Abadan. Though London explained that the cruiser had been sent 'to protect the lives of British citizens', its presence at Abadan was quickly interpreted as a threat to their safety by the captains of the non-British tankers, who sailed forthwith without loading their cargoes.[2] By July 3, production at the Abadan refinery had been reduced by half.

Two days later, President Truman put forward a proposal

[2] Sahebjam, p. 253.

for reconciliation and offered the services of his Special Envoy, Averell Harriman, who arrived in Tehran on July 15. On his arrival, the Tudeh changed its tactics overnight. Until then it had opposed Mossadeq, accusing him of cheating the people with fake nationalisation. Now it declared its complete support for the Nationalisation Law. It staged a massive demonstration in Tehran against American intervention and followed this up with an open letter to Mossadeq. In this it demanded that he send away the American military mission; that he recognise the legality of the Party and release political prisoners; and that he accord diplomatic recognition to the communist government of China. This was the Tudeh's first open and defiant use of the Cold War slogans of the Soviet camp. The demonstration clashed with right wing pro-American elements in front of the *majlis* building, forcing Mossadeq to call in the army and declare a state of siege. As the Shah had expected, the oil crisis had brought the Cold War to Iran.

Harriman completed his talks on July 27 and left for London to persuade the British government to make a last effort to seek a peaceful solution of the dispute. It was largely as a result of this visit that the Attlee government decided to send Richard Stokes, then Lord Privy Seal and Minister of Supply, to Tehran. Stokes arrived at Tehran on July 30, accompanied by Harriman. By this time, throughput at the Abadan refinery had completely stopped due to the refusal of the technicians to continue work.

The Shah, realising that the Stokes mission might well prove to be the last opportunity for obtaining an honourable compromise, appealed for calm in a radio speech and through the Press. However, the news of the closure of the Abadan refinery had aroused growing resentment and anger among the people, and the Tudeh successfully exploited the accumulation of hatred for Britain.

After a preliminary discussion with Mossadeq's advisers, Stokes submitted his proposals. The British government and the Company were willing to recognise, in principle, the fact of nationalisation and the existence of NIOC. The Company was willing to continue with oil operations in Iran as the agent of NIOC and to dispose of all oil produced under such an arrangement after providing for the domestic requirements of Iran. It was willing to make a payment of 50 per cent of the net profit of the sales of such oil overseas.[3] The proposals were quite candid on two points : the Company would not surrender its installations or its oil to the government.[4]

Mossadeq's counter-proposals were equally candid. Iran would not give up its sovereign right to expropriate the Company subject to the payment of compensation, and she was unwilling to share control of the oil operations with the Company. Mossadeq repeated his offer of continued employment for the former staff of the nationalised Company on the same terms. Finally, Iran insisted upon her undisputed control, ownership and disposal of Iranian oil, with a guarantee to supply the previous customers of the Company. Harriman appeared to be more in agreement with Stokes' position than Mossadeq's During the course of the final talks, Stokes tried to impress upon Mossadeq and his advisers that if they gave up the rigidity of their position on nationalisation, the Company would in fact accept it as a matter for negotiation.

On paper the two positions appeared irreconcilable. Yet, there was room for compromise provided both sides were prepared to adopt a flexible approach. The Shah, in daily contact with the progress of the talks, had come to the conclusion that

[3] Marlowe, *The Persian Gulf*, pp. 155–6.

[4] The special feature of these proposals was that Iran would not have to pay compensation to the Company ; until 1966 Iran paid, in instalments, what amounted to several times the amortization of the Company's original capital.

Iran must take a realistic view of the situation. The acceptance by Britain of the nationalisation law as 'a matter of negotiation' in effect meant a definite retreat from the position till then taken by the Company. On the other hand, Iran was as yet not in a position technically to take over the operations of the Company despite her legal expropriation of it. Even Mossadeq had recognised this fact by repeatedly offering to hand over these technical operations to the foreigners whom he otherwise publicly despised. The difference between the Company and the government on the question of the Company acting as agent for NIOC was sufficiently narrow to be eliminated. The Shah conveyed his views to Mossadeq who was in no mood to consider any compromise suggestions, even from his own sovereign. He was triumphant at having brought Britain to a position where it no longer disputed the right of Iran to nationalise the Company, and had to agree to negotiate over the effects of its nationalisation. He and his supporters believed that firmness, not flexibility, was needed. If they refused to give up any of their demands, Britain would be brought to its knees.

This was a dangerous miscalculation on the part of Mossadeq, as later events showed, and as the Shah was always to remember : 'When our oil industry had been nationalised and Mossadeq had first come to power, the British government and the Company had quickly seen the writing on the wall. Completely reversing their former policy, they formally accepted the principle of nationalisation. Soon afterwards, when the British sent the so-called Stokes Mission to Iran, the British agreed on fifty-fifty sharing of the oil revenues. Think of the economic miseries and the political perils that the people of my country would have been spared if Mossadeq had been willing to enter into rational negotiations.' [5]

[5] *Mission*, p. 92.

On September 6, the talks officially ended in failure. With the departure of Stokes and Harriman, the pace of the nationalisation operation increased. The next logical step for Iran was to dispossess the Company of its assets. The Shah took the initiative in making nationalisation really effective now that the compromise proposals had been shelved. He ordered troops to take immediate possession of all the installations formerly owned by the Company. The *majlis* had earlier appointed a committee to undertake the rest of the tasks. The members of this committee arrived at Abadan on September 26. The government notified the British personnel of the Company that on their refusal to take employment with NIOC their residence permits had been cancelled.

The physical dispossession of the Company was a milestone in Iranian history. It brought to a logical conclusion the process which had commenced when Stalin's demand for an oil concession in the northern provinces was resisted by the Shah. It was also a milestone in the British retreat from Asia. A British commentator was to describe this later : 'The fact that a vital British interest in the Persian Gulf had been successfully expropriated, and the fact that the British had not used, or seriously threatened the use of, force for its defence, underlined as nothing else could have done, the change that had taken place in the relationships between Great Britain and the littoral states of the Persian Gulf. The Gulf was no longer a British lake ; British hegemony had been successfully defied.' [6] This was an accurate assessment in all respects but one. Britain had threatened the use of force.

The element of force had formed part of British policy from the very start of the oil dispute. As early as May 15, Morrison had informed the House of Commons that British paratroops were standing by. The dispatch of the cruiser *Mauritius*,

[6] Marlowe, *The Persian Gulf*, p. 158.

ostensibly to protect British lives, was an attempt at nineteenth-century gunboat diplomacy at the beginning of the second half of the twentieth.

As the Iranian flag was hoisted over the Company's former properties a final threat of force was made. Britain moved the paratroops to Cyprus within easy striking distance of Abadan and Khoramshahr, several ships of the Royal Navy moved towards the Gulf ; British military action against Iran again seemed imminent. Many observers in Iran thought, at this juncture, that one of the aims behind this exhibition of force was to divide the government from the Shah. This illusion on the part of Britain, if it ever existed, was soon demolished by the Shah himself, who now challenged Britain's military black-mail. On September 27 he summoned the British Ambassador to an audience. The story of this move, which came as a surprise to many in Britain, has been recorded by the Shah as follows : 'At about this time, Britain announced that she was ordering paratroops to Cyprus and it was rumoured that they were for possible use in Iran. The British cruiser *Mauritius* already lay at anchor off Abadan and there were rumours of further naval movements in our direction in the Persian Gulf. I took occasion to tell the British Ambassador that if his government tried any violation of our sovereignty, I personally would lead our forces to resist the aggressors.' [7] Any hope London might have cherished of 'neutralising' the Shah in the struggle against the nationalisation of the Company disappeared forthwith.

The Shah's response to the British challenge was undoubtedly the primary factor which prevented the Attlee government from making the mistake which the Eden government was to commit in another context five years later. The Shah knew that the threat of force carried much more serious implications for

[7] *Mission*, p. 91.

Britain than it would have done previously. As a rising Asian leader, he was not unaware of the weakened position of British power. All through its long and aggressive relationship with his country, Britain had relied upon the troops and resources of its Indian empire. Seven years earlier, the basis of this policy had collapsed with the dissolution of the empire. However, even if the British government were adventurous enough to risk its own troops and resources in yet another invasion of Iran in peacetime, it would have spelled disaster. The incident would have become an international issue immediately, with the United Nations entering the arena. In the face of an armed resistance by Iran, Britain would also have been exposed to a combined attack by the Soviet camp and the Afro-Asian nations.

Britain, meanwhile, had begun to unfold a well-prepared economic and diplomatic offensive, aimed at the economic strangulation of Iran. Britain advised all potential customers for Iranian oil that it should be treated as the property of the Company; anyone who purchased it from NIOC, it added, would be sued for 'being in possession of stolen goods, knowing them to be stolen'. This threat eventually succeeded in closing the entire export market to Iranian oil. On September 10, Britain froze Iran's sterling balances. Simultaneously, all British licences for the export of scarce materials from the United Kingdom to Iran were revoked. This was a declaration of economic war.

On the diplomatic front, Britain, having already appealed to the International Court at The Hague to have the Nationalisation Law invalidated, called a meeting of the United Nations Security Council on September 30. The Soviet Union and Yugoslavia opposed consideration of the British complaint on the grounds that oil nationalisation and the residence of British experts in Iran were strictly within the competence of Iran's domestic jurisdiction. The complaint, however, was placed on the agenda with the support of other members of the Council. When the Permanent Representative of Iran at the United Nations was asked to attend the Council session, he informed its president that Mossadeq himself was to attend the Council meeting and plead Iran's case.

On October 9, Britain submitted a further petition to the International Court, bringing its case up to date. It no longer wanted merely to have the Nationalisation Law declared illegal. It charged the government of Iran with violation of international law inasmuch as the government had refused to submit its dispute with the Company to arbitration and had abrogated the Company's concession. It further pleaded that with the expulsion of British personnel from Abadan, the matter had assumed a different form.

The British offensive had the opposite effect to that intended. The concerted attack on Iran strengthened, instead of weakening, Mossadeq's position. A small parliamentary minority belonging to the extreme right had opposed Mossadeq. It now abjured its opposition and pledged that it would not weaken the hands of the government in its struggle against a foreign power until the two tribunals, the Security Council and the International Court, gave their verdict.[8] What was more important from Mossadeq's viewpoint was the unreserved support he received from the Shah. The Shah had regretted the breakdown of the talks and feared that Mossadeq had lost the initiative to Britain. This fear proved to be justified. Britain had now begun to call the tune and Iran required national unity above all else. The Shah, despite his own estimate of Mossadeq, therefore fully backed the Prime Minister in the moves he made on Iran's behalf.

Mossadeq, now stronger than ever before at home, left for the

[8] Shamim, p. 90.

United States. He planned to centre the attention of world public opinion on the right of Iran to nationalise oil. He also wanted to seek substantial economic assistance from the United States and secure the co-operation of American oil companies in breaking the British embargo on Iranian oil. Upon arrival in New York, he exhibited his flair for melodrama by making his headquarters at the New York University Hospital. His old age and indifferent health immediately brought him under the glare of publicity.

The Security Council met on October 14, and its proceedings continued for four days. Mossadeq performed effectively. He had a good case and was a powerful emotional orator. He was familiar with facts and figures. He had been the author of the oil policy which had ultimately led to the nationalisation of the Company. The atmosphere also was favourable, since national-isation of foreign assets was becoming a popular platform in the newly independent Afro-Asian countries, many of which had similar problems and sympathised with Iran. The United States did not appear to be particularly unhappy at the national-isation of the British company. Washington knew that Mossa-deq was basically a right-wing politician and the fear that if he were not supported he would be replaced by the Tudeh governed the policy of the Truman Administration. On October 18, the Security Council rejected the British request for immediate action. The Council held that until the Inter-national Court pronounced its own verdict, the British com-plaint should remain in abeyance. The first major move in Britain's diplomatic offensive was thus defeated.

The Shah, who had personally briefed Mossadeq before his departure to the United States, received the news of the British setback from Mossadeq by cable. The Prime Minister was evidently willing to recognise at this stage the Shah's contribu-tion to this triumph, though later he was stoutly to deny it in public. In another cable he said : 'It has always been my wish to pray God for your Majesty's health, long life and success and I confess that whatever and whenever success has been achieved we have been indebted to Your Majesty for your constant support and guidance. . . . I beg once more to express my gratitude for Your Majesty's special attention and favour.' [9]

Mossadeq stayed on in the United States to complete his negotiations with the Truman Administration and the American oil companies. He met Truman and his Secretary of State, Dean Acheson, as well as the directors of several major oil companies. On a number of questions these talks went contrary to Mossadeq's calculations. It became obvious that the American oil companies, keen as they were to enter Iran, were determined not to desert their British colleague and promote the sale of Iranian oil. Secondly, it was also made plain to Mossadeq and his team that these companies would not permit the oil revenues of Iran to be higher than those of other countries in the Middle East. As a result of these discussions, one of the main pillars of Mossadeq's strategy was shaken. He had believed that the western world was so dependent on Iranian oil that he could dictate his own terms. Instead of submitting to his demands, the British and American oil companies had already begun to make good the loss of Iranian oil by increasing production in Kuwait, Iraq, Qatar and Bahrein.

During his visit to Washington, Mossadeq requested a loan of $120 million from the Truman Administration. Truman promised to give careful consideration to his request. The Administration, however, had left no doubt on one point : it was not over-zealous to grant this loan. Mossadeq was disappointed. He still continued to believe that the contradiction of interests between Britain and the United States, specifically expressed in the oil rivalry, was so acute that he could

[9] For the full text of the cable, see *Mission*, p. 93 ; Shamim, pp. 90–1.

count on American support in his fight against Britain and British oil interests. By this time, he was so obsessed with his struggle against Britain and his belief in the importance of Iranian oil to the western world that it did not even occur to him that Britain and the United States were linked in the international alliance critical for successful resistance to what they believed to be aggressive Soviet plans. The larger positive issues over which the United States and Britain co-operated were beyond his political comprehension.

Mossadeq returned home on November 23, to a hero's welcome. At Mehrabad airport, Tehran, he was greeted by hysterical demonstrations. He had brought back with him the reassuring tale of Iran's victories in the Security Council. However, he had nothing else to show. Both government and people faced an acute economic crisis. There was no longer any hope of an early settlement of the oil dispute. On December 12, during a report on his visit to the United States, Mossadeq denounced the very need for a settlement. He told the nation that it was better to stop all oil activity and proceed on the basis that Iran never possessed any oil wells : at least, that would save future generations from being exploited. Simultaneously he announced an era of austerity for the country.[10]

[10] Shamim, p. 90.

CHAPTER NINETEEN

Towards a Civil War

PLEASED as he was with the victory in the Security Council, the Shah realised that Mossadeq was not equipped with the political wisdom to carry the country through this period of new economic crisis. The Sixteenth *majlis* was of little assistance in the undertaking of any constructive tasks. A *majlis* which shared Mossadeq's convictions must now be elected. Therefore the Sixteenth *majlis* was dissolved. Within eleven weeks, the Seventeenth *majlis* was elected and a new period of internal conflict began.

The first warnings of the coming clash appeared when the National Front went to the country in an attempt to secure an overwhelming majority. The Front propagandists marched under the banner of Mossadeq, billed as the sole political leader in the country. For the first time since it was founded, the Front seemed to have acquired the confidence necessary to challenge and defeat the power of the Tudeh. It worked towards this end with the full backing not only of the Prime Minister but also of the entire administrative machinery, including the police. Mossadeq had chosen his own list of candidates, and was determined to eliminate the influence of all parties and individuals who were critical of Front policies and not loyal to him personally.

The Shah warned Mossadeq against the obviously unfair and

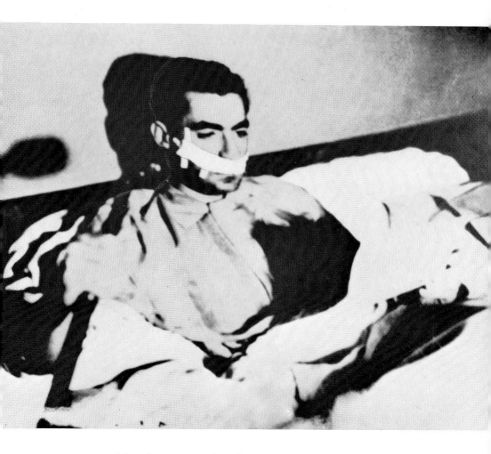

After the attempt: broadcast to the nation

Triumphant return

oppressive election tactics which the Front had adopted. He himself was no less keen to see the defeat of the Tudeh. However, he was wise enough to appreciate the implications of staging national elections with the ruling party making unrestricted use of the administrative machinery and of the police. Mossadeq, heady with the wine of his recent victories, refused to entertain any advice. As a result, Tehran and the major cities became the scene of bloody clashes between the Front and the Tudeh.

Mossadeq, even as he rode his wave of personal popularity, feared that the national elections might not give him the absolute majority he desired, and was proved right when the results began to come in. Of the eighty-one seats for which results had been declared, his Front had won only a few. He at once requested the Shah to suspend the count. The Shah, at this stage, was following the logic of his original decision to support Mossadeq. The old man must be allowed, so the Shah thought, the fullest freedom to execute his policies, even though the Shah's own suspicions about the efficacy of Mossadeq's negative attitude had begun to cause him anxiety. He had to consider the confidence which the people seemed to have placed in Mossadeq's leadership. There was no easy way of making them realise that this faith was misplaced. Only experience could rescue them from their emotional illusions. Mossadeq had to be given the chance to show whether his policy could work.

The elections were halted and the truncated *majlis* began its work on May 29, 1952. Mossadeq was now a changed man. Whatever respect he might once have had for the *majlis*, of which he had been a member for almost four decades, he now despised it. He argued, with some justification, that a substantial number of the deputies were pro-British and were determined to weaken his firm stand against the Company. He therefore wanted to be in a position to disregard the *majlis*, and lost no time in requesting what he called emergency or extraordinary powers. He summoned the *majlis* and the Senate on July 13, to approve and accept his demand, but the *majlis* was in no mood to comply. On the same day, Mossadeq sought an audience with the Shah. He reported that he was unable to carry on the work of the government in view of the obstructionist tactics adopted by a large number of deputies and Senators. He said he required six months, free from the limitations placed on him by the *majlis* and the Senate, to bring his policy to fruition. The Shah must grant him authority to govern the country during that period without recourse to the *majlis*. As the Shah tried to explain to him the undesirability of setting up such an authoritarian precedent, Mossadeq advanced his second demand. He wanted to assume the post of Minister of War. By convention, appointments to this post were a royal prerogative. The Shah, knowing fully the motives which prompted Mossadeq to ask for control of the armed forces, politely but firmly informed the Prime Minister that the latter's request could not be granted.[1] Mossadeq resigned in anger, and the Shah accepted his resignation.

Mossadeq's demand for emergency powers and control of the armed forces was really a prelude to the *coup* which he was to stage nearly a year later. The events that followed his resignation turned out to constitute a rehearsal for this *coup*. Immediately afterwards, the Front took the issue to the streets and the Tudeh, which had fought the Front only a few weeks earlier during the election campaigns, now joined the demonstrations in support of Mossadeq. Meanwhile, the *majlis* had requested of the Shah that old Qavam should be recalled from retirement. This unusual choice was interpreted by many as a move on the part of the pro-British deputies to appease Britain,

[1] *Mission*, p. 94.

since Qavam was believed to be a favourite of the British. Though the Shah did not consider this suggestion wise, he bowed to the will of parliament.

Qavam played his role as expected. As the Front and the Tudeh instigated further riots, he broadcast to the nation. He spoke against popular support for oil nationalisation and threatened to use force against those who would not abide by his policy. His broadcast merely inflamed the anger of a restless population.[2] He was condemned as a British agent who had been smuggled into a position of power to betray the nation's interests. Qavam's government seemed powerless to cope with a call for a general strike made by the Front. The Shah intervened at this stage. As he later wrote : 'Qavam was an old man, and his health was poor ; in fact, he often fell asleep in the midst of policy meetings of the highest importance. It is true that he favoured strong measures, but in conscience, how could I let one of such faltering abilities attempt them ? After only four days in office he resigned at my suggestion.'[3]

The Shah now clearly saw the danger of a civil war. He also realised that there was no statesman in Iran who could oppose Mossadeq. Fate seemed to help Mossadeq's desire for dictatorial powers. On July 22, when he was summoned by the Shah to an audience, the news of the judgement of the International Court reached Iran. The Court had ruled, as Iran had pleaded, that it had no jurisdiction to entertain the British complaint. This, of course, enhanced Mossadeq's prestige, and won him further support. On July 13, he was back in power, with the agreement of the Shah to the demands he had made. On August 2, a bill granting him these powers was approved by the Senate, and by the *majlis* a day later. This was a turning point in the domestic contests generated by the oil dispute.

[2] Shamim, p. 95.   [3] *Mission*, p. 94.

Mossadeq, from this day onwards, adopted policies which aimed at the elimination of the Pahlavi dynasty and the conversion of Iran into a republic under his personal control.

On August 7, Mossadeq, as representative of the nationalised company, advanced several claims against the British government. He asked for the payment by the Company of outstanding debts, amounting to $10 million; the release of Iran's sterling balances; and damages for the delay in paying the debt and for the seizure of the sterling balances. He registered two further claims: for damages caused by the actions of the representatives of the British government and the Company in general, and in particular for damages caused by the British embargo on the sale of Iranian oil.

Twenty days later, Britain replied, but not directly. The answer came in a message from President Truman and Winston Churchill, whose Conservative Party had won the British elections and replaced Clement Attlee's government. They put forward three major proposals. The question of damages raised by the nationalisation of the Company should be submitted to the International Court on the basis of the rights of both parties as they existed immediately before nationalisation, the Court to be the supreme arbiter of all other claims by both parties. The government of Iran and the Company must immediately appoint their representatives to discuss the issues involved, and make arrangements for the flow of Iranian oil to the world markets. If the Iranian government agreed to the previous two proposals, the two Western leaders offered three concessions in return. The oil embargo would be lifted and, on reaching agreement on prices, payment would be made for oil sold abroad; Britain would rescind the restrictions on export of goods to Iran and use by Iran of her sterling balances; and lastly, the United States government would give Iran $10 million to help balance her budget.

Mossadeq reacted violently to the tone and content of the joint Anglo-American message and proposals, which he rejected angrily and absolutely. On October 16, he prepared a report for the *majlis* on this question. Since the *majlis* session could not be held, for want of a quorum, Mossadeq broadcast its contents over the radio. He indicted Britain for preventing the sale of Iranian oil and for attempting economic strangulation. He alleged that British agents had organised intrigues and plots against his government. The conclusion was inescapable : Iran must break off diplomatic relations with Britain. On October 22, this step was taken.

The rejection of the joint Anglo-American proposals brought to the surface the basic contradictions in the political life of the country. A large number of Mossadeq's active followers failed to understand the reasons behind his decision. In their message, Britain had recognised not only the principle but the fact of the nationalisation of the Company. It appeared that even the original British claim for the monopoly of oil purchased from the nationalised Company had been watered down. Further, under obvious American pressure, Britain had agreed to withdraw all anti-Iranian measures. The United States was willing to come to Iran's aid by granting the much-needed foreign exchange. Mossadeq saw in the joint proposals a further weakening of the British position, increasing American pressure and more potential gains for Iran. He hoped that his rejection of the joint proposals would at last open the doors to American purchase of Iranian oil. He clung resolutely to his already discredited belief that he could split the Anglo-American alliance on this question, and did not realise that time was running against him. The United States, still embroiled in the deadlock over the Korean armistice, was about to go to the polls in the presidential elections. The Republican party had nominated General Dwight D. Eisenhower as its candidate and a new hard-line diplomat, John Foster Dulles, was about to rise to a position of great influence.

In December 1952, the Truman Administration, then almost at the end of its term, proposed a formula to Britain which was to have considerable future relevance. It offered the assistance of American oil companies in the exploitation and export of Iranian oil. This American consortium was virtually to replace the Company, on payment of an indemnity, in co-operation with NIOC. The Company was to have a share in the export trade with the American consortium.[4] Not surprisingly, the British government rejected this proposal, which for them was an invitation to suicide. As far as Iran was concerned, the contents of the American proposal were not unpleasant.

Throughout this period the Truman Administration was more concerned with the rise of communism in Iran than with British interests. The Shah was to comment on this policy later as follows : 'American policy throughout the Mossadeq regime had revealed increasing concern coupled with uncertainty as to effective procedures for promoting Iran's stability and development. For the American fiscal year, 1950 (1 July 1950 through 30 June 1951), the U.S. government had made small allotments of $500,000 to Iran under the Point Four technical assistance programme. For the fiscal year of 1951 this had been increased to a still modest $1.6 million but for 1952, after Mossadeq had come to power, the allotment was increased to $23.4 million, most of which was required to make up Iran's foreign exchange deficit arriving from failure to reach an oil agreement.'[5] This period of covert support of Mossadeq by the United States came to an abrupt end with the election of Dwight D. Eisenhower, and the appointment of Dulles as Secretary of State.

There had been some logic behind American policy. While

4 Shamim, pp. 103-4.   5 *Mission*, p. 98.

the flow of oil from Iran had stopped, 'the U.S. Companies in the Middle East had profited hugely from Anglo's discomfiture. Aramco increased production from 200 to 300 million barrels a year in (Saudi) Arabia, and Kuwait shot up from 128 million to 273 million, to fill the Iranian vacuum.'[6]   The comfort which the American companies could draw from the paralysis of the Company had to be balanced with the threat which the Iranian deadlock presented to the international oil cartel.   Iran could market its oil in the special spheres controlled by the cartel and thus undercut the price.   Thus American oil interests commended the policy of the Truman Administration of making haste slowly to resolve the crisis between Iran and Britain.   By December 1952, the American government had arrived at a point when, still in no desperate hurry, it was ready to sound Britain on a partial American takeover of the Company. British resistance, initially strong, was to collapse a year later.

[6] O'Connor, pp. 324–5.

CHAPTER TWENTY

The Second Revolution

EVER since the nationalisation crisis overtook the country in October 1950, the Shah had been under great political strain ; and this period coincided with a time of acute emotional stress in his married life. In 1938 the Shah had married a sister of King Farouk of Egypt. As this marriage had been arranged by Reza Shah, the occasion was without any particularly emotional involvement on the Shah's part. In 1940 a daughter, the Princess Shahnaz, was born. However, as the Shah says, 'for reasons still obscure to medical science, Queen Fawzia bore only one child'. This created a constitutional problem as the Crown must pass by direct line of descent to a male heir. Thus the Princess Shahnaz and the Shah's three sisters were ruled out. The Constitution also debarred anyone of Qajar blood from succeeding, and this eliminated the Shah's half-brothers born of Reza Shah's two Qajar queens. On the recommendation of the Shah's advisers, anxious for a male heir, his marriage was dissolved in 1948.

Two years later, the Shah came to know Soraya Esfandiari, daughter of a Bakhtiari tribesman who had married a German wife. Their engagement was announced soon after, but before the marriage could take place the bride-to-be fell seriously ill, and even at the time of the wedding, in January 1951, the new Empress of Iran was physically weak and fragile. The Shah had planned a trip to Europe with her, but by this time the nationalisation crisis had broken. It was only a few days after the royal wedding that Razmara was assassinated and Mossadeq rose to power. Ever since, the Shah had become more and more deeply involved in affairs of state. As the months went by, he received increasingly disquieting reports of the consequences of Mossadeq's negative policies. All economic and social development had come to a halt, and the Tudeh was infiltrating every aspect of national life. Under these circumstances, the Shah's private life was reduced to the minimum, and his projected tour with the Empress had to be postponed indefinitely.

It was during this period that the Shah prepared to intervene personally. He was under great strain, waiting for the right moment to act. 'I had detailed reports on every phase of our critical situation' he has recorded, 'all necessary information was at hand for me to perceive the exact dimensions of the horrible dangers that faced us as a nation. But my father had bequeathed to me at least a little of his marvellous sense of timing and I knew that premature action might be worse than none at all. To strike too soon might merely seal the doom of the country that was heading towards disaster.' [1]

The Shah waited eight months, allowing his plans for a second revolution to mature. His final decision was taken in January 1953. By this time there could be no further doubt as to Mossadeq's intentions. He had allied himself with the Tudeh which seemed to have become his main support. Together they co-operated with the *ayattollah* Kashani, who as Speaker of the *majlis* frequently interfered in the work of the administration.[2] Having emasculated the *majlis*, Mossadeq got it to pass a resolution disbanding the Senate, and then suspended the functions of the Supreme Court. He appointed

[1] *Mission*, p. 222.   [2] Shamim, p. 105–6.

his own stooges as Minister of Foreign Affairs and to key posts in the armed forces.[3] He ruled the country under martial law, using the police as well as the henchmen of the Front and the Tudeh to execute his schemes.   He abused his authority as Minister of National Defence to interfere in the affairs of the armed forces, forcibly retiring several officers whom he distrusted.   Indeed, when Mossadeq took over there were only 105 officers who were *Tudeh* members ; by the time he left, this number had multiplied several times over, and at least 650 officers were proved to be members of the *Tudeh*.[4] From February onwards Mossadeq, having secured an extension for his extraordinary powers', adopted measures designed to crush all opposition, censoring his critics in the press and imprisoning those who dared to protest.   Deputies of the *majlis* who still showed signs of resistance were beaten up.   A warrant was issued for the arrest of General Fazlollah Zahedi, a senator who had defied Mossadeq from the start.[5]

The Shah could no longer remain passive.   On March 1, he summoned Mossadeq to an audience and told him that he could not permit him to destroy the country.   He reminded the Prime Minister of how he had helped him at various stages of the latter's life.   But this assistance seemed to have escaped

[3] Hossein Fatemi, executed for the crime of treason after the Second Revolution, was appointed Foreign Minister; General Riahi, Commander-in-Chief ; and General Afshar-Tus, Chief of Police.

[4] Several members of this group were tried for treason in August and September 1959 by the Zahedi government after Mossadeq's overthrow. For details, see Shamim, pp. 46–119 ; some Iranian newspapers alleged that General Rodionov, Soviet military attaché, was involved in the conspiracy of the Tudeh officers, but the Soviet government's attitude towards the Tudeh was one of unconcern, see Laqueur, pp. 207–8.

[5] The Mossadeq government charged General Zahedi with plotting against itself in league with a foreign embassy, which was not named, in February 1953, and a warrant for his arrest was issued on February 25, under Article 5 of the Martial Law.

Mossadeq's memory. The interview ended with the Prime Minister threatening civil war, a challenge which the Shah was yet not ready to accept. Instead, in a letter to the *majlis*, he announced his decision to make a pilgrimage to the holy Shiah shrines in Iraq, and later to proceed on a holiday to Europe. Mossadeq and his supporters received this news with unconcealed glee, interpreting the Shah's decision as confirmation of their victory. This proved to be the last in the long series of Mossadeq's miscalculations.

As the news of the Shah's intended departure spread, the real feeling of the people began to crystallise. Those who had been afraid to speak up now took courage. Large crowds gathered at the palace gates and, at their request, the Shah abandoned his plans for travel. The old links between the Shah and his people were now plainly visible, most of all to Mossadeq and his supporters.[6]

The Front and the Tudeh retaliated by calling a general strike. Mossadeq issued orders for the arrest of a number of retired Army officers and others who he thought would stay loyal to the Shah and the Constitution. He then appointed a committee of eight deputies to investigate the possibilities of limiting the powers of the Shah as Commander-in-Chief. Meanwhile eight other deputies who were opposed to Mossadeq had taken sanctuary in the *majlis* building. Mossadeq's committee recommended drastic reductions in the Shah's power, but the *majlis* rejected their report.[7] It was at this stage that London and Washington announced categorically that they would no longer negotiate on the oil dispute with the Mossadeq regime.[8]

---

[6] Shamim, p. 107.   [7] Marlowe, *Iran*, p. 98 ; Shamim, p. 108.
[8] The British Foreign Office statement of March 2, 1953, was blunt ; the Americans conveyed the same decision in a letter from Eisenhower on June 29, 1953, rejecting Mossadeq's appeal for loans.

The moment had arrived for the final *coup* by Mossadeq, supported by his henchmen and the Tudeh. He announced a referendum to decide on the suspension of the *majlis*. Under conditions of terror,[9] the referendum was held on August 10 and, as expected, the government announced a victory for its proposal to suspend the *majlis*, which was formally dissolved. The realisation that Mossadeq was now determined to set up a personal dictatorship had already shaken the faith of many of his supporters. When he announced the referendum, twenty-seven deputies belonging to the National Front had resigned.[10] After the referendum, twenty-five other deputies who had previously lent him their general support also resigned. Kashani broke with him, and Mossadeq was left with the support of the Tudeh alone.

Now the Shah acted. He had waited long enough, and was now determined to launch a second revolution in Iran. Of this long and agonising wait, and his final decision, he has written : 'I could not act alone, or with only a few followers ; I had to feel that the country as a whole was behind me and ready to rally for national regeneration. The rank and file of my people needed time to perceive the danger and to search their own hearts as to what should be done. As the months went by I perceived one powerful trend more and more counterbalanced by another. It was as if the scales of justice were weighing our national destiny. On the one hand the condition of my country went down, down, down. But on the other, my people began to mobilise their energies and their allegiances. It gave me a strange and exhilarating sensation. At the same time that things were reaching their worst, they were getting better. The lowest point was yet to come, but recovery was already on the way. It made me think of my young wife as she had marshalled her courage at the critical point in her struggle with typhoid. And it reinforced my faith that a force stronger than mere mankind

9 Arfa, p. 403.   10 Shamim, pp. 109–10.

was helping to shape our destiny. I concluded that my destiny
had already been designed and ordered by God, and that I
must carry it out. But to carry out anything you must do something, you must act. You must take decisions.' [11]

The Shah took his decision on August 13, at the Caspian
resort of Ramsar. He signed decrees dismissing Mohammad
Mossadeq and naming General Fazlollah Zahedi Prime Minister. He entrusted Colonel Nematollah Nassiri, Commander of
the Imperial Guards, with the task of delivering the decrees.
These moves were the first in a series of events which led to
the departure of the Shah and Queen Soraya. The Shah had
left in the belief that the absence of the monarch from the
country would 'force Mossadeq and his henchmen to show
their allegiance and that thereby it would help to crystallise
Persian public opinion'. [12]

The Shah had made his temporary headquarters at Kelardasht, in Mazanderan, and at Ramsar. Radio communications
had been arranged between the Saadabad Palace in Tehran and
his temporary headquarters. The Shah did not sleep for two
nights as he prepared to leave the country. On August 16, the
Mossadeq regime announced in a broadcast that Colonel
Nassiri had been arrested and was now in prison. The fatal
hour had come : Mossadeq had proclaimed a revolt. [13] The
Shah and Queen Soraya left Kelardasht in a light single-engined
plane for Ramsar, and from there flew on to Baghdad. [14] As

[11] *Mission*, p. 222.   [12] Ibid. p. 104.

[13] The extent of Dr Mossadeq's revolt has been described by General
Arfa : 'All the Shah's pictures in the Government offices, cinemas,
shops, etc., were removed by the order of Mossadeq's government. The
mentioning of the Shah's name in the morning and evening prayers in the
military units was suppressed by the orders of General Riahi. . . .' Arfa,
pp. 404–5.

[14] On arrival at Baghdad, the Iranian Ambassador, on Foreign Minister
Fatemi's orders, tried to have the Shah arrested. The Shah later wrote :
'Our Ambassador in Baghdad went so far as to try to have me arrested ;

the news of his departure spread among the people, the first stirrings of 'the second revolution' proved his strategy right. Mossadeq was now forced to take an unequivocal stand on his attitude to the Shah. He chose to denounce the monarchy and place before the people his long-nurtured aim to eliminate the Pahlavi dynasty. This decision not only robbed him of popular support, but left him a virtual prisoner of the Tudeh.

'The second revolution' ended within five days. Mossadeq and the Tudeh once again overplayed their hand by announcing the establishment of a republic. This was the signal for which the people were waiting: inspired by the example of their fathers and grandfathers who had risen against that other despotic regime in 1911, they fought the supporters of Mossadeq. The police and the armed forces joined the revolutionaries, and by noon on August 19, the rebel regime had crumbled.[15] Three days later the Shah, greatly moved by a heart-warming, tumultuous reception, returned home. An era had ended.[16]

---

but a few days later, as I was on my way back to Tehran, that same Ambassador was to be the first to meet me at the airport in Baghdad!' *Mission*, p. 105.

15 For details see *Mission*, pp. 99–105.

16 Various references have been made to the role of the United States Central Intelligence Agency and the work of the American agents in the overthrow of Dr Mossadeq's rebel regime. That the CIA did some work during those fateful days is not denied: however, all Iranian sources to whom I talked underlined the basic point that if there had not been simultaneous risings in Tehran and other cities, Dr Mossadeq, in control of the armed forces, would have easily crushed the CIA agents. It appears that much of the talk about the CIA's role is part of the CIA mythology which has no basis in facts.

CHAPTER TWENTY-ONE

The Meaning of Mossadeq

CONTRARY to later interpretations, Mossadeq's attempted *coup* had little to do with the oil dispute, although it took place in the midst of it. He had practically no reason for falling out with the Shah over the latter's attitude to nationalisation. The Shah had adopted a firm and unambiguous position on the oil problem from the beginning of his reign by leading national resistance to Stalin's demand for an oil concession in the north. He had unreservedly endorsed nationalisation of the Company, and had lent his moral authority to Mossadeq in the difficult task of making the Nationalisation Law effective. It had been on his orders that troops had been sent to Abadan to dispossess the Company. Furthermore, in September 1951, when Britain threatened the use of force, the Shah had warned the British Ambassador that he would personally lead his army and people to resist any British aggression. Despite the deep differences of opinion between them on tactics, the Shah had gone a long way to keep Mossadeq in power in the hope that the latter might yet achieve beneficial results.

Where, then, lay the motive for Mossadeq's attempted *coup* and for his antagonism towards the Shah? If his motives are not rightly understood, a complete misreading of the events of the second revolution may ensue; frequently these events have been misinterpreted as constituting a fight to the finish between

a 'democrat' and an hereditary monarch; sometimes Mossadeq's attempted *coup* has been interpreted as the work of a
'nationalist' leadership trying to shake off western, and especially American, imperialism.[1] Such distortions have usually
been made innocently, through failure to appreciate Mossadeq's
background.

As a scion of the old landed aristocracy, Mossadeq was a
reactionary in social and political outlook. His vision was
bounded by the intrigues which dominated the life of upper
class Iranians in the nineteenth century. Indeed, he lived in a
world which had been dead for a century. For him there was
only one reality in Iranian politics: the domination of the
country by Czarist Russia and colonialist Britain. The approach he evolved was shaped by this national humiliation. He
believed primarily in the policy of balancing Russian and
British influence to the advantage of what he undoubtedly considered to be the true interests of Iran.[2] He also distrusted any
change in the political, social, economic and cultural *status quo*.
He wanted to protect the economic and social privileges accruing to him and his class from the old system of land tenure.
Since these privileges gave him a specific advantage in politics,
it was easy for him to see any alteration to them, such as the
attempt to modernise Iran, as a moral menace. He was well

---

[1] These reactions have been recorded in several references to Dr Mossadeq in the left-wing nationalist Press and publications in Asian countries,
but seldom in serious studies. The impression that he was overthrown by
the CIA has gained him sympathy from American and other critics of the
CIA. The Soviet attitude, varying at different stages, generally underlined
the reactionary character of his politics, though it also viewed him as a
'nationalist' hero fighting against American imperialism. Dr Mossadeq
himself publicly stated that until August 1953 he had the full support of
the United States since he was at that time their only hope of preventing
Iran from going communist.

[2] Dr Mossadeq was not the author of this theory of 'negative equilibrium': it was rooted in earlier political traditions of Iran.

aware that the process of modernisation first initiated by Reza Shah could not but usher in a social revolution. His fear of modernisation, which in the case of Iran meant westernisation, fired his hatred for the west. This backwoodsman's approach to change was a direct consequence of his instinctive protection of the interests of his own class.

It is only against this background that the several twists and turns in Mossadeq's political career, and his seemingly contradictory policies at different periods, can be understood. His early association in 1919 with the British authorities in Iran, and their confidence in him, were fully consistent with both his nineteenth-century nationalist approach and British policy. It was better, Iranian politicians of this period argued, to maintain good relations with the dominant powers in the country so as to have some influence with them. Mossadeq had collaborated with the British in this belief, and had been prepared to be used by Britain. This type of political thinking was by no means exclusive to Iran in the second half of the nineteenth century.[3] The history of many Asian nationalist movements abounds with examples of politicians for whom such a policy was a justifiable act of faith. It was Mossadeq's fear of change that had conditioned his actions throughout the revolution of 1921. His opposition to the termination of the Qajar dynasty in 1925 was an example of this attitude. His later hatred of Reza Shah stemmed from the fact that the new monarch symbolised the future of Iran.

It was easy for Mossadeq to condemn Reza Shah as a 'traitor' since the first Pahlavi monarch used his unquestioned power and influence with the people in the task of modernising Iran. As the Shah has recorded, Mossadeq genuinely believed that the act of modernisation was equivalent to treason. 'I

[3] A similar attitude was patent in the politics of the founders of the Indian National Congress, established in 1885.

remember one day, Mossadeq told me to my face that my father was a traitor. I asked why. He said because my father had built the Trans-Iranian Railway just to please the British, who wanted to use it to invade Russia. Then I asked if, according to his theory, my father should have built the railway in a different direction. His answer was that my father should have built no railways whatsoever, that Iran did not need them and that she was better off without them. Warming to his subject, Mossadeq went on to declare that before my father's time, Iran had no railways or ports worth naming, you could scarcely call the roads by that name, and in Tehran people had to walk in the dirt and mud because there was no pavement. But at least, said Mossadeq, Iran was independent.' The Shah records a question that he put to Mossadeq : 'I reminded him that before my father's reign, Iran was still under the yolk of capitulations. In that period, half the country was dominated by the Russians and the other half by the British. Law enforcement was then so ineffective that even in the early evening a wise man kept off the streets of Tehran, which were infested by thieves. In what way, I asked Mossadeq, were we then independent ? He had no answer. But I could see that my arguments had not altered the conclusion to which his weird reasoning had brought him.' [4] This strange reasoning undoubtedly flowed from a peculiar approach which identified all science and technology with the west and all ills of national life with western dominance.

Reza Shah's programme of modernisation, limited as it was by the stress of prevalent conditions, was still far too radical for Mossadeq. Compared with his father's approach, the Shah's outlook was even more forthright. If Reza Shah was a radical, the Shah, of course, was a communist. Ever since his return from Le Rosey, the Shah had never concealed his fundamental

[4] *Mission*, p. 84.

thinking on social justice, which had shocked many politicians less conservative than Mossadeq. Of one occasion on which the attitude of Mossadeq's generation was fully exposed, the Shah has written : 'I remember that one cold winter evening soon after I assumed the throne a group of our national assembly deputies, responding to my summons, came for an audience. Bluntly I told them that I could not stand the sight of privileged persons growing rich and sleek and fat, as some of them were, while others of my people remained in dire want. The next day some of the same deputies were spreading rumours that I was a communist. If what I said was communism, then I am one.'[5]

This incident occurred early in the war. During the succeeding ten years, much more had happened to horrify politicians of Mossadeq's stamp. The Seven Year Plan was considered by the privileged classes as new evidence of the Shah's 'communism'. His decision to hand over the Crown lands to the government for distribution among the landless peasants was equated quite naturally by the traditional landlords with Bolshevik practice. Even at the height of the oil crisis, the Shah was constantly advocating change. Time and again he had goaded Mossadeq into the acceptance of measures for improving the abject conditions of the masses. He never failed to stress to Mossadeq that the nationalisation of oil was merely one means to the end of achieving a higher standard of living for the people. This ideological conflict was the salient feature of their relationship, and Mossadeq was well aware of this. He had effectively strangled the Seven Year Plan by creating conditions in which all hopes of financing it were destroyed. He had gone even further by attempting to throttle at birth the very idea of national planning. He had succeeded in diverting the minds of the working people from the basic issues of social

[5] *Mission*, pp. 184-5.

justice and elimination of landlord privileges into hatred for Britain. This enabled him to suppress the proposals for the distribution of crown lands without popular protest.

The one relatively enigmatic aspect of Mossadeq's career was his association with the Tudeh during the last phase of his political career. As a reactionary devoted to the defence of his class interests, communism and the pro-communist policies of the Tudeh should have been anathema to him. He had fought the Tudeh up to 1952, when he began to lose his rightist support, and the Tudeh for its part had not spared him. It had condemned him as a feudalist and as an agent of American imperialism. It was only when their interests temporarily coincided that Mossadeq and the Tudeh had made common cause. The Tudeh needed Mossadeq as a figurehead to push through its own political plans for setting up a 'peoples' democracy' in Iran, a textbook communist manoeuvre. Mossadeq, for his part accepted this support only when he realised that almost all his power was about to collapse. His dealings with the oil interests had shown him to be an inept tactician who constantly permitted his opponents to gain the initiative,[6] and as Prime Minister he had brought his country to the verge of bankruptcy. He had broken all the major promises in his platform : having condemned the isse of paper currency without gold backing, he had brought inflation to a critical point by papering the economy without sufficient gold reserves ; having said he would establish democratic rule and freedom for all, from his first day in office to his last he had ruled by martial law, and had tried throughout to rig every election which was held. Within

[6] The Shah found this particularly annoying. He advised Dr Mossadeq that if a hard line were taken, it must be pursued intelligently and firmly, and cited his own readiness to lead the army against the potential British invasion. He bitterly commented : ' Mossadeq might have shown equal firmness in seeking a constructive oil settlement, but instead he let the oil company call the tune '. Mission, p. 91.

eighteen months he had ceased to be a national hero, and at this stage his nineteenth-century background had once again asserted itself. He had been taught that opportunism in politics was a virtue : he therefore thought there was nothing abhorrent in an alliance with the Tudeh, whose ideology he despised. He believed that he was using the power and influence of the Tudeh for his own special purposes. He had grown old and sick. Blinded by his vanity, he failed to see even his own interests.

With Mossadeq's defeat there ended a whole era in the history of Iran. His epitaph could well be written in the words of an English authority on the modern history of Iran : 'Mossadeq was the last of the old school of Middle East nationalists — composed of people like Zhaghul — who flourished in days before nationalism needed to be equated with social reform, and before local communist parties existed to steal their extremist thunder and drain off their more constructive potential supporters. . . . He had the clown-like aspect of an anachronism, a man born after his time, who acted the histrionics and mouthed the slogans of a past generation.'[7]   Mossadeq lost to the new generation personified by the Shah, but the struggle cost Iran dear. It was, at the same time, a necessary experience : the Shah had successfully defied foreign dominance and unified the country ; he had also to challenge the power of the dominant class in Iranian society if he was to proceed successfully with his plans for social justice. The struggle against Mossadeq was really the battle with this class at its fiercest.[8]

[7] Marlowe, *The Persian Gulf*, p. 164.
[8] Dr Mossadeq was arrested and prosecuted. The Shah used his royal prerogative to reduce his sentence to three years. On release, he went back to his estate at Ahmedabad, near Tehran, and spent the rest of his life in relative peace. He died in 1967.

PART FOUR

A MISSION FOR IRAN

Patience and Victory
  Are friends of one another
Victory a golden youth,
  Patience like a mother.
Patience sedately walks
  Somewhat old and blind ;
Victory superbly stalks
  One step behind.
Unto those who have endured
  He bears a golden cup —
And in the evening, Hafiz says,
That step he catches up.

SHAMS-UD-DIN MOHAMMAD HAFIZ
d. 1389

CHAPTER TWENTY-TWO

Positive Nationalism

WITH the triumph of the second revolution, the Shah was no longer merely a symbol of national life : he could now become its architect. At last he was able to carry out the mission for his country in which he had believed from early youth. For twelve years, between 1941 and 1953, he had had to wage a ruthless struggle to achieve this favourable atmosphere. With the second revolution the political conflict was at an end. However, the Shah, nearing his thirty-fourth birthday, was under no illusion. He realised that he still had to defeat his opponents at an ideological level : only then could the gains of the second revolution be consolidated.

Even though Mossadeq had failed in his bid for personal dictatorship, and the people had celebrated what they genuinely believed to have been their victory, Iran was still suffering from the economic and political wounds inflicted upon her during the previous three years. The flow of oil had stopped, and with it valuable revenue. Inflation, aggravated by Mossadeq's issue of large quantities of paper currency, was rife. The *majlis*, despite the fluctuations in its influence during Mossadeq's tenure of office, had undergone no change in its class composition : it was still dominated by the feudalists, absentee landlords and religious fanatics — most of whom were connected with foreign interests. The Tudeh, battered and broken, had once again gone 'underground'. The National Front, though never an organised political party, had survived the upheaval. The right wing groups and religious totalitarians like the *Fadayan*, could not as yet be written off. In the wake of the second revolution, the once pro-British elements had shifted their loyalty to the United States, willingly offering their services to yet another foreign power.

The political and economic scene seemed dismal, and the Shah surveyed it with a heavy heart. Where should he begin ? What institutions and individuals could he rely upon ? How could he eliminate the lingering evils of years of political anarchy and economic chaos, the heritage left by Mossadeq ? There appeared to be precious little that was positive in the politics of the country. At the outset of his crusade, for a crusade it was that he had in mind, he had only one asset besides his own determination : his links with the common people. These links, the Shah knew, could and must be strengthened. His actions must go far beyond mere advice and consent. He must now ignore the politicians and himself respond to his people's call for leadership.

At least four varieties of nationalism had been propagated besides the negative, feudalist brand which Mossadeq represented. On the extreme left, there was Tudeh nationalism. The party had largely concealed its fundamental belief in the principles of Marx and Lenin. Its propaganda had concentrated on the ideas of national independence, democracy and social equality. Its platform thus had unimpeachable claims on the minds of the younger generation of students, intellectuals, and professional and industrial workers.[1] On the extreme right there were a number of smaller nationalist parties whose general outlook was moulded by Pan-Iranism. Their propa-

[1] For a general survey of the various kinds of nationalism in Iran, see Binder, pp. 79–83.

ganda had been effective largely because it rested on calls to national glory, the need for sacrifice, and anti-communism. Their organisational methods were modelled on the political machines which Hitler and Mussolini had built in Germany and Italy before the Second War. The two Islamic totalitarian groups represented a third category of nationalism which many clergy preached in the mosques. These groups wanted to set up in Iran a *Jafari Shiah* Islamic state. Their methods were medieval and at least one of them, the *Fadayan*, substituted for rational argument the liberal use of the dagger. Finally, a group of politicians who drew their inspiration from the West also posed as nationalists, while advocating that Iran should accept the status of a client state in international relations and give up any idea of social change in internal affairs.

Nationalism as a concept had thus been discredited. To meet this situation the Shah evolved the idea of 'positive nationalism'. This new ideal was to provoke heated debate among every section of the urban population. It was to be condemned by those who saw in it an end to their political influence, but its broad appeal could not be resisted. 'Positive nationalism, as I conceive it', the Shah was to write later, 'implies a policy of maximum political and economic independence consistent with the interest of one's country.'[2] The Shah had chosen to accept 'enlightened self-interest' in preference to the questionable luxury of a set of ideals.

The Shah fully accepted the anti-imperialist features of Iranian nationalism evolved by Reza Shah. However, new circumstances meant that it had to be modified. He rejected a selective approach to different varieties of imperialism. New imperialism, which he equated at that time with Stalin's policies, must be branded and fought in the same way as the old. In dealing with this subject he warned : 'There is nothing more dangerous

[2] *Mission*, p. 125.

for a man or a nation, than to be a prisoner of one's egotism'.[3] He cited his own emotional experiences, which could easily have made him a life-long enemy of Britain. Yet he refused to 'stew in his emotions' like Mossadeq and 'thought of larger interests of the country'. He was willing to co-operate with Britain, despite previous insult and injury, if such co-operation could serve the interests of Iran. He was willing to forgive recent opponents if they in turn were willing to adjust their attitudes to the new situation. This policy initially led to a western alliance but, by 1956, it was also to build a bridge of understanding between the Soviet Union and Iran.

The ideological confusion over nationalism was only partly relieved by this positive concept. 'Nationalism, like imperialism,' the Shah admitted, 'is a tricky notion.' It was therefore necessary to place before the people a set of guidelines. 'First,' he said, 'suspect all who preach negative nationalism.' He did not underrate its initial appeal. 'Anybody can tear down, fewer can build up', he warned : 'By a strange and yet universal weakness, human nature responds more easily to shouts against alleged devils and demons than it does to calls for national building. To destroy is spectacular and emotion-rousing ; construction is a quieter process.' 'Secondly,' he said, 'suspect those who attack only one kind of imperialism for they will prove ultimately to be the supporters of the other kind. Thirdly, compare the pronouncements of the supposed nationalists with those of the foreign groups or powers so as to assess the extent of "genuine indigenous nationalism" in what they advocate. Finally, even when promises are held out for the development of the country, judge these in relation to their feasibility and fruits.'[4]

The real challenge was now the Tudeh. Though Mossadeq had been their figurehead, the real architects of the disaster

[3] *Mission*, p. 126.   [4] Ibid. p. 127.

which had overtaken Iran were the Stalinist leaders of the Tudeh party. The Shah had made a detailed study of the dynamics of the communist movement. He rejected the Dulles doctrine that the battle against communism was a crusade which must be carried out rigidly and ruthlessly. He appreciated that the subversive aspects of the Tudeh must be destroyed, but realised that subversion was a relatively minor symptom of a deeper malaise. Nor did he subscribe to the purely repressive measures advocated by professional anti-communists. 'Nothing could be more shortsighted', the Shah firmly told them 'than to think that police measures alone are enough. To combat communist subversion or any other evil, the Government must enjoy the backing of the majority of the people, and in the long run it would only have this if it provided adequate social justice in the broadest sense.'[5] A policy of repression might be effective for a year or two, 'but eventually the presence or absence of social justice would tell the tale. Even if a country were to exterminate all known communists within its boundaries, the prevalent social conditions might breed new ones as fast as the old ones were liquidated.'[6] This rational interpretation gave the Shah the key to understanding the meteoric rise of the Tudeh. He was therefore prepared to accept the co-operation of those former members and sympathisers of the Tudeh who had been attracted to the banner of the party by their desire for radical social changes. 'Many of them', the Shah was to write later, 'are now making useful contributions to Iran's development. . . .'[7]

The Shah used every opportunity at his disposal to expound the virtues of his positive nationalism, arguing in the concrete terms of Iran's experience. Time and again, he patiently set out the consequences of Mossadeq's negative nationalism during the oil crisis. This negative nationalism was not exclusive to

[5] *Mission*, p. 129.   [6] Ibid. p. 129–30.   [7] Ibid. p. 129.

Iran. Since 1952, it had spread throughout West Asia, and the Shah was not unaware of the dangers of its re-introduction from abroad. Yet positive nationalism alone could not win the ideological battle, and he therefore linked it with his vision of social change as the principal ingredient of democracy. The solution to this problem was as imperative as the solution to the problem of nationalism if the quest for a national ideology was to be successful.

CHAPTER TWENTY-THREE

The Content of Democracy

THE Shah had never accepted democracy as merely the
recognition of the political rights of the individual. He
had, perforce, given considerable attention to the theory and
practice of democratic forms of government. As a student at
Le Rosey he had looked at the question primarily from an
academic point of view. On his return home in 1936, he had
had an opportunity of examining every aspect of democratic
functioning, such as it was, under the rule of Reza Shah. When
he ascended the throne, both the invaders and the invaded
argued in the name of democracy. The Allies claimed that they
were fighting the war in defence of democracy for mankind.
Their justification for the creation of several political parties
during the years of occupation was simple : they did this to
encourage a democratic movement in Iran. The separatists in
Azerbaijan also called themselves democrats, and so did
Qavam's supporters when he formed his own party. Later
still, the Tudeh, the National Front, the Rightist groups and
religious fanatics, all claimed freedom to indulge in their various
activities on the grounds that such was their democratic right.
Even Mossadeq, while organising his *coup*, had justified his
assumption of the office of Minister of War and acquisition of
control over the armed forces in the name of democracy.[1]

[1] Dr Mossadeq had advanced the argument that since in a democracy a
king must reign and not rule, the king must be divested of his power to

227

The deputies of the *majlis* had advocated democracy ever since its first session. The founders of the constitutional movement honestly believed themselves to be the harbingers of a democratic dawn in Iran. They, of course, at the beginning of the twentieth century, had simply adopted the seventeenth- and eighteenth-century definitions of democracy. To them, democracy meant only the right to vote and a form of representative government. Even in their efforts to clarify their understanding, they were handicapped by their desire to integrate basic principles of Islam into a concept which had sprung from a different soil. Thus the dialogue of democracy had converted the country into a veritable tower of Babel. Everyone used the democratic idea to suit his own purposes. Nobody sought to relate it objectively to the conditions of the country and the requirements of its impoverished population.

The Shah, therefore, had to begin at the beginning. He first considered the theory behind the growth of the democratic ideal in the west. It was during this exercise that his earlier rejection of the limited concept of democracy was confirmed. Giving the reasons for the rise of the limited concept in the west, he wrote, 'In former times every man thought of democracy as something primarily political. Thus John Locke, a great seventeenth-century exponent of the rights of the individual, wrote chiefly about political rights. The eighteenth-century American Declaration of Independence also stressed the political rights of the common man. In those days, men thought that if they were politically free and equal, then through individual initiative they could meet their economic and social needs. That view made sense at a time when tech-

---

control the armed forces. Later events established that the reason for this had little to do with the theory of democracy; Dr Mossadeq's acquisition of this power was a step towards a political take-over in Iran.

nology and economic organisation were comparatively simple. A family was the main unit of production, and families with their own hands produced most of what they needed.'[2]

The transformation of society by the machine age, and later the rise of the factory and changes in agriculture with the introduction of sophisticated machinery, widened the horizons of men's thinking. 'The ordinary man', the Shah wrote, 'seemed to be losing control over his economic activities. So I think he was fully justified when he began to demand guarantees of economic as well as political rights.'[3] The Shah saw the implications of the revolution of growing expectations of the poor, both in rich countries as well as less wealthy ones. 'Admittedly the growing impatience of the common man', he added, 'was dangerous but it was also hopeful. Thoughtful people realised that political freedom would mean little when man continued to live in dire economic want.'[4]

Thus, in 1954, when the Shah came to define democracy as part of the national ideology which he was then expounding to his people, he emphasised three features: political and administrative; economic; and social. His ideas on political and administrative democracy had not yet developed to the point which led him, in 1963, to denounce the constitution of Iranian parliamentary democracy as a fraud by which rich and corrupt classes had appropriated the political rights of the common people.[5] In 1954, he still believed that the Iranian

---

[2] *Mission*, p. 162.   [3] Ibid. p. 163.   [4] Ibid. p. 164.

[5] In 1963, the Shah wrote: 'This does not mean that the constitution was not founded on good faith and liberalism, because the founders of the constitutional movement were men of honour who struggled with devotion to put an end to despotism and secure liberty. Unfortunately, however, the parliament that came into being as a result of such self-sacrifice quickly became a plaything in the hands of the aristocrats and feudalists. . . . The parliament of Iran thus became the exclusive preserve of a small minority.' *The White Revolution*, p. 87.

constitution, patterned on that of Belgium, provided adequately for democratic government within the framework of Iran's monarchical tradition. However, his thinking on economic democracy had already taken a definite shape. He rejected pure capitalism, underlining the role the state must play in co-ordinating and controlling national production. At the same time, he did not reject the role of private enterprise, although he was determined to bring its activities under central control. 'My philosophy of economic progress then,' he candidly stated, 'carried with it two basic principles. The first is even greater material prosperity, ever more widely shared, the second is an economy so organised that the individual rights of workers, farmers, managers, scientists and engineers, and everybody else productively engaged, are protected and enhanced.'[6]

These principles would not normally be the credo expected of a king, but then the Shah had learnt his lessons in an unusual school. The rudimentary concept of social justice was part of his inheritance from Reza Shah. His intellectual development in Europe, at the time when free enterpise had broken down during the Great Depression of 1929–1932, and when the subsequent climate of dissent was dominated by the ideals of socialism, inevitably enriched his heritage and altered its nature. 'I could have no patience', he was to state, 'for a society in which the people living in blissful ignorance, pro-duced little and stood still, while the world moved forward. Still less could I countenance a society which, as in so many instances today, produced many things, but under conditions of human oppression.'[7] It was therefore natural that he should accept the principles of economic planning on comprehensive lines from the earliest days of his rule. He had formulated and launched the first Seven Year Plan, although its purpose had been frustrated by political events outside his control.

6 *Mission*, p. 180.   7 Ibid. p. 180.

His philosophy of social democracy was also deeply rooted in his early youth. 'When, as a young man, I returned from my studies in Switzerland,' he was to record later, 'I became acutely aware of the plight of our less fortunate citizens. In spite of the great progress my father had achieved, you could still find people literally starving to death or dying of exposure because they had no roof over their heads and scarcely any clothes to wear,'[8] Such sights had made a deep impression upon him. Although his military post had little or nothing to do with social welfare, the plight of his poor and unfortunate people weighed heavily on his mind. It was not fair, he thought, either to the people or to the future of the country, that their lives should be so wretched and futile. He was an angry young man whose heart burnt at 'the thought that anyone should condone or acquiesce in such conditions', as of course many people did.

Immediately after his accession he had introduced what he described as his five principles of social justice. 'According to my philosophy', was his summing up of these, 'every man, woman and child in this nation is entitled to a decent minimum of these five things : food, clothing, housing, medical care, and education. If anybody can, by honest means, earn more than the minimum, good luck to him ; and of course many do, but, come what may, a man's income should be sufficient for him to secure these things for himself and his family.'[9]

During the decade and more in which he tried to convert the politicians to this view, he was forced to 'hear pompous, over-fed, over-privileged people advance the out-of-date argument that Iran's needy families are in want because they are lazy'.[10] He had no sympathy for the views of such parasites because he believed that the people of his country were industrious and hard-working. Laziness was found, 'more readily among the idle rich than among our ordinary citizens'.

[8] *Mission*, p. 184.   [9] Ibid. p. 185.   [10] Ibid. p. 185.

R   *231*

At this stage the Shah believed that by persuasion and charitable means he could bring about social equality. He still felt that his own example would influence the richer sections of society, who would co-operate with him in making his five principles of social democracy the heart and soul of a new Iran. He was to revise this belief radically within the next five years. However, his zeal to mobilise the latent charity and self-help which constitutes an important part of the faith of Islam was not to abate. He was to set an example which in its scope and results was to inspire widespread admiration both at home and abroad. These principles of democracy were unattractive to several sections of Iranian society. What the Shah was openly trying to achieve was clearly understood by those whose personal and class interests were likely to be hurt in the process of socio-economic change. The resistance thus came from the classes which had monopolised social and economic power.

A special characteristic of the Iranian social structure was the phenomenon of the Thousand Families. Whether or not these families numbered precisely a thousand, it was certainly true that a very few families controlled large areas of economic and political influence. Their power sprang originally from their association with the Qajar monarchy to which many of them were related. They had moved out of Tehran with the rise of the Pahlavis and now lorded it over the countryside through their agents. Many members of this group lived abroad. They owned about 40 per cent of the agricultural resources of the country.

Since they owned and controlled land, and agriculture was the major economic activity of the country, they inspired deference, often by oppressive and terrorist means. Their domination of economic life led to their control over social life in the countryside and gave rise to norms of social behaviour inconsistent with individual dignity.

The clergy too were major landlords controlling vast areas of the country originally entrusted to them in charity under the Islamic principle of *wakf*. They were closely connected with the Thousand Families by economic and social ties. The third element in this trinity of oppressing classes were the tribal chiefs. The existence of nomadic tribes, the absence of adequate communications and the repeated breakdown of the authority of the central government had perforce led to the concentration of inordinate economic power in the hands of the tribal chiefs. They had become, in the course of time, not only the major landowners in the areas in which their tribes moved, but also men who literally controlled every aspect of the lives of their tribes.

Reza Shah had fought against the political power of this trinity of autocrats and had disciplined, by military force when necessary, all three groups. By concentrating authority in his own hands, he had begun to emasculate the Thousand Families politically. With extraordinary determination, he had compelled the clergy to divorce themselves from the politics of the nation. Through repeated military campaigns he had broken the back of the overlordship of the tribal chiefs. However, he had neither the time nor the opportunity to undermine the economic and social power of these classes, which were also traditionally the allies of foreign powers. Both the British and the Russians had patronised them before the revolution of 1921 and, after Reza Shah's abdication, they had revived this practice. During the oil crisis their services had once again been mobilised, but by then new forces had entered the arena and the lackeys of former days had not been able to acquit themselves particularly well.

These then were the classes which found discomfort and danger in the content of the Shah's positive nationalism — the adoption of an international policy consistent with enlightened self-interest and the introduction of democracy as a vehicle for social change. The Shah was not unaware of the challenge he would have to face from these vested interests. However, they did not surrender without a last desperate struggle. They fought with whatever arms were left to them after the triumph of the second revolution. The religious elements again revived the techniques of assassination; the feudal elements tried to exploit the *majlis* to defeat every measure for social change; and the tribal chiefs planned revolt. But all their attempts were confounded by the Shah's decision to make the peasants his partners in the new venture which he intended for Iran.

CHAPTER TWENTY-FOUR

Partnership with the Peasants

THE policy of converting the peasant masses of the country into an army of social revolutionaries was inspired not only by the political demands of the moment. The Shah, from his early youth, was determined to revive the strength of the peasant masses and reform the agrarian society of Iran. As a keen student of the annals of his country, he had learned that agriculture held a sacred and defined existence in the earliest philosophy of the Iranian way of life. The Zoroastrian religious classic, the *Avesta*, had said : 'He who sows wheat spreads truth.' The *Gathas of Benidad*, which recorded the social history of ancient Iran in dialogue form between Zoroaster and Ahuramazda, the Governor of the Universe, had a *gatha* on the basic importance of agriculture : 'Who brings to us the greatest degree of joy ?' Zoroaster had asked, to which Ahuramazda had replied : 'He who irrigates the desert and drains the marshes to make them into fields.'[1]

Despite the place of pride assigned to the peasants by early Iranian civilisation, the condition of the peasantry in the second

---

[1] The first religion of Iran was Mazdaism, also known as Magianism or Zoroastrianism, and its prophet was Zoroaster (Zarathustra) who reformed it about 500 B.C. Its roots are to be found in the tribal worship of the Aryans before their migrations to Iran and India. The Aryan tribes, during their settlement in the area between the Danube and Oxus, accepted the various aspects of nature — sky, sun, wind and storms as supernatural

half of the twentieth century was abominable. At the time of the Shah's first major effort to raise 50,000 Iranian villages out of the quagmire of poverty, jealousy, fear, oppression and superstition, a foreign observer had described the situation in these words : 'The peasant lives for the most part in conditions of grinding poverty ; the landowner, although he enjoys comparative affluence, is in constant fear of being despoiled of his wealth by intrigue, or of being cheated of it by a discontented peasantry ; and the government official, often inadequately paid, finds it difficult to support himself and his family unless he has some source of income other than his pay. Distrust, insecurity and intrigue prevail on all sides.'[2] The Shah knew this depressing picture intimately, and appreciated the need for the rejuvenation of agriculture and of the social structure in rural Iran as prerequisites for any political participation by the peasantry in national life. After consultations with his experts, he evolved an eight-point plan.[3]

This plan was based on a survey of land and its ownership in Iran which showed that of the total land area only 10 per cent was cultivated, 40 per cent was grassland reserved for grazing, 15 per cent was forest and 35 per cent wasteland and desert. The agricultural land was owned by five main classes : private landlords owned 50 per cent ; the government and the Shah 10 per cent ; charitable institutions 20 per cent ; and the

---

powers and deified them, with *Varuna* (sky in *Sanskrit*) as the supreme god. The *Ahura* of Mazdaism is the same as the *Varuna* of Vedic Hinduism. *Ahura*, also called *Ahur Mazda*, with his twin brother *Mitra* (Mithra), the solar god, were the two aspects of the eternal light, identified with goodness. Zoroaster reformed Mazdaism, converting it into a monotheist religion in which *Ahur Mazda* was established as Supreme God. The quotations from the *Avesta* and the *Gathas of Benidad* are quoted by the Shah in *The White Revolution*, pp. 25–6.

[2] Lambton, pp. 394–5 ; quoted in Halpern, p. 85.
[3] For the details see *Mission*, pp. 201–15.

peasants 20 per cent. The barest reading of these statistics was enough to lead any observer to the conclusion that the imperative of any agrarian revolution must be the reorganisation of land ownership. On the Shah's accession to the throne, he had issued a *Firman* handing over his own farmlands to the government, to be administered efficiently and with a stipulation that all revenue accruing from them was to be devoted to helping the peasants and other needy people in the country. This idealistic step did not bring the results he had expected. The government of the day found it easier to use the money received from these farmlands to meet its ordinary expenditure. Nothing was used for the purposes for which the farmlands had been donated. Learning from this lesson, the Shah decided to take back the lands and sell them directly to the peasants who tilled them, on easy terms. But even this proved insufficient. Ownership of land by itself meant little, and in many cases actually worsened the economic plight of the new freeholders who could obtain neither credit nor technical advice. It was at this juncture that the Shah thought of using the money received from the sale of lands to form a bank which could provide the new owner-cultivators with loans and other services.

In 1951, in furtherance of this idea, the Shah issued another *Firman* distributing more than two thousand villages among the peasants, and a year later he established the Bank of Development and Rural Co-operatives, which came to be known as the Development Bank. Actual distribution started in the Pahlavi domain villages in the Varamin plain, a little south of Tehran, but was nipped in the bud during the Mossadeq period when the then Prime Minister stopped the distribution of Crown lands.

The Shah was now in a position to revive this programme of division, distribution and sale of his personal lands. However, he was also experienced enough to know that the problem could not be resolved merely by granting title deeds to the peasants. Land reform, if limited to the transfer of ownership alone, would prove a disaster. It was thus that the eight-point plan — the first point being the transfer of ownership — came to be borne.

In the second point of the plan, the Shah emphasised the need for better training of the peasantry. This involved basic education in general and training in the special requirements of agriculture in particular. 'It is all very well to talk about freeing the Persian peasant from the grip of the landlord', the Shah wrote, 'but once he is independent he must know how to manage his own affairs, to apply the latest techniques, and increasingly to operate and maintain machines. In short, our farmers must, to some extent, become both managers and technicians.' [4] The next point went to the economic heart of the matter, dealing with credit and the terms on which it was to be extended to the peasant. The Shah knew that this was the basic problem in Iran's agrarian life even before any reforms were introduced. It was also the main weapon in the hands of the landlords, who wielded it mercilessly. Of this the Shah has written : 'In the past, the villager has had to rely mainly upon the landlord to tide him over to the next harvest. Payment was usually made in kind when harvest time came, and the effective interest rate ran as high as 50 per cent per annum. It is no wonder, with such fantastic terms, that the peasant found himself in perpetual debt ; and if by chance he possessed any small bit of land or any draught animals, he was likely to lose them.' [5]

The convenient provision of water constituted the fourth point of his plan. The fifth point dealt with the introduction of improved cropping and husbandry practices. The sixth point was related to better methods of processing and storage, while the seventh dealt with plans for improved communica-

[4] *Mission*, p. 205.   [5] Ibid. p. 207.

tions between Iran's 50,000 villages and the urban centres. Finally, he underlined the importance of modernising village life on every level.

The programme for the agrarian revolution was to be one of the three foundations of the Shah's overall national plan. His general scheme for spreading education into every nook and cranny of the country was to be put into practice simultaneously with the beginning of the agrarian revolution. Its aim was to introduce an effective system of free compulsory primary education, and to expand the facilities for secondary and higher training. The Shah had persuaded the *majlis* to pass a law as early as 1943 providing free compulsory education for every child in Iran. Of its results, he was to write: 'In a way, the law was premature, for we still possessed far too few schools and teachers to carry it out; but it provided a good goal for our efforts.'[6] The Second Seven Year Plan was the third tier of the Shah's design. The failure of the First Seven Year Plan had been a direct consequence of Mossadeq's policies. The Shah tried to get the first Seven Year Plan moving again by reorganising and expanding the Plan Organisation, and some results were achieved. At the same time he concentrated on the new plan, and personally supervised its drafting.

This then was the basic framework of the Pahlavi synthesis. Under its terms, nationalism and democracy were laid before the people in their new content of social reform, land distribution, nationalisation of oil, secularisation of political life, and a literacy campaign. However, this was only the beginning. The presentation of a new ideology did not, in itself, eliminate the existence of the old undercurrents of Iran's existence. Obviously, the problems of reconstruction could not be resolved overnight, but the dead grip of the past had been shaken, and conditions created in which the peasant masses could enter the

[6] *Mission*, p. 242.

stage in the near future as principal actors in the drama of national life.

Until the Shah put forward his ideology, a number of definite groups and interests, whose main activities were confined to the urban areas, had monopolised political thought. They treated the rural masses as a reserve force, since they mistakenly felt that the future shape of Iran lay exclusively with the urban population. Now the overwhelming majority of the population was certain to be fully involved. The peasants were at last aware that change was possible.

Between 1954 and 1960 the Shah was instrumental in bringing several other gains to Iran. With an energy which amazed even those who had known him earlier, he threw himself into innumerable projects of reform at all levels of national life. He succeeded in many of them : in several others he laid the foundations for the future : a few of them failed. However, even the collective impact of these enterprises was to have less effect on the future of Iran than his courageous act of bringing the peasant masses into partnership with him in his mission for his country. He had achieved something which had never before been attempted. He had made a bid to bring into the forefront of national life a class which had remained until then the object of exploitation and oppression by other classes.

CHAPTER TWENTY-FIVE

Independence in Alliance

THE position of the Seventeenth *majlis* had become ambiguous after the second revolution. The new Prime Minister, Fazlollah Zahedi, requested the Shah that a new parliament should be elected and that the Senate, 'dissolved' by Mossadeq in the early summer, should be revived. The Shah therefore dissolved the *majlis* on November 19, 1953, and the illegally suspended Senate, on December 17. After the new elections, held in February, 1954, the Eighteenth *majlis* began its work on April 15. This was a memorable occasion, and the Shah used it to address the new deputies on several pressing problems, of which the greatest was to restore the morale of the country:
'It is clear to us that today the Iranian nation is firmly resolved to smooth over the difficulties in its way of progress, and make good use of lost opportunities. After the bitter experience of the past it has discovered the truth, that the attainment of goals is not possible except by relying on the racial virtues and ancient qualities, that is, an adoration of Iran, and unity and self sacrifice. We too will not spare any devotion or self-sacrifice in the service of the country and will always be ready to support and assist you in this service and in safeguarding the welfare of our countrymen and the future generations.'[1]
While the *majlis* began work in a mood of new enthusiasm,

[1] Quoted by Shamim, p. 115.

the Shah personally took over the problem of securing a settlement to the oil dispute, on which he had certain definite ideas. These had been formed long before Mossadeq's rise to power, and had been discussed with his close advisers, one of whom, Hossein Ala, had expressed some of them publicly as far back as 1946, at the time of the crisis between Iran and Stalinist Russia. The Shah's demand for a new deal in oil had been echoed by Ala as follows : 'It would seem that the best method of safeguarding the political and economic interests of Iran, and at the same time enabling the world to benefit from our rich deposits, would be to pool all the oil of Persia, including the area controlled by the Anglo-Iranian Oil Company, and set up an international corporation in which Iranian, American, British, Soviet, French and Dutch companies could have shares. The management might be entrusted for a term of years to the technical experts of a country not a neighbour of Iran. The whole matter might be referred for study to the Economic and Social Council of the United Nations. A special committee of the United Nations is dealing with the atomic bomb ; why should not oil, which is just as explosive, be a matter of concern to our world organisation ?' [2]

The international situation had changed radically since 1946. Stalin had opted out of any such collaboration. Iran too had changed, and was no longer willing to be a mere witness to and beneficiary from the exploitation of her oil wells. Yet the fundamental basis of the concept of an international consortium remained valid. The idea had no appeal for the Company, but attracted the Republican Administration in the United States.

---

[2] *Control of World Oil Resources* (Item 36) : Proposal for the Creation of a United Nations Petroleum Commission under the Authority of the Economic and Social Council, Supporting Document No. 2. Presented by the International Co-operative Alliance to the Fifth Session of ECOSOC, Lake Success, N.Y., July 19, 1947 ; also quoted by O'Connor, p. 327.

President Eisenhower appointed Herbert Hoover Jr. to pursue it and examine its feasibility.

Hoover succeeded in securing the agreement of the five major American oil companies to the idea.[3] He then presented Britain and the Company, as well as the government in Tehran, with a plan for a consortium of western oil companies to explore, produce and export Iranian oil. Negotiations dragged on for a year, but agreement was ultimately reached in September 1954. The terms were very complicated. The first section dealt with the purchase and sale of oil and gas from Iran, and the administration of operations; the second with the payment of indemnity for nationalisation to the Company. The government of Iran, NIOC and the new consortium, consisting of eight western oil companies,[4] were the parties to the first part of the agreement. The second part was a matter between the government of Iran and the Company. The National Iranian Oil Company remained sole owner of the concessions, and of all oil produced. The consortium was granted the rights of exploration, production, refining, transportation and sale of oil in a limited zone, as well as the use of certain existing properties, again within this zone, for a period of twenty-five years, with an option for renewal for three further periods of five years each. The consortium zone included almost the whole area previously controlled by the Company. In compensation for the Company's nationalised assets, and of the claims and counter-claims of both parties, Iran undertook to pay to the Company a sum of £76 million. Iran gave

[3] The Standard Oil Company of New Jersey; the Standard Oil Company of New York (Socony Mobil Oil from 1955 and Mobil from 1966); the Standard Oil Company of California; the Gulf Oil Company; and the Texas Oil Company.

[4] The five Americans and the Anglo-Iranian Oil Company (the British Petroleum Company since December 1954), the Royal Dutch Shell Group; and the Compagnie Française des Pétroles.

control of the nationalised oil installations to two operating companies — an exploration and production company, and a refining company — incorporated in the Netherlands and registered in Iran, while NIOC took over the management of other activities in the southern fields, domestic distribution and a small field and refinery in western Iran. The two new companies undertook to operate the industry and supply crude oil and refined products to the trading companies of the consortium members. The trading companies in turn agreed to buy their share of the crude oil at posted market prices, and pay a nominal fee for refining less a small discount as marketing allowance. The income realised from these activities, including the fees of the operating companies, was to be divided into two equal parts. Iran's share, plus the one-eighth royalty on crude oil, was to amount to one half of the oil income before payment of taxes to foreign governments.[5]

The agreement was arrived at under peculiar circumstances. Iran was at this stage almost bankrupt. The United States had rushed in with emergency economic aid of $45 million. The Eisenhower Administration had, in informal conversations, conveyed to the Finance Minister, Dr Ali Amini, that there would be a continued flow of economic assistance until Iran began to receive its oil revenues. Dr Amini and, to a lesser extent, the Prime Minister, were beholden to the United States for this gesture. The consortium came into existence primarily because Iran was unwilling to accept the return of the Company which, as a monopoly, had defied the wishes of the people and the authority of the government. At the same time, the consortium brought into the picture the Big Five of the American oil industry. They exercised considerable influence on the

---

[5] For detailed terms of the agreement and its analysis see Issawi, Charles, and Yeganeh, Mohammad, *The Economics of Middle Eastern Oil* (London, 1962), pp. 27–8.

United States government, which in turn held the purse strings
as far as Iran was concerned, at least for a time. If Iran were to
continue to receive the much needed foreign aid, it was essential
to take into consideration the views of Hoover, which were
those of the Eisenhower Administration. Although the Shah
did not consider the agreement particularly satisfactory, there
was little that Iran was in a position to do at that stage. He
therefore approved its terms and the *majlis* ratified it on October
21, 1954, the Senate following suit a few days later. Thus the
flow of oil, and revenue, began once again. From a bare
million tons output in 1952, and 1.4 million in 1953, production rose to 3 million in 1954; 16 million in 1955; and 27
million in 1956. In 1957, output surpassed the record established in 1950, reaching 36 million tons. The next year production increased to 41 million, and by 1959 output stood at
45 million tons.[6]

The agreement with the consortium, dictated as it was by
necessity, gave the Shah an opportunity to evolve a radical new
philosophy on the development of oil resources. He took four
specific decisions at this stage and resolved that as the economic
and political strength of his country increased he would put
them into practice without compromise. He recorded his four
principles as follows : 'In the first place, there will be no more
oil concessions in the old sense ; in keeping with the spirit in
which we have nationalised our oil industry, any foreign groups
who come here looking for black gold would either be mere
agents working on behalf of the Iranian government or would
actually enter into partnership with us.' He had insisted upon
the inclusion of the agency concept even in the difficult negotiations with the consortium, and this had been partially accepted.
'Secondly, foreign companies who hoped to produce oil in
Iran would have to show enough faith in my country and its

[6] *Mission*, p. 277.

resources to conduct detailed prospecting at their own risk and expense.' If oil were found in commercial quantities, the Iranian government would participate, both financially and managerially, in producing it. This important principle derived from the Shah's concept of positive nationalism : 'I was determined that never again would a huge foreign company be given untrammelled managerial authority over a vital centre of our economy. My government would constructively participate in the management. The foreign interests would have to assume that since our profits as well as theirs depended upon operational efficiency, we would do our best to help evolve and carry out sound policies.' Finally, the Shah had decided that the scale of royalties had to be improved beyond what had been agreed with the consortium. 'As I saw it, the fifty-fifty split had outlived its usefulness and was out of tune with our national aspirations.'[7]

This new outlook on oil once again provoked opposition from foreign interests, which ridiculed his four principles. They began to encourage their sympathisers to oppose the Shah and divide the country once again on oil policy. These elements were to be found even in the highest echelons of administrative power. The Shah stood firm, however, and instructed the government to carry out his policy when making arrangements with oil interests other than those involved in the consortium. Of this conflict, the Shah said : 'Certain of the oil interests displayed the same unsympathetic attitudes towards our nationalist aspirations that had led to the undoing of the old Anglo-Iranian Oil Company ; and for a time it seemed as if some U.S. officials might repeat in Iran the same blunders that had been committed by the British government in the years prior to our nationalisation of oil. But the arrangements we were proposing were logical and the oil companies found themselves

[7] *Mission*, p. 279.

unable to maintain a united front against them. It seemed that the U.S. State Department also began to change its tune.'[8]

The oil problem having been settled, the Shah turned his attention towards foreign relations. Iran had resumed diplomatic relations with Britain before the oil settlement was concluded. She still faced an acute economic crisis. The problem was twofold; she needed immediate economic assistance to wipe out the deficit in the annual budget, and large scale financial support to implement both the plans for economic development and for improved defence. The outlook and approach of the Zahedi government, and specially of Dr Amini, were western-oriented, and not unnaturally the Eisenhower Administration thought very highly of both these men. The Shah himself was agreeable to the building of close links with the west. There was therefore no difficulty in obtaining a credit of $150 million from the United States. Britain too, made a goodwill gesture by offering a loan of up to £10 million. The American loan was to be repaid in thirty-five years, whereas the British credits had to be liquidated within five years, beginning two years after the date of its grant.

The Shah was keen to strengthen Iran through a western alliance but did not want to antagonise his northern neighbour. He had fought against the policy of Stalin to defend the national interests of Iran, but he was now prepared to reach a new understanding with the Soviet Union. The time was ripe for a positive Soviet response to such an approach. Stalin had died on March 4, 1953, and his death had opened up a new era in Soviet policies. The Shah instructed the Zahedi government to open talks with the Soviet Union to settle several outstanding disputes on frontier and financial problems. A formal agreement on the demarcation of Russo-Iranian frontiers, in the Caucasus region in Iranian Azerbaijan and also beyond the

[8] *Mission*, p. 280.

Caspian in Khorassan, was reached on December 2, 1954. By Article 4 of this agreement, the Soviet Union undertook to pay nearly eleven tons of gold to Iran in settlement of Soviet debts incurred during the Second War. The Soviet Union also undertook to liquidate within one year its debt of nearly $8.5 million in the form of goods, the quantity and the quality of which were to be determined by direct negotiations with Iran.[9]

Meanwhile, the Baghdad Pact had come into existence. In a sense, it was the successor to the Middle East Command proposals, framed by Britain and supported by the United States, which had been rejected by Egypt in 1951. Soon after their rejection Mossadeq had come to power and Iran, under his premiership, would have taken a similar position had the proposals been pursued. By 1952, American interest in the region had been stimulated by the global strategy of anti-communism. The new Secretary of State, Dulles, after a trip to West Asia, submitted a report on the Middle Eastern political and military situation, and recommended a defence organisation of the states of the 'northern tier' who, according to him, 'were the most aware of the Soviet menace, the most likely to do something about it and the best situated to provide protection to the area as a whole'.[10] Under the inspiration of his thinking, Turkey and Pakistan signed a defence treaty on April 2, 1954, which in turn led to the signing of the Baghdad Pact. While Egypt, originally assigned a key role in the new military alliance, rejected the Dulles prescription, Nuri es-Said, who had taken office as Prime Minister of Iraq in the summer of 1954, was enthusiastic about the Baghdad Pact which he signed on February 24, 1955. The acceptance by Iraq of the pattern recommended by Dulles brought the British government into the picture, since it claimed special relations with Iraq, where two

[9] Shamim, pp. 123–4.   [10] Campbell, p. 49.

important British military bases were located. The agreement on these bases was to expire in 1956, and was not likely to be renewed because of popular dislike for them. The new pact offered an opportunity for the continuance of the bases. Britain joined the Baghdad Pact under these circumstances on April 4, 1955. Pakistan and Iran followed suit in October.

Iran's decision to join the Baghdad Pact was taken by the Shah after considerable thought. As a contemporary has written, 'The U.S. authorities strongly advised Iran to enter the Pact, but the British showed themselves reluctant to sponsor this idea, and through their Iranian friends, seemed to advise Iran to stick to its old policy of non-alignment and neutrality.' [11] There was distinct Russian opposition, and public opinion was divided on the question. Historically, Iran had sought her security in neutrality, trying to preserve a balance between the predatory Great Powers by non-alignment and non-provocation. In 1954, however, the Shah felt that conditions had changed. Despite the emergence of the Khrushchev policy of peaceful co-existence and non-interference in the internal affairs of other countries, Iran could not afford to take any risks. The Shah could not ignore the lesson of the history of relations between the two countries. The Russians had for centuries been trying to advance southwards through Iran and, even if Khrushchev's policy contradicted this historical tendency of Russian expansionism, he could ignore history only at considerable risk. [12] In joining the Baghdad Pact the Shah was also guided by more immediate considerations. His military and civil advisers entertained great hopes of the advantages to be derived from membership of the Pact, and which could be harnessed to accelerate defence and economic development.

[11] Arfa, pp. 413–14.
[12] The Shah candidly utlined his thinking to the Soviet leaders ; see *Mission*, pp. 119–200.

These hopes, however, were to prove premature. 'After a time', a contemporary pro-western observer has written, 'it was realised that these aids, which had already been forthcoming before Iran had joined the Pact, were not to be substantially increased or accelerated'.[13]

The decision was a difficult one since it involved consideration of ideological beliefs as well as military and economic factors. The Shah was quite clear in his mind as to what were Iran's interests. He totally disagreed with the Dulles thesis of containment of communism by force of arms, which later degenerated into the hazardous attitude of brinkmanship. His positive nationalism prohibited a selective approach to imperialism. He could not accept the branding of the Soviet Union as an evil expansionist force which must be destroyed through global war. He had occasion to clarify his views both to the American and Soviet leaders in 1956 when, at the invitation of the Soviet government, Queen Soraya and he visited the U.S.S.R. This was his first visit to the Russian capital, where he held frank discussions with the Soviet leaders. He did not try to disguise the motives which had prompted him to join the Baghdad Pact. At the same time, he assured his hosts that while the people of Iran entertained the most friendly sentiments towards the people of the Soviet Union they could not unlearn the lesson of repeated Russian aggressions. Nikita Khrushchev was not a man to let any point of importance remain vague. A friendly but sharp discussion followed. The Soviet Prime Minister conceded that Iran might not harbour any aggressive intentions toward the Soviet Union : however, he went on, Iranian territory might become accessible, through the mechanics of the Baghdad Pact, to some anti-Soviet power, and indeed the western powers had contrived the Pact precisely with this in mind. The Shah has recorded his reply to the

[13] Arfa, p. 414.

leaders of the Soviet government : 'Certainly, I said, we would never allow either the Pact or our territory to be used in further-ance of aggressive designs upon the Soviet Union. I gave Khrushchev my pledge as a soldier that as long as I reigned, Iran would not in any way countenance or take part in any aggressive schemes against his country. Khrushchev and his colleagues generously replied that they believed completely in what I had stated.' [14]

During his visit the Shah broke new ground in Iran-Soviet relations, and paved the way for a series of subsequent agree-ments. The Soviet Union agreed to allow Iranian exports and imports free passage through Soviet territory. Both countries agreed to utilise jointly the waters of the two rivers, the Aras and the Atrak, which flow along their common frontiers, and which could eventually be made to irrigate some 200,000 acres of arable land. Cultural ties were also strengthened. This proved to be a turning point in Iran's relations, not only with the Soviet Union but with the entire Soviet bloc. To quote the Shah : 'Since the 1917 Russian revolution, relations between Iran and the Soviet Union had perhaps never before been so cordial. The same applied to our relations with other com-munist countries.' [15]

Iran thus succeeded where other West Asian members of the Baghdad Pact, Turkey, Iraq and Pakistan, failed. Whatever the aims of the western antagonists of the Soviet Union, the Shah saw Iran as a member of the alliance only in so far as membership served her own interests. In 1956, when the chill of the Cold War had numbed the capacity of most states for a flexible foreign policy, the Shah bravely kept Iran clear of the dangers in international conflicts, and maintained the inde-pendence of his country in foreign affairs even when she was involved in a western alliance.

[14] *Mission*, p. 120.   [15] Ibid. p. 121.

CHAPTER TWENTY-SIX

Towards a New Iran

Iɴ the autumn of 1955, now that the country enjoyed a measure of stability with the settlement of the oil dispute and and with the new orientation of its foreign relations, the Shah turned to his difficult and much delayed work of building a new Iran. General Zahedi had resigned on April 5, having accomplished all he could. By training and temperament he had been best suited to the stormy days which followed the downfall of Mossadeq. The Shah had nominated his trusted diplomat, Hossein Ala, to succeed Zahedi. Ala, who was familiar with the Shah's plans, was to remain in office for the next two decisive years.

The Shah gave priority to the introduction and development of a system of gradual land reform. He issued instructions for the division and sale to the peasants of land owned by the government. In accordance with the royal *Firman* of 1951, which had provided for the sale of the Shah's own land, the work was now resumed without any further loss of time. The *majlis* approved the bill for the sale of government owned lands on November 21. It was a short bill, with thirteen articles and twenty-nine notes. The first article summarised its object: 'The Minister of Agriculture is charged to take steps in accordance with the provisions of the law for the sale of public domains, including villages, farms utilised and unused, subterranean (water) canals, real estate and buildings which definitely belong to the government, with the exception of pastures and natural forests, as well as the domains, buildings and estates which are needed by the government institutions, the list of which shall be submitted to the related committee of both Houses.'[1] Government properties in the towns and suburbs were to be sold to civil servants, while the arable lands were earmarked for sale to the farmers who were actually engaged in cultivating them. The land was to be sold in pieces of ten to fifteen hectares and the peasants were to pay for it by instalments over twenty years.

The new law did not succeed to the extent which the Shah had hoped. Until its passage, the public domains had never been surveyed. The machinery to execute the provisions of the act proved defective. The idea was still new enough to arouse considerable opposition among sections of the civil service. The landlords as a whole were worse than apathetic to it, knowing that it took them one more step towards the Shah's plan for the ultimate distribution of all land to the peasants. Effective, wide scale action on it was delayed for the succeeding three years. However, its psychological effect was tremendous. A contemporary writer commented : 'It was the first blow delivered to the tyrannical system of feudalism and big land ownership, and served as the vanguard of a great transformation. . . .'[2] It led to a new awakening in the villages. The peasants' first reaction was a blend of astonishment and curiosity ; many of them could not believe that the era of serfdom was about to end and that they would soon become owners of the land which for generations their families had tilled. That this should now happen because the Shah was determined to bring the peasantry into full social participation also came to be understood slowly but surely, and the

[1] Shamim, p. 139.   [2] Ibid. p. 140.

Shah's position strengthened among the mass of the people. At last the traditional hold of the feudal landlords and the fanatic clergy over the thinking of the peasantry was on the wane.

As the initial work on the sale of public domains began, the Shah himself directed the work of the Plan Organisation on the blueprint of the second Seven Year Plan. The Plan was geared to new methods of production, increased production and export targets, the provision of social welfare, development of agriculture and industry, exploration and exploitation of mineral resources, improvement of communications, and a new system of public health and education. In short, the Shah's aim was to use the Plan as a means of accelerating the fundamental process of social change.[3]

The Shah was more personally involved in the economics of national reconstruction than in any other of his duties, even military matters,[4] convinced as he was that Iran's progress towards economic democracy could be successful only if the principle of planning on comprehensive lines was accepted. As an enthusiast faced with the economics of an underdeveloped country, he wanted to incorporate the benefits of individual initiative within the scheme of state control on which the Plan was primarily based. He therefore established the High Economic Council as the supreme authority and the Plan Organisa-

[3] The Plan priorities were set out in order of the apportionment of expenditure : 26 per cent agriculture ; 33 per cent communications and transport ; 15 per cent industry ; and 26 per cent social services.

[4] Of his intense interest in the economic development of his country, the Shah wrote : 'And the plain truth is that I derive my chief satisfactions from grappling with complex economic and other problems. . . . I won't go so far as the Englishman who remarked that he would rather share a bed with a copy of *The Economist* than with a woman. But I do find most of my chief rewards in wrestling with difficult economic problems and issues. . . .' *Mission*, p. 140.

tion was strengthened by the addition of an Economic Bureau to work on research studies.[5]

On November 16, 1955, an attempt on Ala's life was made by a member of the *Fadayan*. The Prime Minister was about to go to Baghdad to attend a meeting of the members of the Pact, when he was shot by a terrorist. The bullet only scratched Ala's head and he was able to go to Iraq the following day. Ala's immediate reaction was to forgive the man. However, the Shah wanted the conspiracy behind the attack fully investigated. The battle against the *Fadayan* now entered its final phase.

The investigations established that the attempt on Ala's life was not an isolated event, but part of a scheme of assassinations which the *Fadayan* had plotted. Several political murders were shown to be connected. The first victim had been Dr Ahmad Kassravi, an anti-western, anti-traditional religious reformer,[6] who had been killed in court by a *Fadayan* fanatic. The weakness shown towards the assassins by the Qavam government had led to their increased confidence. The man who killed Kassravi had not been prosecuted, and it was he who shot Hajir in 1949, inflicting injuries on the former Prime Minister from which he later died.

The criminal who made an attempt on the life of the Shah had been connected with the *Fadayan*, which had also killed Ahmad Dehgahn, the editor of a Tehran newspaper and a deputy of the *majlis*. It had made an attempt on the life of Dr Syed Hassan Emami, a religious leader whose politics it disliked, and had succeeded in murdering General Razmara and

---

[5] The Shah wrote in 1960 a graphic report on the achievements of the Plan. *Mission*, pp. 139 to 160.

[6] Kassravi was opposed to adoption of what he called western materialism ; he was also critical of Traditional Islam and the *Shiah* clergy. See Banani, pp. 149–50.

Dr Zangeneh. The murderer of Razmara, Khalil Tahmasbi, had not only been released : at the instigation of the *ayatollah* Kashani and with the support of Mossadeq, the *majlis* had passed a special pardon for him. Indeed, Kashani had gone out of his way to embrace the murderer and hail him as his 'spiritual son'.

Now Mozzafar Zolghadr, who tried to kill Ala, cracked under questioning, and named Tahmasbi and the *mullah* Nawab Safavi as his conspirators. The *mullah* was the recognised leader of the *Fadayan* and at one stage there was some hesitation about arresting him. The Shah was unwilling to show any weakness and ordered that the conspirators should be treated according to the law of the land. The three ring-leaders of the *Fadayan* were arrested, tried, convicted and sentenced to death. They were executed without delay.[7]

The trial and execution of the *Fadayan* leaders showed the people that the *Fadayan* did not represent the true principles of Islam. It was unmasked as a group which had appropriated the principles of Islam to serve its own totalitarian purposes. This exposure also destroyed completely any influence that the Sumka (Socialist National Workers' Party of Iran) held over a small section of backward urban elements. The Sumka had emerged during the Mossadeq period and was part of the National Front. It was founded by a fanatic who claimed to invite the people of Iran 'to the suppression of self and to struggle against communism and the rotten world of democracy'. The Pan-Iranian party, another group with ideological sympathies with the *Fadayan* and the Sumka, also suffered a great setback to its slender political power. This group had called for the unification of the Caucasus, Afghanistan, much of

[7] For a more detailed account of *Fadayan* activities, see Shamim, pp. 126–128.

Turkestan, and other neighbouring areas into a greater Iran and, behind this appeal to national chauvinism, had spread hatred against Iran's neighbours.

The Eighteenth *majlis* was dissolved in the spring of 1956 and, on May 31, after new elections, the Shah inaugurated the Nineteenth *majlis*, which was to last for four years. Ala continued as Prime Minister and, now that the work of consolidating law and order was complete, placed a new and radical programme for economic and social progress before the *majlis*. The hand of the Shah was plain in the various ingredients of this new programme. During the period of Ala's premiership the United States continued to render liberal economic assistance, and consequently held much influence in the country. Ala, for reasons beyond his own control, failed to carry out the programme which he had submitted to the *majlis*. He was faced with opposition at almost every stage from the many conservative deputies who saw the threat to their own class interests in the proposed radical changes.

On April 3, 1957, Dr Manuchehr Eghbal was nominated by the Shah to take Ala's place. In Dr Eghbal the Shah had found an expert who had not been in politics before. Dr Eghbal, later to become chairman of NIOC, was the Chancellor of Tehran University before he appeared before the *majlis* on April 14 to seek a vote of confidence. The deputies knew that the Shah was now trying the new idea of a government composed of experts, unentangled in the web of national politics. Many members of the Eghbal cabinet had been placed in positions of power for the first time. The new Prime Minister was quite candid in his approach to the problems. He had accepted power, he said, to follow the policies which the Shah had advocated. He did not hesitate to admit publicly that he was heading the government as the loyal executor of the Shah's programme of social change.

Dr Eghbal requested the Shah that the two houses of parliament be merged together for the time being into a Constituent Assembly, to enable the revision of Articles 4, 5, 6, 7 and 8 of the Constitution and Article 49 of its Supplement. The Shah readily acceded to this request since he knew that amendments to these articles were overdue. The Constituent Assembly completed its revisions in May, bringing popular representation in the legislature to the correct proportion in accordance with the increase in the population. It further agreed that its own life should be prolonged to four years. The amendment to Article 49 of the Supplement to the Constitution was of some importance. Its motivation lay in a desire on the part of the Prime Minister to expedite the introduction of reforms. On several occasions, obstructionist deputies in the *majlis* had been able to delay the passage of reform measures. The amended Article 49 of the Supplement granted the Shah the privilege 'to issue decrees for the enforcement of laws without causing any delay or detention of the said laws'.

The Eghbal government, which lasted for over three years, began its work on a note of efficiency. Of the numerous administrative steps which it took to modernise Iran and implement the Shah's policies, its efforts to root out corruption were noteworthy. In 1958 it introduced a law (generally known as the 'Where did you get it from?' law), which made it compulsory for all government officials to reveal the sources of their income.[8] Under the Shah's guidance, the govern-

---

[8] This law 'requires all Government employees . . . to make detailed annual declarations of the sources of their wealth and income. We inquire further into any suspicious-looking variations from year to year. Any Government employee who fails to file such a statement, or who includes false or misleading entries in it, is subject to discharge from his position and must pay the additional penalty of confiscation by the Government of his undeclared wealth or income. We call this the "where-did-you-get-it-from" law.' *Mission*, p. 176.

ment completely reorganised its machinery. Permanent under-secretaries were appointed for the first time, and a central co-ordinating committee of these new under-secretaries was established to avoid the usual overlapping of work in the various ministries. In 1958, after more than two years of study, the government prepared comprehensive recommendations for reorganisation which were ratified by the *majlis* in 1959. The overall result was an administrative system based on the American pattern.

The other outstanding development during Dr Eghbal's premiership related to the oil industry. In August 1957, NIOC signed with Agip Mineraria, an Italian company, the first agreement in accordance with the new oil policy the Shah had laid down. This was followed, in April 1958, by another agreement, with the Pan-American Petroleum Corporation, a wholly-owned subsidiary of Standard Oil of Indiana, and a third agreement with a Canadian company, Sapphire Petroleum Limited. The exploration and production of oil envisaged in the three agreements was to be undertaken in areas of southern Iran, along the Persian Gulf coastline and in adjacent territorial waters. Apart from the fact that the field of oil exploration and eventual production in Iran was diversified by these agreements, new ground had been broken in financial arrangements. The Shah later summarised the salient features of the agreement with the Pan-American Oil Company : 'Under the agreements we receive 75 per cent of the total profits and the company takes 25 per cent. The logic here is simple. The agreement stipulates that NIOC and Pan-American are equally to share the profits from oil sales. But this is a fifty-fifty sharing of any profits before taxes. The agreement goes on to state that my government has the right to apply a 50 per cent income tax on all Pan-American's profits in Iran. The 50 per cent tax on Pan-American's 50 per cent profits gives us an additional 25 per cent on the aggregate profits; thus our total share is 75 per cent'.[9]

These agreements established a new precedent. They were the first-ever arrangements whereby an oil-producing country received a higher proportion of profits than was provided in the general formulae then applicable to all other oil-producing countries. When Iran signed them and their terms were published the oil world was shaken. Oil companies already operating in West Asia began to fear that other oil producing nations would now demand revisions in their own agreements. They spared no money and effort in trying to convince the world that the new Iranian terms were not really new. 'I am amused', the Shah was to write later, 'to find that some oil men still try to gloss over the difference between this pioneering agreement and the traditional fifty-fifty ones. They will tell you that the fifty-fifty agreements are not *really* fifty-fifty, that our new agreements are not *really* seventy-five–twenty-five, and actually there is very little difference between the two. In their hearts these men know that such statements will not bear careful scrutiny.'[10]

Dr Eghbal's government had faced the resentment and opposition of the traditional politicians from the very beginning. Its composition and its political allegiance to the Shah had aroused their jealousy and the enmity of those whose economic interests were being threatened by the policies inspired by the Shah and executed by the government. By 1959, this opposition had begun to crystallise. Meanwhile two new political parties were formed with the Shah's approval to counteract the destructive influence of the older parties and politicians. Dr Eghbal had assumed the leadership of the *Melliun* party and Assadollah Alam had become leader of the *Mardom* party. The formation of these two parties was an attempt on the part of the non-traditional politicians to create a parliamentary system in

[9] *Mission*, pp. 281–2.   [10] Ibid. p. 282.

Iran. The programmes of both parties were similar in the sense that both adopted the Shah's reform policy as their sheet anchor. Their differences related to the methods of putting this programme into practice.

By 1960, despite Dr Eghbal's good intentions, his government suffered several setbacks. It had overlooked the mortal danger of inflation, inherent in an expanding economy and especially so in an under-developed economy in the process of change. The cost of living had gone up, and despite the economic progress recorded in the country, the standard of living of the people had been adversely affected. The life of the Nineteenth *majlis* was nearing its end. During these critical months the most dramatic measure of Dr Eghbal's tenure of office was drafted. At the specific instruction of the Shah, a bill was prepared to introduce sweeping land reforms aimed at the destruction of the economic power of the feudal classes. However, it could not be placed before the *majlis* since, on June 1, its four-year term of office ended and it was dissolved.

CHAPTER TWENTY-SEVEN

The Last Resistance

THE election campaign for the Twentieth *majlis* had already become heated by the time the Nineteenth *majlis* was dissolved. Tehran became the focus of a new opposition group, the 'Independents', led by Dr Ali Amini, who had been associated with the oil negotiations in 1954 as Minister of Finance in the Zahedi government. Later he had served as Iran's Ambassador to the United States, but his resignation from his post was shrouded in mystery. What was known, when he reappeared as leader of the 'Independents', was that he was a wealthy member of the notorious Thousand Family group ; that he was a Qajar relative ; and that he had been a severe critic of the Eghbal government. His close and friendly links with the United States were also not unknown.

The rise of the Independents coincided with a sudden change in American policy in West Asia. In the days when Dulles had presided over the State Department, military commitment to the west had been the sole criterion for the receipt of financial aid by west Asian countries. After the fiasco of the Anglo-French-Israeli invasion of Egypt, and United States support of the Nasserite leadership in the Arab world, several earlier Dulles strategies were abandoned by Washington. After the thaw in Soviet-American relations following the meeting between Khrushchev and Eisenhower at Camp David, the United

States appeared to turn away from open military alliances with countries who had thereby risked the wrath of the Soviet Union [1] in favour of growing financial and political support for countries which had proclaimed a policy of non-alignment.

The Shah had conveyed to the United States government his surprise and sorrow at this change which, in a sense, was a betrayal of earlier American pledges. There was little positive response from Washington. At the same time, however, American officials began to criticise his reform policies, taking care to mask their criticism under the guise of objections to administrative inefficiency and the prevalence of corruption. As had become his custom, the Shah laid the issue before his people, publicly expressing criticism of the decline in American interest and in the level of economic and military aid. But this had no visible effect on the progressive decline of economic aid from the western alliance. Whereas for the years 1955–7 inclusive, the total of loans and grants from abroad had amounted to an average of about $100 million per annum, this dropped by about a quarter for the years 1958 and 1959. [2]

This revival of old style politics and the abrupt change in American policy aroused new political tension in Tehran. When the Twentieth *majlis* was elected in August, the new opposition attacked the results as having been rigged by the parties led by Dr Eghbal and Assadollah Alam. [3] The Shah accepted that there was some validity in this criticism, and advised the newly elected deputies to resign. Dr Eghbal

[1] In 1958, Marshal Vershimin of the Soviet Army declared that if Iran continued to be an ally of the United States, she might be destroyed by Soviet missiles. The Soviet government took several other steps, such as permitting a special broadcast against Iran, condemning her because she refused to opt out of the Baghdad Pact. *Mission*, pp. 121–3.

[2] Marlowe, *Iran*, p. 119.

[3] The formation of these parties in 1957 was an experiment by which the Shah hoped to introduce the parliamentary system in Iran. For his own explanation see *Mission*, pp. 172–4.

resigned on August 28, and the Shah nominated Sharif Emami in his place. Emami appointed a committee to examine the electoral law and draw up new regulations for the conduct of elections. While the committee's work was still in progress, the opposition went into action.

The abrupt fall in western aid had led to a crisis in the foreign exchange reserves. On the Shah's insistence Emami introduced a crash programme to stabilise the national economy. Imports were heavily discouraged by a substantial increase in duty; credit control machinery was introduced through the Bank Melli, which was empowered to limit domestic credit; and the purchase of foreign exchange was severely restricted.[4] These measures further angered those wealthy critics of the reform policies who were the most directly affected. They adopted every kind of subterfuge to defeat the programme. Meanwhile, the urban middle class, which had been suffering from inflationary pressures on their standards of living, became involved in the politics of the opposition. The demand for new elections mounted, and these had to be announced before the electoral reform committee had finished work.

The Shah could see that the ghosts of the past were reappearing; yet he was no longer despondent and alone. The heavy burden of his responsibilities was relieved by a new turn in his personal life. The incapacity of Queen Soraya to bear a male heir had once again compelled him to dissolve his marriage, and the divorce had taken place in March 1958. In 1959, he had met Miss Farah Diba, daughter of an Iranian army officer. She was then a student in Paris at the Ecole Speciale d'Architecture. The Shah fell in love with her, and married her on December 21, 1959.[5] In February 1961, Prince Reza Cyrus,

[4] Marlowe, *Iran*, pp. 113–14.
[5] The Shah has candidly related this aspect of his personal life as well as his married life in *Mission*, pp. 222–7.

heir to the Pahlavi dynasty, was born. The birth of his son was a long-awaited moment of joy and happiness for the Shah and his people. Even the critics of his reform policies joined in the nation-wide celebrations.

The election results had brought several opposition leaders back to the *majlis*. The National Front had succeeded in returning one of its prominent leaders, Allahyar Saleh, as a deputy from Kashan. With their return to the *majlis*, the old politicians revived their strategy of obstruction and attack on everything that the government proposed or did, while their agitation outside the *majlis* gave rise to severe discontent among the urban population. The Tudeh and the National Front took the lead in organising fresh agitation in the cities. They threatened strikes on several occasions, and the school teachers of Tehran actually went on strike under the leadership of Deputy Mohammad Darakhshesh. In a protest march led by him in front of the *majlis*, the police resisted the attempt on the part of some of the demonstrators to rush into the building and, in the ensuing clash, one unfortunate teacher was shot dead.[6] The Shah was horrified by this tragic death of a poor teacher who was interested, justifiably, in demanding a rise in his pay. His reaction was characteristic of his general policy. If the Independents as a group could help to solve the economic crisis in the country, he was willing to offer them an opportunity to do so. He invited Dr Amini to form a new government and, in April 1961, Amini was installed as the new Prime Minister.

Before it resigned, the Emami government placed the Land Reform Bill, drafted under the Eghbal government and revised later, before the Twentieth *majlis*. Its fate was doomed from that moment. The Twentieth *majlis* was dominated by land-lords who were determined to defeat the Shah's project. The

[6] Shamim, p. 134.

bill was amended by them to such an extent that its essential purpose was thwarted. The landlords, in their capacity as deputies, gave themselves power under the amended bill to transfer all their property to their legal heirs within two years of the Land Reform Bill becoming law. By another amendment, they opened the way for any landlord to transfer as much land as he could from dry farming into irrigated land, the latter category being excluded from the provisions of the law. However, the amendment which really cut across the entire scheme of land reform gave the landlords power to sell as much of their land as they wished at their own price before the law came into force. The deputies also saw to it that, even after the law became effective, landlords could delay the sale of their land if they did not like the price offered for it. Under the scheme outlined by them, an assessment commission was to be set up in every case where there was a dispute over the price of land to be purchased by the government for eventual sale to the peasants; if its verdict was not acceptable to the landlord he had the power to appeal; another commission, this time at provincial level, was to consider his objection; and even if at this stage the landlord was dissatisfied, he could go to court, and this verdict would be final. This, of course, could mean a delay of several years.[7]

The Shah's plan to introduce effective land reform was now clearly being defied. He had suspected at the time of the election of the Twentieth *majlis* that the landlords might use it to defeat the real purposes of the measure. The bill was his own design; its purpose was to restrict landed estates and limit the landlords' possessions to a fixed farming area. The landlords were to sell their excess land to the government so that the government in turn could divide it and sell it to small farmers

[7] For details of the amendments, see Shamin, pp, 140-1; for the Shah's comments, *The White Revolution*, p. 35.

on easy terms. The Shah had hoped against hope that the bill might have a relatively easy passage, despite the opposition of the big landlords, since it enjoyed national support. As late as 1959, he had felt that the landlords would reappraise the direction of inevitable change. He had had some reason to be optimistic : 'Only a few years ago, these landlords became very bitter when I broached the idea that their vast holdings should be divided, but many have now come to realise that in terms of social justice, their position is untenable. Moreover, with the exception of alternative investment opportunities, landowning as such no longer commands quite so much profit or prestige value as formerly.' He had hoped, with justification, that the landlords would follow his example, and yet he was 'under no illusion that they will be moved merely by the power of example'. If they rejected national arguments and the Shah's precept, what was to be done ? His answer had been simple : 'We shall use stronger measures.' [8]

The sabotage of the Land Reform Bill by the *majlis* had proved that these 'stronger measures' were required. It had challenged not only the Shah, but also the vast majority of the rural population on whose behalf the Shah now acted and unhesitatingly dissolved the *majlis*. At last the new Prime Minister received the opportunity he had asked for. The Amini cabinet approved the bill in its original form on January 1, 1962, and it received the royal assent on January 15. The Minister of Agriculture, Hassan Arsenjani, was asked to execute its provisions without delay. The district of Maragheh, in eastern Azerbaijan, was chosen as the first area where the peasants of Iran were to enter a new age of social equity.

The firm policy of the Shah convinced many of the opposition that the game was up. However, there were some who were unwilling to give up, and staged a last ditch battle. Using

[8] *Mission*, p. 204.

the old shibboleths of 'nationalism' and 'democracy', they succeeded in organising a serious riot among the students of Tehran University, only seven days after the Land Reform Bill had received the royal assent. Many individuals and groups— the National Front, landlords, religious fanatics, and the Tudeh — participated in provoking this riot, which served to show the Amini government's incapacity to convince the younger generation and intellectuals of its sincerity towards the land reform project. The Minister of Finance, Dr Behnia, had resigned in protest and Amini himself was accused of maintaining political relations with the National Front and the landlord inspired political groups. The Shah granted a period of six months to the Amini government to prove its worth. Dr Amini leaned heavily on the United States representatives in Tehran and, after consultations with them, evolved a new policy of reduction of expenditure on economic development and defence. The Shah could not be a party to this retrograde step. Dr Amini resigned on July 17 and Assadollah Alam took his place.

The resignation of Amini provoked resentment among the western powers, and 'the new government received a cool reception in London and Washington'. The Minister of Agriculture, Hassan Arsenjani, who continued in his post in the Alam cabinet, proceeded with his preparations for making a reality of land reform, and this brought the western prophets of doom to proclaim the coming collapse of Iran. 'The retention of Arsenjani', wrote an English observer, 'seemed to indicate a determination to press on with land reform, or perhaps the realisation that the point of no return had already been passed. But the Shah's refusal seriously to face the realities of the financial situation in his insistence on an undiminished military establishment, augered ill for the stability or solvency of the new government.'[9] Neither these prophets nor the

9 Marlowe, *Iran*, p. 121.

reactionary opponents who were awaiting the defeat of the Shah's policies fully realised that the Shah had now cast himself in a different role and was prepared to take on all comers : just as his father had led the first revolution, and he himself had won the support of his people during the second revolution of 1954, he was now determined to launch a third revolution — the revolution of the Shah and the people.

PART FIVE

THE REVOLUTION OF THE SHAH
AND THE PEOPLE

The black of an army,
  Which fronts a soldier's eye,
Should never his brave soul appal
  Nor make him dread or die ;
He should with stouter heart advance,
  Recalling, there and then,
That one real warrior is worth
  A hundred thousand men.

ABOL QASSEM MANSUR FERDOWSI
A.D. 935—1020

CHAPTER TWENTY-EIGHT

The Duties of a Sovereign

THE crisis in the summer of 1962 was at first sight merely another episode in the long series of acute problems which had faced the Shah since his accession. His had been a lonely struggle during the long period when Iran had been repeatedly endangered by external and internal enemies, and her very existence as a free and sovereign society had been in jeopardy. It could not but be an exceptional and emotional strain for one man. 'Only the Almighty knows', the Shah has recorded, 'of the sleepless nights I spent in contemplation and humble prayer for guidance! I used to try and reason out how the intelligent and industrious people of a rich nation with a glorious past should fall prey to such a terrible fate.'[1] Now the decisions had to be made for once and for all. The nation had reached the point where it could not withstand many more such crises. The seriousness of the occasion led the Shah to review the events of the past, so as to verify the conclusions which were to be the basis of his new course.

Looking back, the Shah remembered how, on his accession as a young man of twenty-one, he had found the machinery of government completely broken down as a consequence of the Anglo-Soviet invasion. The forces of reaction and corruption which had been temporarily suppressed by Reza Shah had

[1] *The White Revolution*, p. 8.

benefited from this situation and had mushroomed throughout the country, in the new guises of nationalism, freedom and democracy. They had been supported by the occupying powers and had become their fifth columnists. He remembered the days when he and his people had been subject to the 'frequent vicissitudes of fortune and witnessed artificial scenes, played for their benefit by actors, who, like puppets, were manipulated from the outside'.² He had watched the credulous people of Iran, in their desperate efforts for reform, being deceived by counterfeit patriots whose real political allegiance was known to him, and who publicly opposed the very foreigners whose agents they secretly were.

The principal aims of the foreign powers haunted him ; they had been to create 'an atmosphere of poisonous distrust and pessimism among the people'. To succeed, 'they instructed their agents not only to cultivate suspicion to such an extent that his people would consider foreign backing as the only means of achieving anything in the country, but also to aggravate the inferiority complex which they had deliberately created'.³ They had used five different types of agent : the simple fifth columnists ; the double talking, double-crossing politicians posing as nationalists and liberals ; the feudalists and tribal chieftains ; and, finally, the religious fanatics who, ever since the establishment of constitutional monarchy, had been at the disposal of one particular foreign power. 'All these groups', the Shah knew, 'acted as a deterrent to Iran's progress, for foreign interests depended on a permanent state of anarchy in the country to benefit themselves fully.' ⁴

These agents of foreign domination had fought among themselves on every issue except one : they were always united in their opposition to the power of the monarchy, and especially

---

² *The White Revolution*, p. 6.   ³ Ibid. p. 7.
⁴ Ibid. p. 7.

of the Pahlavi dynasty. It had not taken him long to understand the reason for this antagonism. They were aware that he could never permit himself to be a party to their designs, since his only objective was to serve the true interests of his country. But, until 1954, he had witnessed the fate of his nation isolated and alone, not from inside but from above, due to the nature of his position.

Now, in the summer of 1962, he re-considered his fundamental beliefs about his own course as the sovereign of his country. 'I was not the ruler', he later recorded, 'only of a powerful class of corrupt reactionaries, feudal khans, and deluded or treacherous people who acted as the fifth column in the service of foreigners. First and foremost, I was the sovereign of over twenty million hard working noble citizens, who had placed their hopes in me. I watched them toil and saw the rewards of their ceaseless efforts slip through their fingers into the outstretched hands of a group of parasites whose only abilities were in concluding illegal deals and serving foreign powers. Although perhaps many people thought my personal interests lay in co-operating with this influential class which controlled the government, I myself had no such inclinations still less the right to accept such a situation.'[5]

From this conviction it was only a short step to the decision to assume the leadership of those who believed in social change. He was now in a position to usher in a new movement towards the goals he had set for himself and Iran practically all his life. He was no longer isolated and alone, for his people had joined him. They had seen that during the entire period of his reign he had been engaged in various struggles for the preservation of national independence. They had not failed to see his readiness to sacrifice his own personal wealth : he had begun his work of social transformation by disowning his own estates

[5] *The White Revolution*, p. 8.

first, and dedicating four-fifths of his personal fortune to assist them in their poverty, sickness and destitution. He had done his best to serve them. They had trusted him and now their bonds with him were stronger than ever before. Herein lay the qualitative difference between this and the previous crises.

The Shah realised that he must take every factor into consideration before taking the final decision since he could not afford to make any mistakes which might lead the new movement to setback or defeat. Later, the Shah defined his quest for the answer to Iran's crying needs : 'I looked at Iranian society recognising its weaknesses, needs and potentials ; I studied the structure of other societies and saw how they progressed. I analysed the various philosophies and programmes which had been advocated and implemented.' It was after this exercise that he fixed his new goal : 'The realisation came to me that Iran needed a deep and fundamental revolution that could, at the same time, put an end to all social inequalities and all the factors which caused injustice, tyranny and exploitation.'[6]

Thus was born the revolution of the Shah and the people. Its fundamental purpose was to transform the feudal, oppressive social structure of Iran into one based upon justice and human rights. The moribund traditional economy was to be replaced by one that would be progressive and self-sustaining. This basic social change was to be carried out by democratic and non-violent means. It was because of this that the Shah later called it the White Revolution. However, the democratic measures which he envisaged had nothing in common with the farce to which the *majlis* had been reduced during the previous decades. He wanted the working people of his country to decide upon the change, and exercise their power of sanction to assure its success. His earlier concept was now further enriched with the inclusion of the principle that 'no agent of exploitation must

[6] *The White Revolution*, p. 15.

operate, be it private or governmental or a group which is defending a minority or a class of the community'.[7]

In this design of the new society, the Shah held two principles sacrosanct. He was uncompromising in his refusal to sacrifice the spiritual content of the Iranian way of life for material benefits. For him, reliance on the spiritual principles of Islam was mandatory. He was at the same time equally convinced that progress would be impossible without the strengthening of individual and social freedom. 'No matter how brilliant its progress might be', he knew, 'a society devoid of religious beliefs and devoid of spiritual principles of individual and social freedom is not enduring; moreover, there is no beauty or attraction in it.'[8]

Having decided the general goals of the new society, the Shah worked out a full platform for their realisation. Land reform, geared to the abolition of the landlord and peasant system; reorganisation of labour relations to give the working man a share in the profits of his labour; elimination of illiteracy so as to enable the common people to defend themselves and exercise their rights; universal and effective medical services; the end of the backwardness of the country areas as opposed to the towns; reformation of the political structure of democracy and the recognition of equal rights for women — these were the six points of the programme which the Shah resolved to place before his people.

He laid special emphasis on two aspects of the third revolution. Firstly, it was an Iranian revolution, compatible with the spirit and tradition of the Iranian people. It was not an imported item. The measures recommended to translate the philosophy and spirit of the revolution into practice must also be commensurate with Iranian genius, drawing on the experience of other nations, but not hesitating to introduce new

[7] *The White Revolution*, p. 21.   [8] Ibid. p. 15.

thinking wherever necessary. Secondly, the general principles of the revolution were unalterable and yet the methods of its execution flexible ; Iran should not hesitate to take advantage of the scientific and technical methods evolved in other countries if they helped to speed up social change. The participation of the people at all levels in the third revolution was a prerequisite for its success. The youth, especially, must be fully mobilised. As part of this concept, the Shah laid great emphasis on the co-operative movement.[9] These principles and projects were to become 'the revolution of the Shah and the people'.

9 *The White Revolution*, p. 22.

CHAPTER TWENTY-NINE

The Sixth of Bahman

THE period of eight months between May 9, 1962, when the Shah dissolved the fractious and reactionary *majlis*, and January 9, 1963, when the National Congress of Rural Co-operatives was convened at Tehran, was composed of final ideological and organisational preparations. Superficially the conflict with the reactionary forces was confined to the scope and extent of land reform. However, the Shah knew that reactionary rightists and irrational leftists were storing up their strength to undermine popular morale and prevent the introduction of further reform measures. The Shah used the sense of timing which he had inherited from his father. It was no longer essential or advantageous, he reasoned, to wait ; now was the time to strike at the very roots of social inequality and introduce in one sweep the revolutionary measures which he had planned.

'Frequent revolutions and upheavals', he wrote later, expressing his thinking at this time, 'have shaken the world during the last hundred years. Governments have been deposed, old ideologies discarded. Individuals, who believed themselves to be reflecting the thoughts and hopes of the people, advocated changes through their different ideologies. Some managed to effect these changes by peaceful means, others usurped power and executed their plans through bloody revolutions, but all of

U

them condemned social injustice and expressed the necessity for class equilibrium and equal distribution of wealth.'[1] He shared their goals and was determined to achieve them by peaceful means. There was only one way open to him. He must rouse the peasant masses and create through them a sanction which could not be defied. With their mandate for a revolution, he could achieve a bloodless victory.

Fortunately, political conditions in the autumn of 1962 were ripe for adopting this course of action, because of the initial success of land reform. The bill passed at the Shah's instigation was to be executed in three stages, by the first of which land ownership was now limited to one village per landlord. By its provisions, the landlord could take this up in the form of one-sixth shares in several villages or one whole village, including all its landed property, gardens, orchards, farmlands and water rights. Anything in excess of the whole unit was sold to the government at prices fixed in relation to the declared taxable value of the property. This meant that land which had been undervalued for taxation purposes was bought by the government relatively cheaply. The government paid for the land in fifteen instalments, the first payment to be made on signature of the agreement. The government also undertook to pay 6 per cent interest on remaining instalments. This system had been accepted as inevitable by a large number of smaller landlords. As a result, the large landowners and tribal chiefs had been separated from them, and thus weakened as a political force.

The property acquired through land reform was divided into smaller lots and sold to those peasants who, before the date of enactment of the law, had established themselves as permanent residents on the property concerned. The purchase price of these plots to new peasant owners was subject to a ten per

[1] *The White Revolution*, p. 13.

cent levy which was to be used to finance development projects on the distributed estates. Each purchaser was expected to pay off the price for his land in fifteen easy instalments. However, one major problem still remained. In cases where the landlords chose to retain whole villages, the old landlord-peasant relationship survived. The Shah was determined to end it. In January, 1963, he issued instructions that the second stage of the land reform be introduced without delay so as to limit landholding still further and really free the peasant from these medieval shackles.[2]

The peasants were not slow to appreciate the change in their status. As one landlord after another was divested of his lands, a new wave of enthusiasm spread over the rural hinterland. This growing zeal was channelled into the rural co-operatives. The Agricultural Bank had loaned part of the capital for these co-operatives and the peasants themselves had invested the rest. These new co-operatives had become the new power centres in the villages. They symbolised the liberation of the peasantry.[3]

The Shah resolved to mobilise these new power centres to gather together the forces of progress. He issued instructions for a national congress of rural co-operatives to be convened in Tehran in January 1963. The congress was to be a constituent assembly of the people with the Shah presiding over it. Four thousand peasants, elected by villages all over Iran, had come to attend the congress as its delegates. They saw their king for the first time, without guards and attendants, far from the conservative minority, sitting under the same roof with them. The delegates found their king to be their leader. Their joy at

[2] Shamim, pp. 192–244.

[3] The role of the rural co-operatives while land reform was in progress is a distinctive feature of the land reform measures in Iran. In most Asian countries, the formation of co-operatives was delayed and hence the landlords, finding no popular organisation opposing them, were successful in defeating the measures.

this turn in their fate was equalled only by their sense of loyalty to him.

An air of expectancy loomed over the proceedings. The peasants sensed that the Shah was about to enlarge the ambit of reforms, and so did those who were opposed to them. Confident and happy under the Shah's leadership, they eagerly awaited his call. With their traditional shrewdness they knew that an epoch in their annals and in the history of their nation was about to close for good.

The Shah himself was now a transformed leader. He was aware that his 'prestige and political and moral influence had reached their peak',[4] and knew he was about to act from a position of immense strength. During the preceding eight months, he had perfected his programme of the six principles which were to initiate a social revolution in the country. He had convened the congress of representatives of the peasantry to place before them these principles in a declaration.

As the congress settled down to work, after the usual prayers had been said, the Shah as monarch of Iran, president of the congress and, above all, as leader of the third revolution, addressed the working people of his country through their delegates. He spoke slowly, in his gentle but firm voice, so that every word and each idea of his declaration should sink into the consciousness of his listeners. He told them of his dream, conceived in his early youth, and of the long, bitter and lonely struggle he had waged over the years to make it a reality. He shared with them his inner thoughts and their sorrows and pains. He spoke of the new Iran which he wanted to build for them and through their efforts.

He concluded his historic declaration with these words, which his listeners knew would be remembered for years to come : '. . . by virtue of my responsibilities as Shah and those

4 *The White Revolution*, p. 3.

I took to protect the rights and honour of the Iranian nation, I cannot remain a neutral onlooker in the struggle against the forces of evil, but have taken up the banner myself. So that no power can reinstate the regime of slavery among the villages and plunder the nation's wealth for the benefit of a minority, I have decided, as executive, legislative and judicial head of the state, to refer these reforms to a referendum. In this way henceforth no individual or group will be able to cancel out for their own private interests the results of these reforms, which will free the farmer from the yoke of feudalism, ensure a brighter future based on justice and progress for the noble working class and a higher standard of living for honest and hard working civil servants, members of the guilds and craftsmen.'[5] The peasants applauded him with all their hearts as he concluded. The six principles which the Shah had outlined, and which were to be voted on by the entire nation on January 26, became articles of faith for them. The day of the national referendum fell on the Sixth of Bahman by the Iranian calendar, and thus a tradition grew up later that the modern annals of Iran had opened on this day.

The first of these six principles, naturally, affected the lives of the peasants. It implemented the abolition of the system of master and serf through the ratification of the land reform already approved by the government on January 9, 1962, together with the new rules and conditions made in January 1963. By the second principle all the forests and pastures in the country were declared to be national property. The third principle was concerned with the ratification of the system which had been organised to finance land reform and by which the landlords were given shares in government-owned factories by way of compensation. The fourth principle embraced the life of the industrial workers, making it compulsory for their

[5] Quoted in *The White Revolution*, p. 36.

employers to share their profits with them. The electoral system was completely overhauled and women granted franchise for the first time in Iranian history by the fifth principle. By the sixth and final principle, a Literacy Corps was to be organised, to be staffed by recruits volunteering for it in lieu of military service, to eliminate illiteracy completely.

On January 26, the nation voted with great enthusiasm for the adoption of the six principles of the third revolution. Women went to the polling stations with the greatest enthusiasm of all because this was the first time that they had been granted effective participation in decisions which were to affect not only their own future, but the future of Iran. Considering that most of the adult population had never had the chance to vote before, it was remarkable that over 5.5 million votes were cast for the ratification of the Shah's programme, representing an overwhelming majority in favour. The Shah responded immediately, on January 28, in a message to his people. The positive answer which had been given to his call conveyed in an explicit and decisive manner the wishes of the people and their true understanding of the significance of the revolution he was now leading. For him, this was a great moment of fulfilment and joy.

'My dear people', he told them 'today we have turned a new leaf of our history together.' He referred to the past glories of the people of Iran and distinguished the new stage from the old. Never before had the foundations of Iranian society been 'so fundamentally transformed to assume a new form based on social justice'. He then outlined the future : 'With God's will and your enterprise, we will make such a country in this part of the world that it shall rival the most advanced countries in every aspect. We will make a country that shall be the land of free men and women where the genius of the Iranian can manifest itself and its eternal originality which is the secret of the survival of this country and nation more fully than ever before, and in a rich environment free from corruption. For the chains of slavery have now been broken. . . .'[6] On January 29, the Shah issued a royal *Firman* in which he instructed the government to implement the principles approved by the referendum.

The Shah had warned the congress of peasants that forces inimical to the reforms would attempt to sabotage their principles. He was proved right within weeks. The landlords and tribal chieftains reorganised their depleted forces, now augmented by the extreme left, who felt robbed of their own power to influence the peasantry. Immediately after the referendum, large-scale terrorism on the part of the landlords and these leftist elements began, and in some cases they succeeded in murdering peasants who had received land. By June, 1963, these forces had organised a revolt in the south and riots in Tehran, but the tribal chieftains were no longer in a position to dictate to the central government. In 1963 they neither commanded the power of life and death over their former subjects nor could hope to receive aid from foreigners. They were disciplined by the Shah who sent the army to the south. The riots in the capital were incited by a religious fanatic. He used the old, discredited language of the *Fadayan* and laid stress on the new rights granted to women, condemning them as un-Islamic. The Shah had taken great care all through the period of propagation of the six principles to explain to his people that the reforms were not only consistent with Islam but were in fact enjoined by their common faith. The riots were easily suppressed.

The absolute victory of the Shah made the reactionaries desperate. For the next two years they constantly sought a means of rousing the people against the third revolution. When they could no longer ignore the fact that they had lost, they organised an assassination plot against the Shah. On the

[6] Quoted by Shamim, pp. 180-1.

morning of April 10, 1965, as the Shah was on his way to his office in the Marble Palace, a guardsman attempted to assassinate him with a burst of machine-gun fire. Miraculously, the would-be assassin missed his victim. It seemed incredible that a burst of machine-gun fire at that range could fail.

'But the will of God,' the Shah wrote later, 'which had saved me on several previous occasions, snatched me from the jaws of death.'[7]   The attack by the would-be assassin had led to a short encounter. Two loyal guardsmen had fired to save the Shah. They lost their lives but not before they had shot the killer dead. The case history of the dead guardsman was investigated. The real instigators of the attempted assassination were arrested. Their confessions revealed the reasons for the plot. 'Their object in killing me', the Shah recorded, 'was to disrupt the existing order of the country, to instigate a civil war, especially partisan warfare in the mountains and forests of the country, so as to force the great powers to intervene in Iran.' The men who plotted the assassination were educated in Britain and themselves claimed to be followers of Mao Tse-tung.[8]

In the midst of these events, the nation went to the polls under the new electoral system of effective adult franchise to elect the Twenty-first *majlis* and the Fourth senate. The new parliament was dedicated to the principles of the Sixth of

[7] *The White Revolution*, p. 38.

[8] Ibid. p. 38 : 'The Marble Palace Plot', as the conspiracy came to be known, was masterminded by Ahmad Kamrani, Ahmad Mansuri and Parviz Nikkah ; the would-be assassin was Reza Shamsbadi. Kamrani and Mansuri were sentenced to death, but the Shah commuted this sentence to life imprisonment Nikkah's sentence of life imprisonment was reduced to 10 years. The author met the Shah soon after these men were sentenced. The Shah explained his action thus : ' They had committed a crime against me personally ; I had therefore a right to commute their sentences.' He also related how the men had told him all the details of the plot in the same room in which he was talking to the author. Four of the other plotters were freed on the eve of the Coronation on October 26, 1967.

Bahman. Many deputies were ordinary workers and peasants ; several women had been elected and the rising new middle class was fully represented while the landlords had lost their hold over it. A new political party, too, had been formed in support of the third revolution. It was led by Hassan Ali Mansur, a youthful intellectual. Two years later, he was to become yet another Prime Minister to lose his life at the hands of assassins. However, unlike previous occasions, his murder was nationally condemned and his memory preserved as that of a martyr.

The new Iran Novin Party worked under the direct guidance of the Shah. Of its origins, Mansur's successor, Amir Abbas Hoveyda, was to say later : 'On March 8, 1963, our country was on the threshold of a profound revolution. . . . There was complete readiness to rebuild the nation ; but the economic, industrial and agricultural machinery of the country required a complete overhaul. The social values which had come into being since January 1963 needed new impetus so that the Iranian society, as envisaged by our Shahanshah in his revolution, could lead a life of freedom, of pride and of comfort. To achieve this the need was felt for an organisation of dedicated men and a proper platform.'[9]

Besides the rise of the Iran Novin party, the Sixth of Bahman principles led to a major shift in the political balance of the country. The leaders of the extreme right condemned it as a 'socialist or bolshevist programme' while the extreme left saw in them an 'unholy compromise with the capitalist system'. However, the bulk of the urban population, which traditionally supplied these two groups with their main activists and followers, welcomed the Shah's declaration. The National Front proved to be the first group to disintegrate under its impact. Many independents and intellectuals

[9] From Mr Hoveyda's report : Iran Novin Party, First Congress, Tehran, May 14, 1967.

supported it. Even within the ranks of the Tudeh, it led to a major debate. A section revolted against the old diehard leadership. Soon afterwards, the Tudeh split into two groups, one supporting the general aims of the third revolution, the other preferring the extremism of the strict Maoists.[10]

The Shah kept in close contact with these political developments, influencing them whenever possible in order to help forge national unity. He welcomed constructive criticism and received the critics whenever they requested an audience. He discussed with them their objections and suggestions. He was willing to welcome all who were ready to be soldiers of the revolution. He analysed the recent political past without rancour with the former members of the Tudeh and helped them to see their mistakes, offering an opportunity to them to redeem themselves through work in the service of the people.[11]

Simultaneously, he continued to take measures to strengthen the agrarian foundations of the revolution. The principle of land reform could not be limited merely to the break-up of large landed estates and their distribution among the peasants. With his experts' assistance, he prepared to launch the third stage of the reforms, by which the peasants were encouraged to implement the mechanisation of agriculture. He expanded his original eight-point agrarian programme into a twenty-point plan in order to introduce correct methods of irrigation, promote greater use of chemical fertilisers, encourage protection of crops from disease and train technical experts.[12]

[10] Though the split in the Tudeh was a consequence of the break-up of the communist camp, the author was told by several Tudeh members that the issue of support of the Shah was an important factor in the debate preceding the split.

[11] During several conversations with the author, the Shah mentioned the good work done by the former Tudeh members, pointing out in some cases the record of each individual official with a Tudeh background.

[12] *The White Revolution*, p. 39.

The daily routine of work increased enormously, always hard, sometimes back-breaking, often disappointing. The Shah had trained himself to face this with zeal and interest. No problem seemed dull and devoid of interest to him, for he saw in their solution the guarantee of the success of the Sixth of Bahman principles.

CHAPTER THIRTY

The New Deal

THE second of the Sixth of Bahman reforms was a direct consequence of the Shah's radical ideology. It decreed the nationalisation of forests and pastures. The word 'nationalisation' revived for many memories of the Mossadeq period ; for others, it evoked the ghost of communism. The Shah, aware of these misgivings, patiently explained his outlook : 'This revolutionary step was taken not only in accordance with the national interests of Iran but according to the teaching of Islam.' He reminded them of the Prophet's saying : 'Muslims have equal rights of water, fire and pastures.' He added : 'Islamic law denies the principle of private ownership of forests and pastures since in Islam land ownership is based on the principle of the work done to the land, and that is why in the early days of Islam pastures were common land in which the entire community had equal rights.'[1] This Islamic principle was consistent with his own ideology of social change. The nationalisation of forests fell within the pattern of the new social revolution which was based on the principle that a man could benefit only from his own efforts, and clearly nobody could justify exclusive rights over the forests of Iran. 'The forests are a divine gift,' he said in a speech, 'for which no-one has laboured except nature, and it is perfectly logical that something

[1] *The White Revolution*, p. 62.

which nature has bestowed on a country should belong to all inhabitants.' [2]

The immediate effect of the measure was to deprive the landlords of their titles to the forests and pastures. The situation was particularly acute in relation to the pastures. These were owned by big landlords who had allowed them to deteriorate to such an extent that they were capable of sustaining only half the number of livestock that grazed on them. The shepherds lived at the mercy of the landlords who exacted heavy fees for grazing rights. 'After this natural source of wealth had been nationalised', the Shah later recorded, 'the power was removed from the influential landlords, who had done nothing to deserve this source of wealth, the pastures were allotted to the shepherds by the responsible government organisations, and charges imposed by the former owners for grazing and water rights abolished. The abolition of these charges, and the insistence of scientifically correct methods of pasturing, have helped to raise the standard of living of the shepherds and, at the same time, have prevented a needless rise in the price of animal products.' [3]

The Shah knew that the land reform measures would create a large number of subsidiary and complex problems.[4] The landlords' compensation placed a huge new money income in their hands amounting to just over seven per cent of the value of their estates each year for the next fifteen years. They were also to receive additional amounts by way of annual interest during the same period. By an irony of fate, some of them were now

[2] *The White Revolution*, p. 58.

[3] Ibid. pp. 62–3.

[4] The author is grateful to Clifford German for his research on the financing of land reform and the new industrial revolution in Iran. Much of the material here is drawn from his two essays, titles ' Financing Land Reform' and ' The New Industrial Revolution', numbers 4 and 5, published in *The Revolution of The Shah and the People* (London, 1967).

receiving a higher income than they had derived from their estates. Left to themselves, a substantial number of them were content to spend the compensation money easily or use it for speculation. The compensation provision, on the other hand, placed a tremendous strain on the treasury and this too presented a serious problem. The third of the Sixth of Bahman principles was evolved to deal with this situation.

The Shah had studied the sad experience of several Asian countries where land reform projects had not only failed, but had proved detrimental to the solvency of their economies. He saw that the failure to find an effective and practical solution to the dual problem of the accumulation of capital in the hands of landlords, who did not know how to use it, and of the unbearable burden the principle of compensation laid on national budgets had caused an economic chain reaction. It had also led to a recession in the process of social change.

The Shah was determined to see that Iran did not become a victim of this growing malaise, and his remedy lay in the third principle of the Sixth of Bahman programme. He resolved to liberate the capital which compensation had placed in the hands of the landlords, and to encourage investment designed to increase the pace of industrialisation. He offered the landlords an opportunity for investment which was sound as well as lucrative. The state owned a number of factories opened in the reign of Reza Shah, and manufacturing or processing sugar, textiles, cotton, silk, chemicals and foodstuffs. The Shah converted 55 of them into joint stock companies and offered shares to the landlords. The shares thus became securities for land reform and helped to finance it.

This third principle served the primary purpose of providing a source of capital to cover the heavy costs of initiating the land reform before the peasants could pay their first instalments. The only other way the government could have defrayed this cost would have been a liberal use of the printing press to increase paper currency, which would have inevitably triggered off a new round of inflation. The second principal result of the conversion of the government factories into joint-stock companies was an increase in their efficiency, resulting from larger capital and new shareholders to keep a close watch on their management.

The Shah accompanied the new association of the former landlords with existing industry by a new industrial development programme. The conversion of the government factories into joint-stock companies was one of the many steps taken in this direction. The Shah was resolved that a major change in the balance between agriculture and industry should be effected by diversification and selective growth of new industries with the aid of domestic and foreign capital and skills. His approach was pragmatic and flexible, completely free from doctrinaire rigidity : 'To speed up the rate of industrial development, the government has generated two policies. On the one hand, it is creating industries in the public sector and, on the other hand, it is creating favourable conditions for private investment which it is encouraging and protecting. In some cases, the government is engaged in industrial activity to prevent the risk of monopolies and to ensure the supply of good quality goods at moderate prices. In the remote and under-developed parts of the country, which seem unattractive to private investors, the government is taking steps to develop industries that can utilise local resources and lead to an increase in economic activity and to a higher income in the region.'[5]

To ensure the success of both public and private industrial development, the Shah instructed the government to undertake basic capital investment in ports, roads and other means of communications, power supplies, and the provision of basic

[5] *The White Revolution*, p. 68.

commodities such as building materials and, where necessary housing facilities for workers. Within this infrastructure the Shah made the necessary provision for investment of money, time and skills in schools, education, training of technical personnel, and the establishment of an intensified programme of industrial research and development. Finally, with a view to infusing the new industrial system with the necessary combination of stimulation and competition, a scheme of adequate tariff protection, together with access to relatively cheap development finance on easy terms, tax exemptions to encourage initial investment, export guarantees both against expropriation and to protect the right to repatriate capital and profits in hard currency, was evolved.

The objective of this scheme was to absorb most of the increase in the labour force, inevitable with the growth of the population and a larger number of women seeking employment. The Shah was aware that, with the introduction of mechanisation in agriculture, a certain portion of the labour used on the farms would also become superfluous, and he wanted this section to be absorbed in industry. He was convinced that such a process, if successful, could ultimately eliminate the difference in social and cultural levels between the rural and urban centres.

The Shah viewed the planning and practice of industrialisation as a means toward his major aim of higher and better standards of living for the working people in the country. It was thus that he decided that from the very beginning of the new industrial revolution the working class must possess a definite stake in its growth and development. Therefore, he introduced profit-sharing in industry as the fourth of the Sixth of Bahman principles, with the idea of giving Iranian workers the same sense of pride and participation in their work, and the same interest in and responsibility for the success of their efforts, as land reform had provided for the formerly landless peasants and serfs.

The Shah held strong views on the question of the exploitation of the working class : 'The history of labour is one of the saddest and most poignant chapters in the saga of mankind. Throughout the centuries, workers' rights have been usurped, their efforts so exploited, and this noble and hard working class has made so many sacrifices of various kinds, that the final reckoning cannot but be extremely disquieting to the human conscience.'[6]   In consequence of this belief, he had taken several measures since 1944 to establish and protect the rights of labour within a legal framework.   After setting up the Department of Labour, which became later the Ministry of Labour, he had in 1946 inspired the passage of the first labour law in Iran, which reduced the working day to eight hours and the working week to forty-eight.   Two years later, upon his instructions, the government had introduced a fund to pay for the treatment of, and compensation for, the sick and injured workers, the capital of which came from contributions by both workers and employers.   In 1958, further legislative measures were introduced.   However, the efficacy and the range of these measures were limited, and the Shah realised that they were inadequate : 'In spite of the measures taken to protect the workers, the basic problem had not been overcome.   He could still not be confident that his labour would not be exploited and that he would not be treated simply as a hireling.   He could only be sure that such was not the case if he knew that he had a share in the work he did.   Such participation would not only be important to him in material terms but, and this was of special importance, it would make him really feel that his personality and his labour were being and would continue to be respected.'[7]

[6] *The White Revolution*, p. 72.   [7] Ibid. p. 79.

When the Shah expressed this belief to his advisers, he found them worried. They argued that, if the principle of the participation of the working class at all levels in industry was introduced, private investors would be frightened away. The Shah could not accept this argument. Apart from the inherent justice in his proposal, he was confident that this would work out in practice to the benefit not only of the workers but also of the employers, who would gain from better labour relations. 'Every employer must realise', he told them, 'that work carried out in an atmosphere of oppression and duress or of mutual suspicion and lack of confidence was unprofitable.' [8] The Shah added : 'Furthermore, let us not forget that in this age when it is realised that every human possesses a personality and human dignity of his own, and no privilege, except that of merit and capability, should rightfully be admitted, economic problems should not be divorced from social and moral problems. Economics can no longer be regarded as it was in the past as an abstract mathematical reality. Today, research must ensure that social justice and a better life for all become basic goals of economic policy and, in the distribution of wealth, laws based on morality and humanity must complement economic laws.' [9]

The initial, unwilling acceptance of the fourth of the Sixth of Bahman principles by the employers was balanced by the support it received from the workers, intellectuals and professional men. Even the employers, after a time, came to recognise the essential force of the Shah's arguments. Whether they were convinced of the ideological promise of his New Deal or not, they were satisfied when production began to increase in their factories.

[8] *The White Revolution*, p. 80.   [9] Ibid. p. 81.

CHAPTER THIRTY-ONE

Liberation of Women

THE revolution of the Shah and the people was conceived on an all-embracing national scale. The cardinal requirement for its success, besides a dynamic and enlightened leadership, was the full, free and voluntary participation of the people in its fulfilment. The requisite sense of belonging could not originate merely from the economic and cultural transformation which would be the consequence of the great economic and literacy revolution.

To ensure that the people of Iran could make their own revolution, the Shah introduced political democracy as an important point of the Sixth of Bahman reforms. To say that political democracy was a weak point in previous Iranian history is to make a ridiculous understatement. Even though, sixty years before, Iran had adopted a Constitution, no political observer could honestly say that the Constitution reflected the true content of political democracy. The Shah himself was acutely aware of this vacuum in Iranian national life: 'Sixty years have now passed since the establishment of the Constitution in Iran, and we could confidently state that until 1963 this Constitution was devoid of any true meaning.'[1]

Before the Shah could introduce any measures in this context, he had to define democracy, and the problem was not

[1] *The White Revolution*, p. 86.

simple. Democracy, as it is popularly understood, had existed for a century and a half and yet, even in western Europe, which is believed to be its cradle, it was practised in a very limited sense. The franchise had been restricted and in many countries it was merely a democracy of 10 per cent of the population. Even in those countries of western Europe which claim to be closely attached to democratic principles, adult franchise has been of recent origin. Even today, in some countries of Europe, women have been deprived of the right to vote.

Thus, the Shah had to determine the content of democracy not only in relation to the special national characteristics of his people, but also keeping in mind the mixed fortunes of the democratic apparatus in western Europe. 'What is the real meaning of democracy?' he asked himself. His answer to this crucial question can be summarised in his own words: 'First and foremost, it means that every citizen should have the right to express his opinion and to vote on questions concerning his own fate.'[2]   He then added: 'Our revolution is not one of constraint: it is, on the contrary, a revolution based on the freely given co-operation of every individual with a full understanding of its real meaning. The complete fulfilment of its principle demands that every citizen should have as wide and deep a knowledge of the revolution as possible, and should voluntarily take part in it inspired solely by a belief in the propagation and execution of these principles, the objectives of which are only the safeguarding of his real interests.'[3]   If Iran's revolution was to be carried out in its true sense, argued the Shah, and if, as was the principal objective of the revolution, it was to be a democratic transformation in harmony with the true sense of the Constitution, then it was clearly necessary to create a parliament that was representative of the whole nation.

[2] *The White Revolution*, p. 86.   [3] Ibid. p. 101.

The Shah, who had watched in sorrow the mockery of the constitutional process in Iran ever since he was Crown Prince, has described the tragic role of the helpless common people in these farcical elections : 'In all these elections the vast masses of agricultural and industrial workers were no more than tools. Their votes, or more correctly, the votes made in their name, were cast wholesale into the ballot boxes, although they themselves had no idea of what was going on. In those days the peasants and a large number of agricultural workers had little self respect and therefore showed no interest in voting. Besides, they were well aware that it did not matter in the slightest who went to the *majlis* on their behalf, because whoever it was would not champion their rights, but merely those of the ruling class.' [4]

The electoral law itself never guaranteed the interest of the majority of the nation. Both groups of the working class, urban and rural, were beyond the pale. One of its regulations stipulated that supervisory electoral bodies should be constituted ; but these were to consist exclusively of landlords and the wealthy. This stipulation gave the latter complete control of election procedure, and they ran the proceedings in the interests of their own class. They stuffed the ballot boxes with bogus votes. When, despite this, some ballot boxes showed results contrary to their desires, they declared the entire process null and void. The regulations for election were so framed as to give rise to a new breed of professional election agents. These men were employed by the land-owning feudal classes and foreign agents working openly or behind the scenes, and specialised in every manner of collusion and interference, openly and secretly, both at the time of polling and counting of the votes.

However, the most repugnant feature of the electoral law

[4] *The White Revolution*, p. 89.

was its Article 10 which laid down that half the population of the country, the women, should not be permitted to express their wishes on their own fate. It stated : 'Those deprived of the right to vote shall consist of all females ; minors and those under guardians ; fraudulent bankrupts, beggars and those who earn their living in a disreputable way ; murderers, thieves and other criminals punishable under Islamic law. . . .'[5]

In these circumstances it was essential to fulfil two conditions if political democracy was to have any meaning for the Iranian people. The electoral law had to be radically reformed. The new innovations had to be aimed at the corrupt practices of the influential people and their professional agents. Only such measures could enable representatives of all classes of society, especially industrial and agricultural workers, to get elected to the *majlis*. Secondly it was necessary that in the new electoral system, the women of Iran should enjoy equal rights with men, including the right to vote, and to stand for both houses of parliament.

The first condition was fulfilled with the approval of the principles of a radical electoral reform, submitted to the nation as part of the referendum of January 26, 1963. The grotesque anomaly of the disenfranchisement of women was removed by a decree of the Council of Ministers on March 7. In this manner, for the first time in the history of the Iranian Constitution, conditions were created in which elections could be held in a democratic manner and parliament could emerge without the domination of the landlords and alien powers.

The bill to reform the electoral law was introduced on February 8, 1963. The regulations which received legal sanction through this bill were of extreme importance to the success of the entire scheme of parliamentary reform. These laid down that by producing evidence of identification and entitlement to

[5] Quoted in *The White Revolution*, p. 92.

vote, every person should be issued with a voting card. In order to avoid the rigging of elections, it was also laid down that they should be held simultaneously on the same day throughout the country. The system of professional election agents was abolished. Finally, it was provided that the members and alternative members of the electoral supervisory bodies should consist of representatives of guilds, agricultural and industrial workers, small landowners who worked on their land, merchants and religious leaders.

The thinking of the Shah on the second problem, that of the franchise of women, was based on the following premise : 'If we consider the important role played by Iranian women in every material and spiritual aspect of the nation's life we can better comprehend how a continuation of the legal prohibition of women's right to determine their own destiny and that of the country by voting and by being elected to parliament was not only oppressive but illogical and against the best interests of the nation.'[6]

In the Iranian Constitution as it existed before January 16, 1963, an illiterate man was legally entitled to vote, while an Iranian woman engineer or doctor was prohibited from participating in national elections. Ever since Reza Shah introduced higher education for women a large number of Iranian girls had qualified with distinction as physicians, engineers, lawyers and university professors. This section of the new Iranian intelligentsia was precluded from participation in political activity. The Shah believed that, in a society in which the work done by every individual forms part of the gross national product, enlightened monarchy cannot accept that half the work force of the country be deprived of its legitimate rights. It was on this basis that on February 27 the Shah issued a decree by which equal electoral rights for men and women were announced.

[6] *The White Revolution*, p. 98.

The decree received enthusiastic and almost frenzied support from the women of Iran. Multitudes of women from all walks of life went to the Marble Palace in Tehran to express their gratitude to their king. The Shah was touched by this : 'I feel that in doing this', he has written, 'I discharged one of the greatest duties expected of me by the Iranian nation.'

The decree once and for all put an end to a state of affairs that was contrary to the true spirit of Islamic law, and contrary even to the constitutional law of the country which explicitly laid down : 'Every citizen is entitled to, and shall participate in, the ratification and control of public affairs.' The Shah addressed his nation on this historic occasion in the following words : 'Let us thank God that this final shame on our society has now disappeared, and this humiliating and enslaving chain has been removed from the necks of half the population and smashed to pieces.'

The Shah pointed out that in Iran women went to school and university side by side with men. How then, could anyone expect that a woman who has passed these stages of education should be included among a group of criminals and insane, and be prevented from expressing her opinion even on how the streets of her city should be cleaned. He went on to say : 'Such a woman, like her male equals, in the name of nature and the principles of civilisation, has the right to express her opinion not only on matters connected with her family and home, but on those affecting the country, its economics and its politics.'

The Shah addressed specially those who were still under the influence of old and outworn social norms. In his characteristically simple and yet penetrating fashion he asked them : 'How can a man give the rights to himself yet deprive his mother or sister of the same rights ? How can a man say that this mother who has given him his very life, is in the same category as lunatics and evil doers? This is against nature, humanity and civilisation.'

In conclusion, the Shah expressed his confidence in the contribution which the liberated women of Iran were certain to make to the conversion of the Iranian social structure to a new society. He said : 'I am convinced that the women of Iran, now that they have equal rights with men, are ready to manage the affairs of the country. Because they are a hitherto deprived class they will from now on play a far more enthusiastic role in the activities of our society and will take their new responsibilities seriously. Moreover, this doubling of the number of active people in the country will soon pay handsome dividends in every sphere of national life.'[7]

[7] *The White Revolution*, pp. 99–100.

CHAPTER THIRTY-TWO

The Three Corps

IN 1963, neither the political parties nor the administrative machine were capable of linking the various sectors of society during the process of transition. The Shah knew that, unless an agency were found to play this role effectively, any efforts in the direction of ultimate and permanent change would be foiled. He had experimented with the two party system and it had failed. The record of the civil service was not such as to inspire confidence. Much more than mere conveyance of the principles of the revolution had to be accomplished. What was needed was an army of dedicated men who believed in the principles of the revolution and who would devote all their energies to its successful implementation in every sector. The Shah, in his search for such cadres, evolved the sixth of the Sixth of Bahman principles, which aimed at utilising the services of youth in the country's cause.

As in other countries, the urban youth had fallen prey to the political designs of ambitious politicians and foreign powers who wanted to subvert them to their own purposes. Time and again, these impressionable young men had been carried away by appeals to nationalism, democracy and, occasionally, to socialism, and had swelled the ranks of angry demonstrators in the streets. They were honest and sincere in their desires. They had watched the various governments' failure to solve fundamental problems, including their own. Urban unemployment among the educated had defied solution. Educated young men were unwilling to take work which they felt to be inconsistent with their qualifications, but the narrow basis of the economy and the limitations of social class did not permit them to secure the jobs they sought. They grew frustrated, angry and desperate. In this state of mind, they became ideal raw material for unscrupulous agitators who used their explosive passions to help undermine their opponents.[1]

The Shah solved the dual problem of finding a unifying force on the one hand and of harnessing the fervour and energy of youth on the other. In late 1962, he had already set in motion this process by bringing them into the battle against illiteracy in the country. On January 26, 1963, the people had approved this experiment in the referendum, and the Literacy Corps was founded.

Under the law which created the Corps, young men of conscript age were enabled to serve in it in lieu of normal military service.[2] Twice yearly, secondary school graduates of twenty-one and over were recruited into the Corps. These recruits were then sent to one of more than 20 training centres where they underwent courses in military and non-military subjects. Their military training included basic weapon and tactical training ranging from drill and map reading up to the role of the individual in atomic war, and they were taught by staff officers of the Imperial Army.

The remaining two-thirds of the training period was devoted

---

[1] These views were expressed by the Shah to the author in 1966 ; since then he has taken several steps to draw Iranian students living in Europe to join him in the work of national reconstruction.

[2] The author is grateful to David Missen for much of the material in this chapter, which is to be found in his two essays, the ' Literacy Corps ' and ' The Health and Development Corps ', numbers 7 and 8 in *The Revolution of the Shah and the People*.

to non-military subjects. These included conventional teacher training programmes in classroom procedure; methods of teaching Farsi, arithmetic and science; and educational psychology. The corpsman, however, was to be trained not merely as a school teacher; he was to be a harbinger of the revolution in every household he entered. His training programme included a wide variety of subjects, such as health, sanitation, first-aid, agricultural education, community development, rural sociology and village law. The cost of training in these subjects was borne by the Ministry of Education. Once trained in this manner, the corpsman was ready for assignment to the villages.

Two important principles governed the Ministry's assignment procedure. No corpsman was sent to a village unless the village had first requested his assistance and had undertaken, for its own part, to provide a suitable school building. Whenever possible, the corpsman was sent to villages in his own district where he would be more familiar with the dialect and customs of the people, and therefore better able to take his place in the life of the community and gain the confidence of the villagers. He remained for a year and a half in the village to which he had been assigned. He could then return to civilian life, his duty discharged, but the Shah knew that if his scheme worked properly, a substantial percentage of the discharged corpsmen would volunteer to continue with their work as full time employees of the Ministry of Education in the villages.

The scope of the problem was enormous, as the Shah realised. Like other developing countries, Iran had been caught in a vicious circle of illiteracy and low productivity. On the one hand, literacy and a reasonable standard of education were prerequisites for the efficient use of natural resources, the development of agriculture and industry, and the smooth functioning of the administrative machinery. On the other hand, illiteracy not only acted as a brake on the speed with which these aims were accomplished, but resulted also in low productivity, and hence a shortage of the very funds needed to finance its elimination. Thus a 70 per cent majority of the population was responsible for producing no more than a third of the country's gross national product.

Besides the shortage of funds, the Shah had to overcome another major difficulty: the lack of trained staff willing to work in rural areas. About 70 per cent of the population of Iran lived in some 50,000 villages scattered over 628,000 square miles. About 76 per cent of the teachers were concentrated in the towns, leaving only 24 per cent for the greater needs of the rural population. Several efforts, such as publicity campaigns to popularise teaching and salary increases ranging from 20 to 80 per cent, had failed to counteract the disinclination of professional teachers to work in remote isolated villages, lacking in urban amenities and amusements. As a result, the children of the rural population were denied proper education.

The immediate necessity for a literacy campaign in the rural areas was sharpened by the need to convey the principles of the revolution to the rural hinterland of the country. Nobody was more aware than the Shah that there could be little point in taking land from educated, if reactionary, landlords and dividing it amongst the peasants unless the level of their education could be raised to enable them to make the fullest use of their new possessions. The nationalisation of forests and pastures would also have had little meaning.

The corpsman's primary duty was the formal education of children. He was also trained to conduct classes in adult education, and to set up small village libraries to circulate reading material amongst those who became literate. He was to organise recreational and youth groups, and to act as general adviser, teacher and elder to the village on questions of social change.

The Literacy Corps was a uniquely unorthodox idea. To the Shah, it was inconceivable to evolve a solution to Iran's own illiteracy problem without sharing its results with other countries and making available to them the lessons learnt in the early days of the experiment. Indeed, the problem of illiteracy in Iran was a part of the general malaise in Africa and Asia, where the average rate of illiteracy in 1963 was 90 per cent. In some areas of the two continents, only one person in a hundred could read and write. The international significance of the problem lay in the fact that, of the total population of the world, only some 700 million adults were literates. The Shah realised the necessity of linking his crusade against illiteracy with that throughout the world : 'If, in keeping with the spirit of our revolution, we were prepared to eradicate the curse of illiteracy from Iranian society and yet to look on as passive by-standers while such an unhealthy state of affairs continued in vast areas of the world, we could scarcely claim to have carried out the true meaning of our revolution.' He was convinced that basic social reforms carried out in one part of the world must have repercussions elsewhere. 'This fact was particularly true in the case of the principle of our revolution relating to eradication of illiteracy because, whereas the other principles of the revolution such as land reform, improving the lot of workers, the nationalisation of forests and pastures, and the electoral law reform were primarily of an internal nature, the campaign against illiteracy was first and foremost a world problem. With this point in mind, I felt that if we wished to carry out this principle completely, we must not confine its execution to the national and geographical limits of Iran, but test it in a wider theatre.' [3]

[3] *The White Revolution*, p. 118.

The Shah therefore proposed that a World Congress on the Eradication of Illiteracy should be convened in Tehran, under the auspices of UNESCO. At this conference the Ministers of Education of UNESCO member countries would have the opportunity of discussing the world campaign against illiteracy and of arranging effective means of international co-operation to further it. The delegates would also have the chance of seeing for themselves the methods of the Literacy Corps in Iran. This proposal was made after the Literacy Corps had been active in the villages for two years, and met with the unanimous approval of the general conference of UNESCO.

The Congress was convened in September 1965. In his opening address the Shah advanced another proposal true to the revolutionary spirit of the Literacy Corps. Of this he was to write later : ' This proposal was a recommendation that the countries of the world should set aside a defined proportion of their annual military budget and that this money should be made available to UNESCO to help the world campaign against illiteracy in order to help achieve victory in one of the greatest battles humanity has ever fought.'[4]

A year before the Congress was called, the Shah had already extended the horizons of his reforms by adding three more principles to those approved by the referendum of January, 1963. Two of these dealt with the creation of the Health Corps and the Reconstruction and Development Corps, and the third with the Houses of Equity. The two corps resembled

---

[4] The Shah took the 1962 figure of world military expenditure at $162 billion ; one-thirtieth of this figure would be enough to teach 700 million people to read and write. The military expenditure of the world, at 1962 levels, amounted to $13 million every hour. 'It would therefore be enough', the Shah concluded, 'for every country to give up military expenditure of only a few hours and for this credit to be invested in one of the most profitable projects in history, the safeguarding of mankind's peace and prosperity.' *The White Revolution*, pp. 122–3.

the Literacy Corps in that they were revolutionary solutions to those problems of Iranian life which required immediate attention. Instead of health and development remaining the indirect responsibility of the people through taxation, the creation of these two new corps made these vital sectors their direct task. These two new corps were to translate the policies of the Ministries of Health and Agriculture and of the Plan Organisation into everyday rural terms and to show how each individual citizen could contribute to the progress of health and agriculture through optimum use of national resources.

The principle of the Houses of Equity was derived by the Shah from ancient and Islamic precepts.[5] Its immediate inspiration, however, sprang essentially from the long exploitation of the legal system by the propertied classes: 'Unfortunately, throughout the ages the powerful have tried many different ways of using the operations of the law to serve their own interests. The law thus tended to become the means of protecting the privileges of the ruling class and depriving the rest of the population from the true benefits of its spirit.'[6]

The Shah's thinking on the problem of justice started from the premise that in a really progressive society, a judicial system by itself was not enough to secure the rights of the people. The theory of equality before law had been formally adopted in Iran in 1907 and integrated in the judicial system a little later. But in practice, this system helped the strong and the influential. Under it the landlord, for example, could easily take advantage of expert legal advice and assistance, whereas a poor man was left almost defenceless. The legal luminaries engaged by the rich client could weave a web of interpretations around the real issue. The illiterate peasant

[5] For full treatment, see 'Houses of Equity', in *The Revolution of the Shah and the People*.

[6] *The White Revolution*, pp. 140-1.

Land Reform

Campaign against illiteracy

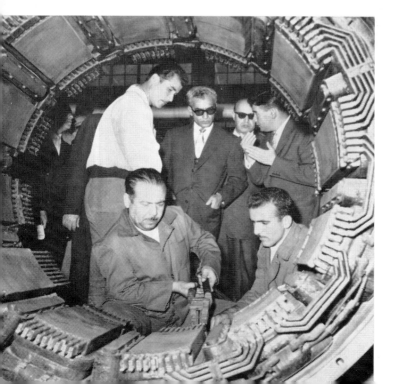

The new industrial revolution

could not even follow the meaning of what was being argued. The result, more often than not, was a gross miscarriage of justice. The root cause of this perversion of the principles of justice lay in the inequitable structure of society, and in the survival of the landlord-peasant system. The Shah had come to the conclusion that whatever the theory of law, its practice would result in injustice and tyranny if the judicial system was not founded on the principles of social justice.

Once success had been achieved with the land reform measures, the problem of judicial reform became more pressing. The Houses of Equity were created in order to make the villagers, peasants and farm labourers, the poor and illiterate, equal in the eyes of the law with townspeople, the educated and the rich. The Shah had to make a detailed survey of the problems of the rural population so as to make this equality effective in practice. It appeared to him that the problem had two facets. Firstly, a means of justice had to be brought within the physical reach of the villagers. It was not uncommon for the villager to be unable to spare money or time to travel to distant cities where the courts were held, and there was no such thing as a village court. Secondly, it was essential to consider the actual character of the disputes that normally arose in the villages. His survey showed that these were related, by and large, to the problems of land, water and grazing rights.

The new system of rural justice was based on the conclusions of the survey. The Shah wrote: 'The solution was not so difficult as it seemed. It was simple to realise that no-one could understand the problem of a villager better than another villager. Things which a distinguished lawyer might have difficulty in grasping would appear crystal clear to a village elder who, acting as an arbitrator, could solve the difference in a way that would be acceptable to both parties since he was familiar with the precedents involved and the whole substance of the dispute, and would speak to the two parties in a language they would both easily understand.'[7]   Under this system, five judges were elected to each House of Equity, their election to take place under the supervision of the provincial court, and the appointments to last three years.   Often a member of the Literacy Corps would be appointed as a clerk to this people's court.   The principle of arbitration thus became the decisive factor.   The law came into force in December 1963, and the first House of Equity was set up at Mehyar, near Isfahan, shortly afterwards.

[7] *The White Revolution*, p. 146.

CHAPTER THIRTY-THREE

The Emergence of Iran

'WHEN there is a revolution in Iran', the Shah had once said, 'it will be I who will lead it.' Under his direction, the nation was now engaged in transforming the old society. But it could not proceed effectively with the task if the relations of Iran with the world were not revalued and adjusted to the changing conditions both at home and abroad. A foreign policy must now flow from the principles of the third revolution, and their practice. The world had moved a long way from the days of 1954.

In 1963, the Shah saw that old traditions and beliefs that could no longer keep up with the needs of the era were giving way to new criteria: 'Today, the use of force does not solve any problems. Conflicts and crises have to be solved, but only by discovering their origin and by obtaining the close understanding of their source can they be overcome. I believe that there are only two rational solutions open to us: first, instability and disruption must be uprooted by establishing social justice. Second, the advanced and developing countries must bridge the gap through closer co-operation. But, before this can be done, these two disparate groups must be given a suitable position in relation to one another. Each nation like each individual must profit according to the responsibility it assumes and the contribution it makes to the social and economic structure of the world. The age of aggression has passed and today the forces of humanity declare war only upon ignorance, poverty, hunger and social and economic discrimination.'[1]

From these convictions were borne the basic principles of a new foreign policy : 'We seek peace, co-existence and better understanding with other nations, whatever their ideologies may be. We will always support any endeavours for the establishment and furtherance of social justice. We will assist the efforts in bridging the gap between the rich and poor nations of the world ; and will support any plans in international co-operation and campaigns against illiteracy, poverty, disease and other contemporary social ills.'[2]

In the direct context of this thinking, the Shah had to decide upon his relations with the two power blocs. He knew that sections of the western Press had treated Iran as a kind of western pocket in the Middle East. When this charge was put to him during an important Press interview, he replied : 'Let me put it this way : if in the past we walked along the same path as the West, it would not be because we were their camp followers. No, of course not. We believe in the philosophy of humanity, liberty and similar values as the West and, hence, we work in co-operation with them. Now let me return to this business of Iran being a western pocket in the Middle East. The answer is a categorical no. I would say never. You must know that my father was exiled by the West. When I succeeded him, they did not give me an easy time. They made innumerable mistakes in Iran and in this region, and I had to face them and put up with them. Putting it mildly, these created many new problems for me, and yet I must add that this cannot change my outlook and philosophy. I would say this ; I am independent, or as independent as anyone can be.

[1] *The White Revolution*, pp. 164–5.   [2] Ibid. p. 165.

You must remember that we have to face many handicaps. Our geographical situation is peculiar and it has its own logic. Then we have some liabilities stemming from the under-developed nature of technology in the country. Let me conclude by saying this : if I had more engineers, I would feel even freer than I feel today.' [3]

The actions of the western Alliance had on many occasions depressed the Shah. His main dispute with them concerned the ambivalence of western relations towards allies : 'The West treats those who are their friends as a negligible quantity', he commented and added bitterly : 'As to the others who bully them, they lick their boots. There is a kind of masochist complex with the West.' [4] This attitude was partly a consequence of the western oil policy. In the autumn of 1966, differences with the consortium on production levels reached the proportions of a major crisis. The west was worried that the Shah would not hesitate to take over the entire machinery of oil production and distribution in Iran, built up by the consortium since 1954. The London *Economist* summarised western feelings as follows : 'Foreign oil companies could be facing their worst crisis in Iran since Mossadeq's two year nationalisation crisis in the early 1950s. In the *majlis* last week, the Prime Minister, Amir Abbas Hoveyda, made a further threatening speech. He pointed to the revolutionary agreement recently negotiated between Iran and the French state company ERAP (in which ERAP effectively acts as an exploration agent for Iran rather than a concessionaire) and implied that the western operating consortium could be stripped of much of the concession area granted to it in 1965.' [5]

The dispute with the West in this sector had begun as early as

[3] From an interview given to R. K. Karanjia and the author, see *Blitz* (Bombay, May 28, 1966).   [4] Ibid.

[5] *The Economist*, October 29, 1966.

the autumn of 1965. The Shah had asked that the consortium should increase the production of oil substantially, doubling it to 200 million tons a year by 1970. The consortium replied that it could not do so since its markets could not absorb the new increase. Early in 1966, the Shah repudiated this argument. The revenues earned by Iran in hard currency, he argued, were spent in the western world at a rate of over $800 million a year for the import requirements of the country. If the western oil companies could not find it convenient to increase oil production and thereby increase revenues for Iran, the Shah gave a clear indication that he would have to turn to other export markets. This clearly meant that the Shah was willing to rely partially upon the Soviet Union and its allies for the fulfilment of Iran's growing need for machinery and allied items.

The consortium, at this stage, put forward different arguments. If the western oil companies were to increase oil production in Iran, they would be compelled to do so in every oil producing country. The Shah met this argument by the force of statistics. He stated that the case of Iran must be judged on the basis of its population and its development needs, and expounded his views in a Press interview : 'You know that the same people extract oil at other places in this region. There is a small place, which I shall not name, with a population of 360,000. Iran has a population of more than 22,000,000 but, strange as it may sound, they like to extract more oil in that small place. What is the result ? They are creating a terrific disparity in wealth. In that small place, the oil companies are creating wealth which amounts to $2,000 per annum *per capita*, while in Iran, it works out at the paltry sum of $25 *per capita*. Obviously, this cannot go on. We cannot permit the creation of a monster. We must have at the same time better utilisation of our natural resources, our people must gain from our wealth. That is what I told the oil consortium. Iran is not prepared to put up with the present situation any longer.'[6]

The consortium appeared to remain insensitive to the Shah's warnings, nor did western governments see their true significance. He therefore entered into a series of commercial agreements with the Soviet Union, by which the Soviets undertook to supply Iran with a steel mill, later to constitute the foundation of a steel complex based at Isfahan, a machine tool plant, and a north-south pipeline network, projects which would cost $800 million. In return, the U.S.S.R. undertook to buy at least $200 million worth of gas from Iran. The consortium had no use for this gas and, because of its refusal to utilise it commercially, Iran was compelled to flare it off every day at a rate of 100,000 million cubic feet. Once this agreement was concluded, the Shah visited Yugoslavia and Rumania. Rumania agreed to purchase $40 million worth of Iranian crude oil, to occupy their surplus refining capacity, in return for Iran's purchase of their tractors and farm equipment to the same value. Similar barter agreements were arrived at with other communist countries of eastern Europe, except Albania, and the Shah himself went to each of these countries on state visits. Asked whether this presaged a new policy of close and intimate economic and political relations with the countries of the communist bloc, he replied in the affirmative and added : 'My country is geographically closer to these countries. We have the facilities to build easy and inexpensive communication with them through the Caspian and the Black Sea. Naturally, we would like to build close economic relations with these countries, but that is not all. The terms offered by these countries are most attractive and very competitive. The interest they ask on the loans they advance is 2½ per cent and the time for repayment is ten years. This is very good. Further, it is

[6] *Blitz*, loc. cit.

better to keep a balance in a divided world. One should not place one's eggs in one basket. It is better to put them in more baskets than one. Naturally, these economic relations improve political relations. What I said about a balance in the economic field applies equally and with the same justification to political relations also.'[7]

The conflict with the consortium did not, in itself, give rise to a new foreign policy : it only highlighted its birth and application. It gave the Shah an opportunity to announce that Iran was to judge each international issue on its merits and was determined to play an independent role in international relations. Still, the Shah had one reservation : 'At the same time, you must bear in mind the history of the hundred and fifty years of Russian-Iranian relations. True, there have been some changes in recent times. I have, myself, been to the Soviet Union but we cannot wipe out the memories of our experience.'[8]

The Baghdad Pact had been re-named the Central Treaty Organisation after the overthrow of the government of Nuri es-Said in 1958. Iran had continued its membership despite the exclusion of Iraq. Now this membership appeared an anachronism in the light of the new foreign policy. The Shah was willing to concede that membership of CENTO and an independent national foreign policy appeared contradictory. But he was still convinced that, in the broadest context of international relations, the value of Iran's membership of CENTO could not be challenged. No progress towards real disarmament had been made. Military pacts like the North Atlantic Treaty Organisation and the Warsaw Pact still continued to be facts of international life. The great powers had advanced no guarantees for the defence of the smaller countries like Iran against aggression either by conventional means or nuclear

[7] *Blitz*, loc. cit.   [8] Ibid.

weapons. 'And yet I have often thought of CENTO', he was willing to concede, 'as a toothless organisation. There are no serious military provisions in that treaty. Some people call it a farce. Maybe they have reasons for saying this, good reasons. My own view now is quite clear : it is good to have allies but you cannot depend upon them.'[9]

The Shah had made common cause with King Faisal of Saudi Arabia and King Hussein of Jordan in the formation of a bloc of Muslim countries. This step was both apparently inconsistent with the secular policies he followed at home, and seemed to indicate that he was being party to a trade union of Middle Eastern Monarchs with medieval and obscurantist aims. When faced with this criticism, he replied : 'Let me first tell you that the idea of the Islamic bloc is not new. Once King Saud and President Nasser discussed it. In any event, the idea to which I have subscribed is devoted to the study of ways and means to promote the standard of living, national economy and cultural revolutions of the Muslim countries. . . . Iran will have no part of a reactionary obscurantist approach to this question. We do not want to go back, we want to go forward. Iran will have no sympathy with the Islamic bloc if it is going to be a feudal combination or a gang to protect the feudal interests. I want to go a step forward and say that the Islamic bloc, when and if it is formed, should not be limited to the level of Heads of State. Let the scholars, scientists and others from these countries meet and devise ways and means of improving the living conditions of the people which is the main purpose of this body. . . . Finally, the Islamic bloc has no military significance.'[10]

In the winter of 1967, the consortium, after two months of secret negotiations, yielded to the Shah's demands. It agreed to provide for much more than a mere increase in oil production. It agreed to deliver to Iran oil for marketing in eastern

[9] *Blitz*, loc. cit.   [10] Ibid.

Europe, and also to return and restore a sizeable part of the area under its control to the government of Iran for the latter's exploration. The negotiations in the later stages were conducted by the Shah himself. John Addison, general manager and one of the chief negotiators for the consortium, commented : 'I have no hesitation in admitting that the agreement is a sizeable victory for His Imperial Majesty, the Shahanshah, Aryamehr, and his country'. By the new agreement, the western oil companies were compelled to terminate the system by which they unilaterally decided upon the level of production, irrespective of the needs of the producing country. The agreement also established the right of such a country to insist upon participation in the planning of production targets. However, the article providing for sale to Iran of large quantities of oil at a price lower than the market price, for resale to the markets which the western oil companies did not or could not exploit, was the real landmark. For the first time, the Shah had succeeded in breaking the monopoly in oil marketing.

By April, 1965, the principles of the revolution began to yield results which astonished not only the sceptics but also its supporters. The Shah then sat down to prepare a progress report for his people as well as the world. Iran had proved, once again, a living textbook on political and social processes. His report, published in book form, was distributed all over the country, and created a stir throughout the world. An expert on Iran's affairs wrote : 'His Imperial Majesty the Shahanshah has won. The Persians have again proved their ingenuity and ability to accomplish the impossible. . . . Certainly, the Shah, Mohammad Reza Shah Pahlavi, and his people have become one to a degree not known since Shah Abbas ruled Persia in the early Sixteenth Century.' [11]

[11] Peter Avery in his review of *The White Revolution: Tehran Journal* (Tehran, April 22, 1967).

It was then that the Shah began to prepare for an occasion which had been delayed for over a quarter of a century. Now that he had redeemed the pledge he had taken at his accession, he agreed to crown himself as Shahanshah of Iran at a full and formal coronation ceremony.

CHAPTER THIRTY-FOUR

The Coronation

M ANY years before the third revolution, the Shah had been requested by his advisers to crown himself formally. His accession to the throne in September 1941 had come about under abrupt and sad circumstances. There was neither the opportunity nor the right atmosphere for a traditional coronation. The Shah had replied that the time had not yet come : he did not want to be crowned a 'ruler of a nation of beggars'.

Now in 1967, he had accomplished in substantial measure the task he had taken upon himself at the age of twenty-one. Iran was no longer a nation of beggars. The great transformation had taken place. He could now say with relief, confidence and happiness : 'It is not a source of pride and gratification to become a king of a poor people. So in the past I had felt that a coronation ceremony was not justified. Now I am proud of the progress we have made.' His people fully endorsed his view. Even those who had watched his philosophy of the revolution with scepticism were won over, both at home and abroad. The western critics of the third revolution, who had lamented the fall of the Amini government, had now come to recognise his achievements and the successes of his people.

The critics and sceptics of yesterday now agreed that the Shah was 'a monarch better than his Crown';[1] some of

[1] *The Financial Times* (London, October 26, 1967).

them now described him as 'Persia's revolutionary on the throne'; [2] while still others compared his coronation with that of Napoleon Buonaparte to contrast it in favour of his legitimate right. 'When Napoleon Buonaparte seized the crown from an outraged Pope in Rome in 1804', wrote Edwin Leane in *The Scotsman*, 'and jammed it squarely on his own head, the arrogance and blasphemy of the act shocked the entire world. But when the Shah of Iran crowns himself, it will be both just and proper — the prerogative of a ruler whose heritage stretches back 2,500 years. For Mohammad Reza Pahlavi, King of Kings, Light of the Aryans, is the heir of Darius, whose world empire stretched from the Sind to the Danube, from central Asia to the heart of Africa.' [3]

The Shah was keenly aware that coronations, like birthdays and New Years, could degenerate into occasions for the expression of pious hopes which largely go unfulfilled. He wanted his coronation to be quite different. In 1967 the difference was this: he was not going to hold out the usual set of royal 'election promises'. Instead, his coronation would set the seal on achievements which could be seen and felt not only by the people of his country, but the entire world. Iran had emerged as the pacesetter of economic progress among the developing nations, recording a remarkable 12 per cent growth in national income in 1966. Set against the troubled background of West Asia, of economic disruption and failing development plans, Iran seemed a prodigy.

The targets of the third revolution had been fulfilled and transcended. The standard of living of the people had risen appreciably; most of the population was now literate, and well cared for from a medical standpoint. The co-operative movement in the cities had succeeded in keeping the cost of

[2] *The Daily Telegraph* (London, October 26, 1967).
[3] *The Scotsman* (Edinburgh, October 1, 1967).

living under strict control. While inflation hit national incomes in almost every country, in Iran prices had increased by only 0·87 per cent in 1966.[4] The prosperity of Iran could be seen not only in the cities like Tehran, Isfahan and Shiraz, but also in its fifty thousand villages and hamlets. Certainly it was not a nation of beggars which the Shah now led. It was a segment of humanity which was fortunate to have a sound ideological base for its development plans and a true leader to carry them out. Now it was their right as much as his to stage the coronation ceremonies, for it was as much the crowning of the revolution that was involved in the occasion as his own. They decided that the formal and true crowning of their king would take place on October 26, his forty-eighth birthday.

That day dawned amidst jubilations throughout Iran. The Shah had decided that a new precedent should be established. For twenty-five centuries, no woman had ever been crowned. Now that women had been accorded equal status with men in every sphere of life, the Shah saw no reason why the Empress Farah should not sit by his side and be crowned likewise. He also decided that his eldest son and heir, Prince Reza Cyrus, should be proclaimed Crown Prince.

The ceremonies in the Hall of Mirrors in the Gulistan Palace were conducted in splendour. It was a moving as well as fantastic experience for everyone of the selected group of five hundred men and women who witnessed it. R. K. Karanjia, a leading left-wing Asian journalist, described it in *Blitz*: 'Entering the Coronation Hall one halts bewildered, overwhelmed, almost blinded by the flash and glitter of a myriad fractured mirrors. Have we penetrated the heart of some enormous

---

4 Much credit for this is deserved by the distributors' co-operative movement, launched and carried out by Seiffullah Rashidian under the guidance of the Shah. For a detailed study see Rashidian, Seiffullah, *A Plan for Economic Well-Being* (London, 1967).

diamond, or are we watching a giant crystal in the final throes of formation ? Here an Iranian poet comes to our rescue. He compares the third revolution and Mohammad Reza Shah Pahlavi to a growing crystal which history has fashioned with great artistry and mighty patience, till the climatic moment arrives when the crowded spheres are generated into a creative flash and the crystal emerges in the perfect form of an epoch.

'Even as the poet invokes this beautiful imagery, its truth is vindicated by the arrival of the Royal procession. This is the dramatic moment of compressed formation in the history of contemporary Iran when the royal crystal, now finished and symmetrical, scintillates to the lights of a thousand suns as the regal monarch, his ecstatically beautiful Empress and the utterly charming Crown Prince arrive upon the stage in separate processions, to the fanfares and trumpets and choruses of hallelujah.' The ceremony is brief as it is brilliant and dazzling. The Shahanshah walks to the bejewelled Nadir throne, then he turns to face the audience with the Empress on his right and Crown Prince on his left. The Royal belt, sword, cape, sceptre and crown are brought to the King of Kings by ordinary conscripted soldiers as representing his people, and His Majesty solemnly lifts and dons them with his own hands, in all pride and dignity becoming a Sovereign. Here Iran's Shah departs from the convention obtaining in other monarchies. He has no Pope, Bishop or *mullah* to help him with the Sceptre and Crown. He assumes them himself by the right of popular sanction in the twenty-five century old tradition of Iran.

'Next comes the most enchanting moment of the drama, when the Shahanshah places another crown, blazing with regal jewels, on the head of his Queen, proclaiming her Empress and future Regent. He also announces Prince Reza to be the heir apparent to the throne.

'The ceremony ends with the kissing of the Holy Qoran by the Monarch, followed by a brief address from the Throne, as 101 guns boom a thundering salute and trumpets and cymbals raise a fanfare which pierces the heavens, together with the *muezzins* calling the faithful to prayer from atop thousands of minarets all over Iran.'[5]

During this ceremony the Shah spoke to his people of his pledge in a few moving words : 'My only goal in life', he said, 'is the ever increasing ascendance of the land and people of Iran, and I cherish no other wish than to safeguard the independence and sovereignty of this country, helping the Iranian nation to catch up with the most progressive and prosperous communities of the world, and reviving its ancient grandeur and historical glories. Towards this end I will not spare anything, not even my life, just as I have not spared it in the past.'

He then underlined the new departure in the Iranian tradition and added : 'Now, as I sit wearing the crown of the world's most ancient monarchy and now that for the first time in history the Iranian Shahbanou has also been crowned, I feel myself more than ever beside my beloved, honourable and patriotic nation. . . . It is a source of happiness and pride for me today to feel that my nation and I are linked together by an unbreakable tie of the heart, and to feel that we are marching forward hand in hand on a road that guarantees the grandeur, progress and happiness of Iran.'[6]

The Shah's voice merged, as he concluded his new pledge to his nation, in the rejoicings of his people. As the blazing sky re-echoed to a 101-gun salute, happy cries of *javid-Shah*, 'Long Live the Shah', rose from the festive multitudes in the streets of Tehran. Then the coronation procession began. If an Asian, Karanjia, could be moved by its sight, so could an English-

[5] *Blitz* (Bombay, November 4, 1967).
[6] For full text see *Kayhan International* (Tehran, October 27, 1967).

Coronation: the Shah's speech from the throne

With his family

woman, Gerda Paul, trained in the art of restraint and under-statement. She wrote in the London *Daily Telegraph* : 'When crowned and caped and sworded and belted he emerged from the Golestan Palace like a figure in some splendid Persian paint-ing to ride in triumph through the streets, crowds burst over the crush barriers and through police cordons to get a better view and shout their blessings. As the Shah and his lovely Empress Farah, crowned too and appointed Regent, sat side by side in a blue and gold coach, every street along the three mile route went wild. The Shah who had been grave through-out the hour and a half ceremony smiled for the first time. This was the reward he wanted.'[7]

It was the moment of his fulfilment and rededication. He had kept his tryst with destiny.

[7] *The Daily Telegraph* (London, October 27, 1967).

CHAPTER THIRTY-FIVE

Aryamehr

I

IN 1951 there were ten kings in the seventeen sovereign countries from Morocco to Pakistan, almost all of them the final authority in the State. In 1963 only six of them were left, and their power was, in most cases, diminished. Mohammad Reza Pahlavi has proved an exception to this law of declining monarchy in the Muslim world. Despite challenges to his power and position he has not only survived but also strengthened his position in Iran to such an extent that now, for all practical purposes, it is impregnable. It is in this typically Iranian combination that the secret of his success is largely concentrated.

When the Aryan peoples migrated from their original home, probably in Central Asia, at a period variously estimated as from 2500–2000 B.C. to 1500–900 B.C., and arrived at the upland plateau below the Caspian Sea, they called their new home Iran to emphasise that it was the homeland of the Aryans. The people of Iran were never to forget these racial origins in the succeeding millenia. Though later they embraced the religion founded by the Semite tribes of Arabia, their pride in their Aryan origins remained. The civilisation which their ancestors built during the Achaemenian, Seleucid, Parthian and Sassanian periods between 550 B.C. and A.D. 640 remained the bedrock of their consciousness, and the glory that was Iran remained a source of undying inspiration for them during the periods of decline and defeat.

It was thus that when the Shah ultimately succeeded in reviving and enriching the proud traditions of ancient Iran, they joyously and gratefully bestowed upon him the title 'Light of the Aryans': *Aryamehr*. The Shah warmly appreciated this token of their deep affection for him, for although, like any king, he possessed a number of hereditary titles, nothing could ever surpass for him this title, which his people spontaneously bestowed on him. In it he recognised their belief that he belonged to the tradition of the great monarchs of former days : Cyrus, Darius, Xerxes and Shah Abbas the Great who had made Iran magnificent and the people strong and prosperous.

The Danish Iranologist, Christensen, has said that : 'The ideal King in Iran is not so much the political head of the nation as a teacher and leader. He is not only a person who builds roads, bridges, dams and canals, but one who leads them in spirit, thought, and heart.'[1] This had been the Shah's guiding principle for twenty-five years : the bestowal of the title *Aryamehr* by his people was their recognition of the fact.

II

Mohammad Reza Pahlavi is of middle height, broad shouldered and slim waisted, with clear intelligent eyes and regular features. He is fortunate in having inherited the dignity and charm of his race. His physical appearance has hardly changed, despite the stresses of the two and a half decades of his reign, except that his hair is prematurely white. In other respects,

---

[1] Quoted in *The White Revolution*, p. 2.

this acutely intelligent and dignified man scarcely differs in physical appearance from the Crown Prince who, in 1941, took upon his young but broad shoulders the responsibility of raising Iran from the quicksands of corruption, conquest, and degeneration.

The Shah's chief relaxations are music and sport. Music is his great love and, though he likes Iranian music, he prefers western classics, which he finds more attractive in their variety. He especially enjoys the Romantic composers, but finds light classical music such as Strauss waltzes agreeable, and jazz amuses him. As a keen sportsman, he enjoys swimming, tennis, volley ball and walking, but his speciality is ski-ing both on snow and water. He hunts and plays golf and, as a pilot, he enjoys the speed of his aircraft as much as he does the pace of his sports cars. Of all games, chess is his favourite : he could at one stage play on three boards against three adversaries simultaneously.

The Shah takes a childlike delight in electric trains, and every so often he himself operates, for his own amusement and the pleasant wonder of his children, several of these which he continues to buy whenever he is in Europe or America. In his secondary school days he learnt carpentry and woodworking, and has not neglected his skill in these crafts. He is a voracious reader, although he has little time now to spend on fiction, which he enjoyed immensely in French during earlier days. In the realm of the cinema, his preference lies with the British, French and Italian films for their exceptional acting and direction, over those produced in the United States, despite their excellence in production techniques. Above all, he enjoys relaxed conversation, whether during audiences when he receives people of special status, or whether he is amongst modest and unassuming people engaged in their daily chores. He will listen to them patiently and courteously, asking occasional questions which touch upon the human qualities of the men and women with whom he is dealing.

The Shah is a family man. He enjoys nothing more than spending hours with his Queen and children. His relatives normally gather each Friday at his Palace to join him for lunch. The Queen Mother, to whom he is deeply attached, and his twin sister Princess Ashraf, are by his side on all important occasions whether they are of a personal or political nature. Many of his childhood friends still visit him, and spend hours talking to him on an affectionate and easy informal basis.

Yet the Shah is a man who is isolated from his fellow men by his role as Head of State and leader of his people. This isolation is accentuated by his reluctance to employ advisers, and by his habit of taking the final decisions alone. He has made it a principle that, except in trivial matters, he will not even discuss affairs of State with his close relatives. Isolated as he is, he is not a lonely man. 'My affection for my wife and children', he has recorded, 'and for my people as a whole, and for nature, helps to prevent that. Furthermore I really love my work, the challenge it offers and the satisfaction it brings. Visible signs of progress greet me wherever I go in my country, and these tell me we are on the right road.' [2]

These links with his people often make the Shah appear sentimental : 'A sight of our pretty schoolgirls trooping along the streets, chattering and laughing, drives away loneliness and brings me a more cosmic sense of rapport'. Although both a monarch and an intellectual schooled in western Europe, he thinks of the future of these girls like an oriental father : 'Thus inspired, it is no wonder that I look towards the days when I can institute a Government dowry for every Persian girl when she is married at the legal age. The marriage of many of our girls is delayed for economic reasons and I consider that unjust.

[2] *Mission*, p. 326.

In the same way I cherish a plan for creating really spacious and beautiful Government homes for all our older people who wish to live in them. The twilight of life should be a time of happiness and peace, and we can make it so.' [3]

Finally, Mohammad Reza Pahlavi, like all men who have guided the destiny of their people, is sustained by his faith in God. It is his conviction that 'God is guiding me and that I can rely upon God's support' that prevents him from ever becoming lonely. 'I have my assurance of His direction', he said with humility, 'and it makes me in no way arrogant or fanatical : instead it gives me a quiet confidence of somehow being in tune with the Universe. Besides saying my daily prayers, sometimes I call on God to help me. Without claiming any sort of telepathic communication with the Divine, I can simply say that these calls do not go unheeded and I find it difficult ever to be lonely.' [4]

III

Few monarchs in the long annals of Iran have attained the stature of the Shah. As the acknowledged leader in the crucial era of Iran's transition, only a handful of Afro-Asian leaders in our century can compare with him. He did not inherit a kingdom, for his country was then occupied, but he did inherit a right to rule and has worked incessantly to convince his people that he was worthy of that right. One has only to remember the limitations on his power at the time of his accession to appreciate his record of achievement, as exemplified in the position of total leadership that he now enjoys. The battle was all the more difficult in that he had nobody to stand by his side during the troubles of two decades, and the two revolutions which he led to overcome these troubles. Had

[3] *Mission*, p. 326.   [4] Ibid. p. 326.

Reza Shah's plan of abdicating power to him in the early 1940s
become effective, he would have had his great father to stand by
his side as an elder statesman to guide and advise him, but this
was not to be.

He sustained himself on his lone journey by making himself
accessible to every one of his citizens. He had seen Reza Shah's
reliance upon a narrowing circle of advisers as one of the few
mistakes his father had made. Reza Shah was fierce and hence
flattered, with no one willing or capable of telling him the truth.
In this system, based upon a narrow circle of advisers, corruption was inevitable. 'My system is entirely different,' the Shah
has recorded : 'I know that advisers, no matter how technically competent they may be, sometimes make the national
interest subservient to their own. Further, they are prone to
try to funnel all information through themselves and to seal off
independent intelligence channels.'[5] This thinking has led
him to obtain information from as many sources as are available
to him, and only then make decisions. As a result, he has made
mistakes, but only rarely. The refusal to rely for advice on one
particular group was a new feature in the tradition of modern
Iranian monarchy. It aroused antagonism among those who
were deposed from positions of power, and criticism from
foreign observers. The Shah has explained to his critics the
reasons for adopting this novel system : 'Let me add that in
no way do I regard myself as the one true repository of knowledge and enlightenment. On the contrary, I use my multiple
intelligence channels to draw upon the judgement of many wise
men.'[6] He invariably enlarges this network of information
sources when he is faced with an unusually serious and complex
problem. This system has worked, yet he is candid enough to
assign credit where it belongs : 'Thanks largely to the contribution of other people, in my system the decisions usually turn

[5] *Mission*, p. 322.   [6] Ibid. p. 322.

out to be right for Iran, and especially for our ordinary people whose welfare must come first'.[7]

His reliance upon informal contacts and audiences does not exclude the normal functions of the Council of Ministers and the High Economic Council. The expertise of the members of these two bodies is used to the full both in making decisions and carrying them out. These meetings in the Marble Palace help him to clarify his own judgement and strengthen it. Once the decision is taken, 'remorseless following up is required' and here too he has evolved a new system. He believes that many personal contacts are needed. 'Some western administrators talk blandly', he has said, 'of a limited span of control under which the leader or executive regularly sees no more than eight or a dozen key aides ; but such a system in no sense fits our cultural situation, and furthermore it would be dangerous in its limitation of channels of information and intelligence upon which I regularly depend. A tremendous range of contacts is required for me to keep fully informed of the needs and problems of my people and the same principle applies if I am to fulfil my obligation of perpetually expediting and accelerating my country's progress.'[8]

IV

Iran, under the *Aryamehr*, has achieved the unique status of being a politically stable land which has left its neighbours far behind in terms of prosperity and social justice. This is an achievement which the rest of the world should not ignore, and the man who made it possible is no longer only a national leader, for he now reserves part of his energies for the problems which the world has to face.

In the Shah's view, a nation should not rely upon aid from

[7] *Mission*, p. 322.   [8] Ibid. p. 325.

other nations either to sustain or to expand its own strength. This conviction was the starting-point of a new approach to international relations and problems. The Shah was a shrewd observer of the interplay of national and ideological factors and realised that the division of the world into two camps in 1946 could not survive the emergence of new international forces, and especially the rise of China. As early as 1959, when most governments and students of international relations thought of the communist camp as an ideologically united monolith, the Shah went on record to state that such was neither the present reality nor the future likelihood. He was among the very few to predict the coming split in the communist camp and the conflict between the Soviet Union and China : 'To the public applause and secret distress of the Russians, the Chinese will acquire nuclear weapons and missiles to deliver them. They will seek to impose ideologically as well as militarily, leadership upon the entire Communist world ; and, even if covertly, the clash of ideas between the two powers will become exacerbated.'[9] Nor was he sanguine about the unity of the western camp and its relations with the nations of Afro-Asia and Latin America for, he added : 'New ideological competition will arise as the Western powers modernise their own idea-systems into something more palatable to the newly developing societies'.[10]

In this world of changes, the *Aryamehr,* has laid down a credo for himself and his people which speaks for itself : 'So precipitate is the world's metamorphosis that it has become easy for any society to lose its moorings. I think the recent dramatic advances in my country show that we welcome constructive change. But at the same time we stand fast in support of certain superior values that I believe to be characteristically ours. We cherish the gardens and the poetry and the family

[9] *Mission*, p. 316.   [10] Ibid. p. 316.

life and the hospitality of Persia. We acclaim this land of deserts and snow-capped mountains, of cedars and plane trees and rivers and fountains and tiled water courses, and roses and orange blossom and nightingales, and we are proud of our political and social institutions.' [11]

[11] *Mission*, p. 328.

Text of the Anglo-Persian Treaty of 1919

PREAMBLE: In virtue of the close ties of friendship which have existed between the two Governments in the past, and in the conviction that it is in the essential and mutual interests of both in future that these ties should be cemented, and that the progress and prosperity of Persia should be promoted to the utmost, it is hereby agreed between the Persian Government on the one hand, and His Britannic Majesty's Minister acting on behalf of his Government on the other, as follows:

1. The British Government reiterate, in the most categorical manner, the undertakings which they have repeatedly given in the past to respect absolutely the independence and integrity of Persia.

2. The British Government will supply, at the cost of the Persian Government, the services of whatever expert advisers may, after consultation between the two Governments, be considered necessary for the several departments of the Persian Administration. These advisers shall be engaged on contracts and endowed with adequate powers, the nature of which shall be the matter of agreement between the Persian Government and the advisers.

3. The British Government will supply, at the cost of the

Persian Government, such officers and such munitions and equipment of modern type as may be adjudged necessary by a joint commission of military experts, British and Persian, which shall assemble forthwith for the purpose of estimating the needs of Persia in respect of the formation of a uniform force which the Persian Government proposes to create for the establishment and preservation of order in the country and on its frontiers.

4. For the purpose of financing the reforms indicated in clauses 2 and 3 of this agreement, the British Government offer to provide or arrange a substantial loan for the Persian Government for which adequate security shall be sought by the two Governments in consultation in the revenues of the Customs or other sources of income at the disposal of the Persian Government. Pending the completion of negotiations for such a loan the British Government will supply on account of it such funds as may be necessary for initiating the said reforms.

5. The British Government fully recognizing the urgent need which exists for the improvement of communications in Persia, with a view both to the extension of trade and the prevention of famine, are prepared to co-operate with the Persian Government for the encouragement of Anglo-Persian enterprise in this direction, both by means of railway construction and other forms of transport ; subject always to the examination of the problems by experts and to agreement between the two Governments as to the particular projects which may be most necessary, practicable, and profitable.

6. The two Governments agree to the appointment forthwith of a joint Committee of experts for the examination and revision of the existing Customs Tariff with a view to its reconstruction on a basis calculated to accord with the legitimate interests of the country and to promote its prosperity.

Signed at Tehran, August 9, 1919.

Text of the Tripartite Treaty of 1942

HIS IMPERIAL MAJESTY THE SHAHANSHAH OF IRAN on the one hand, and His Majesty the King of Great Britain, Ireland and the British Dominions beyond the Seas, Emperor of India, and the Presidium of the Supreme Council of the Union of Soviet Socialist Republics on the other :

Having in view the principles of the Atlantic Charter jointly agreed upon and announced to the World by the President of the United States of America and the Prime Minister of the United Kingdom on the 14th August, 1941, and endorsed by the Government of the Union of Soviet Socialist Republics on the 24th September, 1941, with which His Imperial Majesty The Shahanshah declares His complete agreement and from which He wishes to benefit on an equal basis with the other nations of the World and :

Being anxious to strengthen the bonds of friendship and mutual understanding between them and :

Considering that these objects will best be achieved by the conclusion of a Treaty of Alliance ;

Have agreed to conclude a treaty for this purpose and have appointed as their Plenipotentiaries ;

His Imperial Majesty The Shahanshah of Iran :

His Excellence Ali SOHEILY, Minister for Foreign Affairs,

His Majesty the King of Great Britain, Ireland and the

British Dominions beyond the Seas, Emperor of India ; for the United Kingdom of Great Britain and Northern Ireland :

Sir Reader William BULLARD, K.C.M.G., C.I.E., His Majesty's Envoy Extraordinary and Minister Plenipotentiary in Iran,

The Presidium of the Supreme Council of the Union of Soviet Socialist Republics,

His Excellency Andre Andreevitch SMIRNOV : Ambassador Extraordinary and Plenipotentiary of the Union of Soviet Socialist Republics in Iran, Who having communicated their full powers found in good and due form, have agreed as follows :

ARTICLE I

His Majesty The King of Great Britain, Ireland, and the British Dominions beyond the Seas, Emperor of India, and the Union of the Soviet Socialist Republics (hereinafter referred to as the Allied Powers) jointly and severally undertake to respect the territorial integrity, the sovereignty and the political independence of Iran.

ARTICLE II

An Alliance is established between His Imperial Majesty The Shahanshah of Iran on the one hand and the Allied Powers on the other.

ARTICLE III

(1) The Allied Powers jointly and severally undertake to defend Iran by all the means at their command from all aggression on the part of Germany or any other Power.

(2) His Imperial Majesty The Shahanshah undertakes :

(a) To cooperate with the Allied Powers with all the means at His command and in every way possible in order that they may be able to fulfil the above undertaking. The assistance of the Iranian forces shall however be limited to the maintenance of internal security on Iranian territory.

(b) To secure to the Allied Powers for the passage of troops or supplies from one Allied Power to the other, or for other similar purposes, the unrestricted right to use, maintain, guard, and in case of military necessity, control in any way that they may require, all the means of communication throughout Iran, including railways, roads, rivers, aerodromes, ports, pipelines and telephones, telegraph and wireless installations.

(c) To furnish all possible assistance and facilities in obtaining material and recruiting labour for the purpose of the maintenance and the improvement of the means of communication referred to in paragraph (b).

(d) To establish and maintain in collaboration with the Allied Powers such measures of censorship control as they may require for all the means of communication referred to in paragraph (b).

(3) It is clearly understood that in the application of paragraph (2) (b), and (d) of the present article the Allied Powers will give full consideration to the essential needs of Iran.

ARTICLE IV

(1) The Allied Powers may maintain in Iranian territory land, sea and air forces in such number as they consider necessary. The location of such forces shall be decided in agreement with

the Iranian Government so long as the strategic situation allows. All questions concerning the relations between the forces of the Allied Powers and the Iranian authorities shall be settled so far as possible in cooperation with the Iranian authorities in such a way as to safeguard the security of the said forces.

It is understood that the presence of these forces on Iranian territory does not constitute a military occupation and will disturb as little as possible the administration and the security forces of Iran, the economic life of the country, the normal movements of the population and the application of Iranian laws and regulations.

(2) A separate agreement or arrangement shall be concluded as soon as possible after the entry into force of the present treaty regarding any financial obligations to be borne by the Allied Powers under the provisions of the present article and of paragraph (2) (*b*), (*c*) and (*d*) or Article 3 above, in such matters as local purchases, the hiring of buildings and plant, the employment of labour, transport charges et cetera. A special agreement shall be concluded between the Allied Governments and the Imperial Iranian Government defining the conditions of any transfers to the Imperial Iranian Government after the war of buildings and other improvements effected by the Allied Powers on Iranian territory. These agreements shall also settle the immunities to be enjoyed by the Allied forces in Iran.

ARTICLE V

The forces of the Allied Powers shall be withdrawn from Iranian territory not later than six months after all hostilities between the Allied Powers and Germany and her Associates have been suspended by the conclusion of an armistice or armistices, or on the conclusion of peace between them whichever date is the earlier.

The expression 'Associates' of Germany means all other Powers which have engaged or may in future engage in hostilities against either of the Allied Powers.

ARTICLE VI

(1) The Allied Powers undertake in their relations with foreign countries not to adopt an attitude which is prejudicial to the territorial integrity, the sovereignty or the political independence of Iran, nor to conclude treaties inconsistent with the provisions of the present treaty. They undertake to consult the Government of His Imperial Majesty The Shahanshah in all matters affecting the direct interests of Iran.

(2) His Imperial Majesty The Shahanshah undertakes not to adopt in His relations with foreign countries an attitude which is inconsistent with the Alliance nor to conclude treaties inconsistent with the provisions of the present treaty.

ARTICLE VII

The Allied Powers jointly undertake to use their best endeavours to safeguard the economic existence of the Iranian people against the privations and difficulties arising as a result of the present war. On the entry into force of the present treaty discussions shall be opened between the Government of Iran and the Governments of the Allied Powers as to the best possible methods of carrying out the above undertaking.

ARTICLE VIII

The provisions of the present treaty are equally binding as bilateral obligations between His Imperial Majesty The Shahanshah and each of the two other High Contracting Parties.

Appendix B

ARTICLE IX

The present treaty shall come into force on signature and shall remain in force until the date fixed for the withdrawal of the forces of the Allied Powers from Iranian territory in accordance with Article v.

In witness whereof the above-named Plenipotentiaries have signed the present treaty and have affixed thereto their seals.

Done at Tehran in triplicate in Persian, English and Russian all being equally authentic, on the twenty-ninth day of January one thousand nine hundred and forty-two.

The Philosophy of the Revolution

The following extracts are taken from the introduction to The White Revolution, *His Imperial Majesty's personal account of the philosophy behind the revolution of the Shah and the people.*

FREQUENT revolutions and upheavals have shaken the world during the last hundred years. Governments have been deposed, old ideologies discarded. Individuals, who believed themselves to be reflecting the thoughts and hopes of the people, advocated changes through their different ideologies. Some managed to effect these changes by peaceful means, others usurped power and executed their plans through bloody revolutions, but all of them condemned social injustice and expressed the necessity for class equilibrium and equal distribution of wealth. The degree of their success has been relative, yet even the least successful of the progressive countries has managed to alleviate these evils which are still the source of unrest in some areas of the world.

Historical development and the evolutionary course of human society have in our time caused deep and fundamental changes in several ancient societies, in different ways but with a similar effect. With the growth of education and the development of the social, scientific and economic thinking of the present generation, the old social order which has prevailed for centuries, in which class privileges and class distinctions are more or less considered in the nature of things, is no longer acceptable.

After the defeat, in the most devastating war in history, of the latest attempt to impose the principle of racial mastery on the world, the United Nations was established, on the principle of equal rights for all races, nations, religions and individuals.

Even the church, which owing to its attachment to spiritual concepts has the right to consider its institutions permanent, has voluntarily set about deep and extensive change and is trying to harmonize itself with the social needs of the day. Fortunately, the true spirit of Islamic law has always been in harmony with these evolutions and changes.

Consequently, if our nation wished to remain in the circle of dynamic, progressive and free nations of the world, it had no alternative but to alter the old and archaic order of society completely, and to build its future on a new order compatible with the vision and needs of the day.

. . . . .

In building a new society in place of the old one we had to find the way which was most beneficial for us and which would be in harmony with the Persian spirit and character, with the needs of our continent, our geography and history. Only then could we reach our goal rapidly, and our goal would be as great as that of any of the most advanced nations of today.

In all these designs two principles must remain constant and holy for us. One is the reliance on spiritual principles and religious beliefs, which in our case is the religion of Islam. Our people and our society are devoutly attached to their religion and beliefs, and the sublime truth of religion is the governing power and the consistent factor of our moral and spiritual order. The second is the preservation of individual and social freedoms, and the strengthening of these freedoms so that they become stronger than ever before in our history.

No matter how brilliant its progress might be, a society devoid of religious beliefs and devoid of the spiritual principles of individual and social freedoms is not enduring ; moreover, there is no beauty or attraction in it. The absence of spiritual values is a great handicap, a handicap that must be intolerable for a society.

When after deep study, I reached the conclusion that such an all-round social revolution was imperative to save the country and to elevate it to the ranks of the most progressive contemporary nations and societies, I felt very keenly where my duty lay.

When I remember the various episodes when I had had miraculous escapes from death, and noted the fact that during my reign my country had also miraculously been saved from ruin, I became aware that my mission to my country was not completed yet. I will frankly confess that I was convinced that God had ordained me to do certain things for the service of my nation, things that perhaps could not be done by anyone else. In whatever I have done, and in whatever I do in the future, I consider myself merely as an agent of the will of God, and I pray that He may guide me in the fulfilment of His will, and keep me from error.

In 1963, after many vicissitudes, I was in a position to act. My people trusted me, and the bond of spirit and heart, to which I have already referred, was stronger than ever between my people and me.

The Iranian nation had seen that throughout my reign I had been engaged in various struggles for the preservation of Iran's independence, one of which was the recovery of Azarbaijan. They had seen that with the distribution of my estates to farmers and with the dedication of 80 per cent of my personal fortune to charity or for the advancement of the country, I had done my best to serve my country and my people.

Since I relied on this complete trust and confidence of my people, and my goal in bringing about the revolution was simply to increase their prosperity and welfare, and since I was sure the intelligent people of Iran realized this, I presented to public opinion the sum total of my studies in a revolutionary programme and offered it to the nation for approval.

On January 26, 1963, the people of Iran, with a resounding majority, gave decisive approval to this programme, and in this way the great social revolution of Iran came into existence in a completely democratic fashion.

What was the philosophy and spirit of this revolution? As already stated, this revolution was essentially an Iranian revolution, compatible with the spirit and tradition of the Iranian people. We had not delivered this revolution to the people as an imported item. For it would be beneath the dignity of a nation which had for several thousand years been the pioneer of thinking, philosophy, and religion, to wear anything borrowed. We had adopted measures commensurate with the Iranian genius, utilizing all the experiences of others but not hesitating to introduce new thinking wherever necessary.

It is as if Emerson had our revolution in mind when he wrote : 'Every project in the history of reform . . . is good when it is the dictate of a man's genius and constitution, but very dull and suspicious when adopted from another.'

In our noble revolution, the two sacred principles already mentioned, emphasis on spirit and religion and preservation of individual and social freedom have been fully observed, as has the general principle that every kind of exploitation that benefited the interests of a limited group but acted to the detriment of the majority must be discarded.

To realise these goals it was essential that land reform should take place and the feudal landlord and peasant system be abolished ; that the relationship between workers and employers should be regularized so that labour should not feel exploited ; that women — who after all make up half the population — should no longer be included with lunatics and criminals and deprived of their social rights ; that the scourge of illiteracy should be taken away so that illiterates who did not know how to defend themselves would understand and become familiar with their rights ; that nobody should die of disease or spend their lives in misery and wretchedness through lack of treatment or care ; that backwardness in the villages should be ended, and the undeveloped villages connected with the main centres of the country, and a general condition in harmony with today's civilized world prevail.

In utilizing the potential wealth of the country, we had to observe the principles of logic and justice. The God-given resources of the country, which no citizen had himself created, such as oil, mineral deposits, the fish in the sea, forests and great natural pastures, should not fall into the hands of individuals or corporations. Nor should the heavy industries, which determine prices and become cartels and trusts. For such people or institutions would, in practice, become the successors of the former feudal minorities or past ruling classes. If this happened, the new society in Iran would be afflicted with a new ruling class of industrial capitalists.

We thus recognized that industries and resources vital to the interests of all citizens had to be nationalized. Railways, posts and telegraphs, airlines, the oil and steel industries, and the like must be put at the service of all the people, and remain in their control. Also the forests and pastures of Iran, the fisheries, dams, rivers, and other items of this nature belonged to the people, and no one had the right of personal possession of them.

In the case of dams and rivers, and in general all our water resources, it must be noted that these have a direct bearing on our national life and destiny, and for this reason their significance is so great that the nationalization of these resources will form the tenth article of our revolution. Full explanations will be given in the chapter on Land Reform.

While we declare that these resources as well as the heavy industries are national property, the philosophy of our revolution underlines individual and social freedom, so that we wish to encourage individual initiative and enterprise in various social and industrial fields.

The general principles of Iran's revolution are unalterable, but if in details or in the method of execution of these principles corrections or amendments are found necessary and better scientific or technical methods present themselves, we shall naturally take advantage of them.

.   .   .   .   .

We believe that the era of rigid, inflexible ideologies has passed, and many ideologies as presented in their original form cannot answer the needs of a society that is permanently in a state of revolution. And so we witness the change and gradual evolution of these ideologies.

What human society needs today is to follow principles that are not based on vindictiveness, jealousy, greed or animosity, nor on exploitation and the protection of the vested interests of a minority to the detriment of the majority. Today, more than ever, humanity needs understanding, friendship, affection and love for one another.

True political or spiritual leaders of societies have no right to encourage men to tear one another apart, to exterminate each other. They must teach them to co-exist, to co-operate. They must create conditions resulting in greater friendship among individuals and societies, so that all members of the great human family can, with each other's help, move the caravan of civilization towards universal progress.

Our revolution has taken shape in this way and on the holy principles of love, friendship and understanding. In this way we are the followers of those high religious, ethical and mental principles which for thousands of years have been the distinguishing marks of pure Persian culture. Be it the ancient teachings of Zoroaster or the principles and supreme tenets of Islam ; or the thinking and teaching of philosophers, thinkers, poets, and writers of Iran. They have all taught us that the important ingredients of the life of every real society are love, friendship and understanding.

We have always known injustice, lies, avarice and egotism to be the signs of evil and darkness, and have always promoted justice, truth, and humanitarianism. We believe that human society can only prosper and reach sublimity and progress in the wake of these principles.

None of the ideologies based on enmity and antagonism and on crushing a class or classes for the gain of other classes, or on the exploitation of individuals or classes by other classes or individuals can be acceptable to us, because these ideologies are essentially contrary to our national spirit, culture and way of thinking.

. . . . .

The Revolution : New Dimensions

The dimensions of the revolution of the Shah and the people were broadened on October 6, 1967, by the Shah as the leader of the revolution. In the Speech from the Throne delivered at the opening of the newly elected parliament, the Shah assessed the achievements of the revolutionary programme of Nine Principles; and to the original nine, added three further points :

'BY The Grace of God, We open the twenty-second session of the *majlis* and fifth session of the Senate.

The term of the last *majlis* and Senate will definitely be known as one of the proudest terms of Iranian legislative history because it coincided with the start of the revolution of the Shah and the people, and the beginning of a great social movement which is now clearly visible in all intellectual and material aspects of our country. It was this revolution which destroyed the old foundations of Iranian society and replaced them with the most progressive ones in this modern world.

Perhaps it may not be necessary to discuss at length the nature and depth of this revolution because of the obvious results, but it will not be useless to review briefly the consequences of the Iranian revolution and its achievements in this short period.

One of the most important results of this great upheaval is certainly the introduction of the land reform programme and the freeing of huge masses of Iranian farmers who form sixty-five per cent of the total population. With this measure, the era of feudalism and large land ownership was ended for all time in our country and, as you know, in the first phase of the land reform programme more than 600,000 farming families became landowners. In the second phase of this programme a law was passed by the *majlis* under which landowners who had rented out their properties to farmers could sell them to the government which would in turn sell to the farmers working on the properties — with long and easy instalments to enable them to become landholders. This part of the law is even now being enforced in part of the country.

With the introduction of the first two phases of the land reform programme the grave injustices which existed in the field of land ownership were abolished. Now the next stage requires arrangements which will ensure maximum exploitation of the land under cultivation, and creation of a standard of ownership of land to show how many hectares of land are needed so that a farmer can live a reasonably comfortable life. The creation of agricultural units with shareholders is a new and important experiment which we are now undertaking. We hope that we will succeed equally in this new experiment as we have done in all other work so far undertaken.

These agricultural, limited companies are being set up so that the new landowners, who obtained their properties under the Land Reform Law, and are not capable of undertaking modernisation and mechanisation plans individually, can do so through co-operating with others and form units on which mechanised farming can be feasible. Also these will ensure that the lands are not subdivided into even smaller plots through inheritance. Only shares can be inherited or transferred, leaving the agricultural unit itself unaffected.

Under this plan every farmer has the right to join the company formed by himself and others like himself no matter what the size of his property, whether purchased from the government or rented from the landlord. He will benefit to the extent of his contribution. At the same time, the farmer will be entitled to wages in addition to his share of profits if he works in the fields.

The government will certainly co-operate with these new companies for some time in providing them with guidance in the management and running of their affairs so that the country can raise crops which it needs most or which are most suitable to local conditions.

Obviously, both in connection with these and other agricultural lands, mechanisation of farming, extensive use of chemical fertilisers and introduction of the latest and most modern techniques are of prime importance to us.

According to the latest figures the legal status of more than three million farming families involving more than 14 million people has been clarified since the introduction of the Land Reform Law. The law has been enforced in nearly 50,000 villages and on 18,000 farms.

On the other hand, in order to ensure that proper working conditions, whether from the point of view of capital or technical facilities, were placed at the disposal of these farmers, steps were taken to establish co-operative societies all over the country — which now exceed 7,000, in number with a membership of more than one million. Efforts are being made to establish as many co-operatives as are needed by the country. The Agricultural Bank of Iran has so far contributed nearly twenty billion rials either to these co-operatives or as loans to individual farmers.

Expansion and strengthening of co-operatives not only in agriculture but also in other fields of Iranian social and economic life are some of our main and basic aims because these co-operatives and social insurance plans are the best answers to the requirements of our own society, as well as, I think, of any other society no matter what its régime.

Our revolution, which is based on social justice, on the one hand requires that economic democracy — which should complement political democracy — be based on these co-operatives ; i.e., co-operatives for production, co-operatives for distribution and co-operatives for consumption without middlemen who do not perform any positive work. On the other, the same revolution requires that the welfare of every Iranian should be ensured from the day he is born to the day he dies through various kinds of insurance such as against disease, accidents, retirement, old age and others. This is an objective for which careful efforts will be made.

The second principle of the Iranian revolution is the nationalisation of some twenty million hectares of forest and pasture lands which are part of the national wealth, and in the creation of which no human being has played a part. Up till the Sixth of Bahman Revolution, this huge and natural wealth was being wasted and gradually destroyed. Now with the nationalisation of the forests and pasture lands, and the measures that followed for their protection and safety, it can be hoped that this vast national resource may be utilised for the common good of the nation. Our hope is that not only those areas which, according to history were once covered with forests, but all others where planting of forests is feasible will one day regain their lost greenery. Perhaps the results of these efforts will not be visible for several years because it takes a long time, sometimes as long as a hundred years, for a tree to grow. But the work has to be started now because every day that passes will be a loss to coming generations of Iranians.

The third point of our revolution was the sale of shares in government factories to provide financial backing for the land reform programme. The main objective of this measure was to provide the landlords, whose properties were taken over under the land reform programme, with an opportunity to invest their capital in industrial and productive work and through this play a greater share in the economic activities of the country. In accordance with this law, a Factories Company has been established with thirty-two factories, the shares of which are available for public sale.

In practice this point was expanded and completed by several plans and new programmes in the sense that to assist in the industrial expansion of the country a new organisation called 'The Organisation for Expansion and National Industrial Reconstruction' was established, so that simultaneously with the encouragement of individual industries, a concerted effort could be made to create new industries, specially heavy ones. With the necessary powers and free hand granted to this organisation under law, efforts will be made to introduce a new order and discipline in the establishment and management of large industrial units. Government industries will be created with the joint efforts of the people so that a greater interest is created among the people to participate in industries of this kind. The profits of these units will thus be shared by a large number of people.

On the other hand, the Organisation for Expansion and National Industrial Reconstruction is required to undertake wide measures to overcome one of the most chronic difficulties faced by industry — weak management. Specialised and experienced management cadres will be created to run industries whether public or private. The effects of these efforts will be visible within a very few years. Obviously, if it is found necessary, shares of other industries will be sold in the same manner as those which are now put up for sale.

The fourth and definitely the most important point of the revolution was profit-sharing by workers in the factories where they worked. This revolutionary measure not only gave a better income to the labourer for his toils but at the same time it gave him the human dignity and personality which was his birthright because he felt that he was no longer being exploited. He felt that he was a shareholder in the factory where he worked. For the correct enforcement, and to make sure that the Iranian labourer gets his twenty per cent share of profits, legislation will be brought in as and when necessary.

The fifth point in the revolution of the Shah and the people was amendment of the Electoral Law, to abolish discriminations which altogether favoured the influential class and which prevented entry of other people into parliament. Perhaps one of the most important results of this programme was the freeing of Iranian women from many unfair restrictions and granting of rights to them equal with men. We all know that until the amendment of the Electoral Law, the Iranian woman was treated in the same manner as the mentally unbalanced or financially insolvent and was deprived of her right to vote or contest an election. This meant that nearly half the Iranian population had no say in its own affairs. Our revolution gave millions of Iranian women their human and natural rights : so much so that even in this gathering there are a number of women sent in by the nation to sit beside their brothers and discharge their national duties. At this point it is not out of place to recall one of the most important laws passed by the outgoing House. That is the Family Protection Law, which I hope, will play an effective role in stabilising the family and provide our society with needed security.

Perhaps it is not necessary to say much about the Literacy, Health and Development Corpsmen who bear the proud name of the Soldiers of the Revolution, because these soldiers have truly won respect for Iran in foreign countries. The Soldiers of the Revolution represent the highest ideals of civilisation and progress : learning, health and creativity. They take these to the farthest corners of the country and it is only just that the Iranian nation should be proud of its selfless, sincere and responsible sons. Perhaps it will be sufficient to cite these figures to show the output of work by these young men. At present nearly half a million children or adults are going to more than 7,000 rural schools run by the Literacy Corpsmen. So far nearly 40,000 Literacy Corpsmen have served in the countryside.

It should, however, not be forgotten that the efforts of these young men are only part of a much wider campaign going on in Iran for the eradication of illiteracy. It will, therefore, not be out of place to mention that at present 2.5 million students are attending more than 15,000 primary schools, 600,000 students are attending 17,000 secondary schools and about 40,000 students are going through university education. The number of technical and vocational schools, which did not exist a few years ago, now exceeds one hundred which provide education to more than 17,000 young men and women.

We are firmly determined that in our country, where more than eighty per cent of the people were illiterate until recently, we shall eradicate illiteracy completely in a few years. Not confining ourselves to this country alone in this highly humanitarian field, we have decided to join with other nations in removing the scourge of illiteracy from human society. The first step was holding a Literacy Congress in Tehran in 1965. Our efforts and the results obtained from the work of the Literacy Corps led to the recognition of Iran by UNESCO as a pioneer and model country in the drive against illiteracy. You are aware that we have decided to make financial contributions from our own budget to UNESCO.

In order to ensure faster progress in the eradication of illiteracy, it is necessary that, like male Iranians serving in the Literacy, Health and Development Corps, a number of educated women should be required by law to teach illiterates or help in the improvement of health facilities in the cities and towns where they live. Studies have been launched to determine the best way.

The services of the Health and Development Corpsmen are laudable in their own fields both in view of the heavy responsibilities that were entrusted to them and the manner in which they discharged them. Let it be sufficient to say that at present 500 medical groups forming the Health Corps are working in more than 13,000 villages for more than six million people. Similarly, 2,500 Development Corpsmen are working in some 1,000 villages.

The ninth principle of our revolution was the establishment of the Houses of Justice and Arbitration Councils. These courts transformed the complicated, and often cumbersome and unnecessary, legal procedures by solving ordinary disputes simply. This eased pressure on the Ministry of Justice as well as saving considerable time and expense for the litigants. They gave the villagers an opportunity to spend their money in more productive fields. At present nearly 1,000 Houses of Justice are operating in the countryside while fifty Arbitration Councils have been established in the cities. These institutions have jurisdiction over about 1.5 million villagers and about the same number of city dwellers.

All the achievements dealt with here briefly show the consequences of the revolution over the last five years. What is important at this stage is to say that to fulfil the revolution we should maintain the spirit which has been the main moving force behind the changes, and work for increasing it. It is for this reason that we have decided to add three other points to our nine-point reform programme so that the changes in Iranian society can move faster and in many directions.

One of these three points is the nationalisation of water because our physical and atmospheric conditions do not allow us to waste even one drop of water. We must make sure that modern science and techniques assess our sweet water resources, both underground and surface. Then with maximum economy we should determine the priorities for the uses of water on the basis of returns for domestic, urban, agricultural and industrial consumption. However, because we have little water in our country, we must use it in the first place on land which is the most productive, so that agricultural centres can be created across the country. Obviously, we shall participate with interest in activities now underway all over the world for the desalination of water and take maximum advantage of any new developments in this field.

The second point which must be added to our revolution is the launching of a nationwide programme of reconstruction to provide a better life for Iranian families. These programmes should be launched in both the villages and cities and should be compatible with Iranian social conditions, aiming at the utilisation of our vast natural resources and manpower, for which I hold a high opinion. To achieve this objective our entire resources, intellectual and material, should be brought to bear with the same spirit of change which is necessary for the accomplishment of such a programme. No talent should be left unused.

Document Two

The third point relates to an administrative and educational revolution which will meet the requirements of present day society. The meaning of this reform is that any person employed in administration and working in government agencies whether in high or low position, should discharge his duties with complete honesty, sincerity and responsibility. The spirit of time wastage, paper work and bureaucracy should be eliminated. Every worker should know that in the first place it is his duty to attend to callers who approach him with work and help solve their difficulties quickly, through correct interpretation of law and without personal bias. It is these people who pay the worker's salary through their taxes. Our offices should be cleansed of the spirit of time killing and indecision. On the other hand, unreasonable and illogical centralisation of work in the capital should be eliminated and officials in the provinces and districts should be given an opportunity to show their talent and enterprise in their work. It may even be desirable that service in the capital and other big towns may be made inter-dependent with service in the villages.

Similarly, basic and profound reforms are needed in the educational plan of the country. Iranian youth should be given the opportunity to show their talent which should be used in the sphere to which it is best suited. Jobs should be given to people according to their specialisation and experience. It is for this reason that the government has been ordered to launch wide-ranging studies as to the changes required in the educational system in view of the increasing need for trained personnel and top-flight managers. The main aim of the education reform is that the sense of self-reliance and personality of our youth should be developed so that they can shoulder national responsibilities later. In fact, our society should change itself constantly to keep pace with new development and other developed societies, and to walk ahead of them, if possible.

In foreign policy we continue on our well-defined path : we follow a national independence policy based on international co-operation and understanding, protection of our own national rights and respect to those of others. We firmly believe that this international understanding and co-operation is a vital prerequisite for all societies, anywhere in the world and with any kind of government. In this field we not only believe in co-existence but also in peaceful co-operation between nations of different regimes. The success achieved by us in many spheres of national rights speaks well that we are on the right and wise path.

From the point of view of international relations, we continue to abide by the principles and regulations of the U.N. Charter, and although recently signs of weakness have been visible in the world body, we firmly believe that it is still the best body to solve international disputes. We hope the day will come when the world organisation is able to make decisions and enforce them. As one of the founder members of the United Nations, we reiterate our allegiance to it and sincerely back it. It is for this reason that we believe that any country recognised by the U.N. should have the right to exist and no other country should threaten its destruction.

We support non-proliferation of atomic arms, declaration of atom-free zones and complete and general disarmament through controlled supervision. But at the same time, while guaranteed disarmament is not a reality we have no option but to strengthen our defences to safeguard our territorial integrity despite all the friendship pacts of which we are members.

Unfortunately, recently events occurred in the Middle East which have hurt our feelings based on Muslim brotherhood. Naturally our sympathies were immediately aroused. We announced immediately and repeat today that occupation of any country's territory by another country is unacceptable. This truth should be understood clearly : the days of speaking through force and military adventure are over for ever. Quick military victories should have no intoxicating or blinding effects.

. . . . .

We hope that this House of Parliament, which will consider the Fourth Development Plan and witness the 2,500th Anniversary of Iranian Monarchy, will have as much success in its work as the previous one. We hope that the Fourth Plan will prepare the ground on which the Fifth and later plans can be drafted, and within the course of one generation we may catch up with other advanced countries of the world. The government will undoubtedly discharge its duties for the achievement of this goal and I am confident that Parliament will also endeavour to do its duty fully aware of the responsibility that rests on its shoulders.

At the same time, however, we firmly believe that it is the Iranian nation which will work with greater will, faith and confidence in the promotion of the movement which has shown its effects within a few short years in the political, social, economic, intellectual and material fields. We are glad to say that during the last three years the annual economic growth of our country has averaged over eleven per cent while the cost of living has been almost stationary. However, it must be understood that this was quite exceptional. We will try to maintain this rate in the future so that an average rate of nine per cent per annum should be maintained in economic growth.

We must pay special attention to agriculture because by doing so we will be performing two jobs. First, we shall be able to improve Iranian food in the sense that every Iranian will have more and better to eat as compared to the past or present. Secondly, we will be fulfilling our duty to humanity and other people who face food shortages. Let us not forget that by the end of this century the world will have passed through a most serious food situation unless nations from the start co-operate, so that remedies may be found before it is too late. The special attention that we are giving to agriculture and the plans which we have for development require that the Ministry of Agriculture should be broken into a number of other ministries.

I would like to take this opportunity to recall one basic measure that was taken recently to ensure continuity in the regime by the Constituent Assembly.

We pray to God Almighty to keep this ancient nation under his constant mercy and provide us with all opportunities to maintain through hard work on the basis of the revolution the high ideals of Islam.

I wish you all success in the grave responsibilities that you shoulder as representatives of the nation.'

The New Industrial Revolution

INDUSTRIAL development is vital if Iran is to make the best use of the country's natural resources : the products of the mines and the soil and the efforts of the country's farmers and herdsmen. Just as land reform must harness the energies of the rural population, industrial development is essential to make the best use of the farmers' output, to create a market for his products and provide a source of money incomes to generate further investment in the land.

Industrialisation requires heavy capital investment in order to initiate projects and carry them to the point where they become self-supporting. Land reform also is an expensive project. The temptation to finance both by printing money and causing inflation must have been very considerable. To a great extent, however, both land reform and industrialisation have been made self-financing. The government is buying out the former land-lords by instalments over a period of fifteen years. The peasants in turn are repaying the government. There is inevitably a considerable shortfall in the government's receipts, which is being made good by the offer of shares in state industrial concerns to private shareholders, in many cases the former landlords. The landowners are in fact being given the oppor-tunity to convert their investments in land into investments in rapidly growing industrial activities. This investment in turn gives a productive outlet to the cash and income which the former landlords have acquired.

Initially of course the only opportunities for immediate investment of these funds were in existing industries owned by the state. For this reason the industrialisation plan was supported by a decree providing for the sale of shares in government-owned factories as security for the land reform, and vesting the responsibility for putting the law into operation in the hands of the government. In the words of H.I.M. the Shah, 'Under the law govern-ing the sales of these shares, fifty-five government factories manufacturing or processing sugar, textiles, cotton, silk, chemicals and foodstuffs were

2 B

incorporated as joint stock companies, and their shares were used as security for the land reform measures. The issue of these shares enabled landowners whose estates were sold in accordance with the land reform law to invest their capital in industrial enterprises by buying these shares. Instead of standing idle or being invested in harmful speculations this capital was therefore used for useful productive purposes.'

The reform has been administered through a new organisation, the Government Factories Corporation. This corporation was formed by the factories themselves, after they had been converted from state enterprises to joint stock companies. The Corporation's capital is spread through half a dozen industries, of which sugar refining and textiles are by far the most important. In fact, sugar factories make up 43 per cent of the share value of the Corporation, followed by textiles with 38 per cent, cotton and silk processing with nine per cent, a variety of building material industries with 7 per cent, and chemicals and food processing with a modest 3 per cent between them.

The total value of these factories was 7,700 m. rials, or just over $100 m. (perhaps 20 per cent of the country's industrial sector). They were allotted into 154,000 shares each of 50,000 rials. The dividend paid to shareholders has been guaranteed by the Agricultural Bank of Iran on behalf of the government at a minimum rate of 6 per cent a year. The new companies have an obligation to modernise their equipment and production techniques and keep down the cost of their products to reasonable levels. The rejuvenation of these industries is, however, only part of the wider programme of selected industrial development and diversification which is being undertaken.

The government is in fact carrying out two separate policies. On the one hand it is creating industries in the public sector, and on the other it is creating favourable conditions for private investment, which it is encouraging and protecting. In some cases the government is deliberately engaging in industrial activity parallel with the private sector in order to discourage monopoly conditions and raise the quality of output. In remote parts of the country also, the government is investing direct.

This dual programme is being backed, as all successful industrialisation projects must be, by a programme of basic capital investment, in roads, ports, power supplies, water, housing, education and technical training and an intensive programme of industrial research and development.

Iranian tariffs and taxes have been adjusted to allow industry to enjoy the advantages of the local market in fair competition with bigger suppliers outside the country, and to avoid monopoly conditions while preserving opportunities for local capital. Special efforts have been made to attract foreign capital. Raw materials for industry, heavy machinery, which features prominently in the needs of new industry, and a variety of communications equipment can be imported at tariff rates of usually no more than 10 per cent.

General machinery, vehicles and semi-manufactured items considered essential by the Iranian authorities attract duties of 10 to 25 per cent. Foreign investment is offered special tax terms. Any firm qualifying as a productive enterprise obtains a 50 per cent exemption on net profits in the balance-sheet or profit and loss account. With this advantage it is claimed that the average foreign enterprise finds its net corporate tax less than 25 per cent.

Complete exemption from company tax for a period of five years may be obtained by new businesses set up more than 60 kilometres from Tehran. All enterprises qualifying under this law are exempt from customs duties on the import of machinery and raw materials needed to start production. Unlike the situation in most other developing countries, these duties do not first have to be paid and then reclaimed.

The Law for the Attraction and Protection of Foreign Investment in Iran provides for the repatriation of the original capital invested and of accrued profits upon three months prior notice and in the same currency as the originally imported capital. Wage rates in Iran are attractive to employers compared with those current in industrialised countries. They range from 84 rials a day to 140 for unskilled workers and 100 to 300 rials for semi-skilled workers.

The industrial sector in Iran is still relatively small, employing perhaps 2 or 3 per cent of the labour force, but already accounting for about 12 per cent of the value of production, and growing fast. The development which has taken place is almost entirely the work of the past four decades, and especially of the last decade. With the exception of a sugar refinery, a match factory and a number of small metal workshops, Iranian industry even 40 years ago consisted almost entirely of handicrafts such as silk, weaving and the internationally known handmade rugs and carpet trades.

In the fifteen years before the outbreak of the Second World War, a programme of industrialisation was begun on the orders of Reza Shah. The main aim was to make better use of the country's own natural resources. Because the commercial classes in Iran were little prepared for the problems and risks inherent in industrialisation, the leading role was taken by the government itself. State cotton, woollen and silk textiles factories were set up, especially in the province of Mazanderan and the cities of Tehran and Isfahan.

Sugar beet was introduced to the country virtually for the first time and eight state-owned refineries were set up in various parts of the country to process the bulky crop as it was harvested. The processing industries were also improved. Grain stores, bakeries, plants for fruit drying and pack-aging were established, together with rice cleaning mills, slaughterhouses vegetable oil refineries, breweries, wineries and distilleries. In addition, a number of light manufacturing industries, mostly state-owned, were developed. These included soap, cigarette, glass, paper and match factories.

Developments were slowed down as a result of the Second World War and again by the financial crisis of 1952–4 which followed the confrontation with foreign oil interests. But the solution to this crisis, the renewed flow of investment, the resumption of oil exports, and a substantial influx of overseas aid and investment set industry once more on the road to expansion.

In 1956 when the Law for the Attraction and Protection of Foreign Investments was introduced, Iranian industry was still mainly concentrated on the processing of local raw materials and the service of local markets, making cotton, wool and silk textiles, and processing foodstuffs. This was augmented by sugar refining, although sugar was still imported to supplement local output, and building material manufacture. Capital equipment and even consumer goods industries featured scarcely at all in the still embryonic industrial structure.

Between 1956 and 1960, however, both local and foreign investment doubled, imports of capital equipment increased six times, and the number of mechanised factories, as opposed to workshops, multiplied four times. Among the new industrial activities which have emerged in the past decade are chemicals, pharmaceuticals, fertilisers, car and lorry tyres, food canning, paper and plastics, the assembling of buses, lorries and, in 1967, of passenger cars. Dry-cell batteries, steel rolling, lead, zinc and chromite mining, plate glass, soap and detergents, and a variety of miscellaneous industries, have also been attracted to Iran.

Even in 1960 food processing industries accounted for 45 per cent of the invested capital in industry, nearly $250 m. out of $545 m. Within this total flour milling was the most important single sector, followed by sugar refining, vegetable oil refining and ice making. The next largest section was textiles, with 34 per cent of total capital invested : cotton textiles accounted for the overwhelming share. Building and construction ranked next with 6 per cent of capital, with cement already more important than the traditional brick and tile.

Wood and paper industries absorbed another 3 per cent of industrial capital, and leather products 1 per cent, a clear indication of the small amounts of capital involved in the labour intensive industries. The infant chemicals industry already accounted for 3 per cent of the capital, however, divided almost equally between rubber, pharmaceuticals and plastics. The metal goods industries, including repair shops and small metal working shops using small lathes, accounted for another 5 per cent.

The spread of industry has been comparatively wide, in view of the small scale of a great deal of the output, and the wide distribution of the food processing industries in particular. Nevertheless, Tehran itself is the main centre of the engineering and chemicals industries and, with Isfahan, is one of the two big textile centres. Tehran also has 6 of the 16 canning factories in the country.

Canning is a non-traditional industry, but once the local preference for fresh or dried food is overcome canning is likely to grow rapidly to serve local and export markets. Dried fruit is already an important export, but with greater application of capital, modern methods, and modern techniques of grading and packaging, a substantial export trade of fresh and canned fruit is likely. Iran can produce and will be able to market fresh, canned and dried fruit, nuts, tobacco, wines, dairy products, and especially meat.

In addition, heavy emphasis is being placed on a local steel industry to be based near Isfahan and built with Russian technical help, and on petrochemical industries. These two basic developments will help supplement older industries and provide a broader base for the next phase of secondary industrialisation. This in turn should see Iran equipped with a variety of basic industries which will supply the semi-processed goods, and support the sophisticated engineering and chemical goods industries, which Iran will need to augment the oil industry as a source of export earnings in the years to come.

Profit-sharing in Industry

PROFIT-SHARING is being encouraged in Iran's small but expanding industrial sector in order to give Iranian factory workers the same enhanced sense of pride in their work as land reform has given to the formerly landless peasants. At the same time it is intended to preserve the craftsman's traditional sense of pride and responsibility which will become increasingly important as the mass-production industries grow. Another objective is to prevent the development of class antagonism.

The distribution of bonuses is traditional in Iran, but has always been arbitrary, voluntary and dependent on the whims of the owners of industrial enterprises, some of whom gave bonuses on religious feastdays, at *Now Ruz*, or to celebrate weddings or the birth of children. The decree introducing profit-sharing, or more accurately one of several forms of profit participation, is intended to formalise the situation and link bonuses specifically to improved performance. In this way the interests of the emerging industrial class will be identified with the national interest.

Employers and workers in Iran were given a choice of four main types of profit participation which they could apply to their factory or workshop according to preference and suitability for their particular type of work. Article II of the law gave employers a period of three months in 1963 to work out with a trade union or workers' representatives an agreement to pay bonuses 'proportionate with gross profits, reduction of costs, reduction of wastage, or a provision of a share in the net profits, or a combination of two or more of the above'. If agreement was not possible a government scheme was to be prepared, and if this too was unacceptable the problem was to go to arbitration.

If this was not acceptable to the employers, a proportion of the concern's profits were to be set aside for distribution by a committee representing both workers and owners, together with three government ministries. A further regulation was introduced to ensure that if the average income of workers in state-operated industries and state monopolies was less than the average income in comparable private businesses, the balance was to be paid to the workers in the form of bonuses. Similar forms of profit-sharing were also introduced into state industries parallel with their competitors in the private sector. Once agreements had been put into operation it was made illegal for employers to reduce or revoke concessions made to their workers. Employers had to undertake to send their balance sheet annually to the Ministry of Labour and Social Services.

The workers' share of the profits comes as first claim on the operating profit of a firm, subject only to the requirements of the firm's reserve fund. As soon as the reserve fund amounts to 10 per cent of the company's capital, the workers' share takes first place absolutely. Within four months of the balance sheet being approved by the Ministry the employer has to deposit the workers' share in a bank account in four equal monthly instalments. The funds paid in must then be shared out within two months among the workers in proportion to their basic daily wages and their length of service reckoned together.

Each worker is allotted a profit co-efficient of one to five based on his length of service, and one to five based on his earnings. For example, a worker with less than one year's service receives a profit coefficient of one. One to five years' service earns a coefficient of three. Five to ten years' earns four, and more than ten years' the maximum of five. The scale for earnings gives a coefficient of one for workers earning up to 35 rials a day, three for between 35 and 60 rials, four for 60 to 80 rials, and five for workers earning more than 80 rials a day. Each worker is entitled to the sum of his two coefficients. The total share of each worker is determined simply by dividing the total number of points earned by the total labour force into the total profit fund and paying a bonus in appropriate multiples of the basic value of a share.

The most popular system of profit participation at present is that based on gross production of the factory or workshop, and accounts for almost half the 1,100 agreements which had been signed up to the middle of 1967. The system is based on gross production rather than profits as such, or any more abstract formula. Its great attraction is its relative simplicity. In a country where output falls short of potential demand there is little danger of producing an unprofitable glut.

A slightly more sophisticated type of agreement is that based on increases of production above an agreed norm. This type has been chosen in about one-ninth of the agreements to date. If production fails to meet the norm, no bonus is paid at all, but every increase in production carries a higher rate of profit participation for the workers.

A third and again rather more sophisticated method is related to savings made by the reduction of waste. Savings in reduced waste and better workmanship are to the unmistakable advantage of both workers and owners. The system is particularly useful in many of Iran's traditional craft industries, from pottery, glass, mosaic and tile making to gold and silver work, where expensive raw materials are used.

True profit-sharing, based on the distribution of a percentage of the net profit of the firm, accounts for about 12 per cent of all agreements signed so far. Net profits reflect not only gross production and production costs but also the more complicated factors of the cost of marketing, distribution and promotion, and the market price. This is an idealised situation, but even in countries with a long tradition of factory employment the net profit is based on so many factors outside the workers' control that it loses effectiveness as an incentive and may be regarded with suspicion.

Combinations of these methods are quite common. In addition, a variety of other methods were in fact put forward as model schemes by the Ministry of Labour and Social Services, in order to give the widest possible choice, and inspiration, to workers and employers. A number of them, however, were rejected because of the relative difficulty of assessing and explaining the system proposed. This was a material obstacle because of the high cost of the accountants and statisticians needed.

A further refinement of the system requires that in all cases where payment cannot be related directly to the production or productivity of a specific individual, but can only be calculated on the efforts of a group, that group has to be as small as practicable in order to preserve as large as possible a link between individual effort and individual reward.

Up to the end of June 1967, a total of 1,101 factories, employing 103,046 workers (a little over 70 per cent of the total number of industrial workers in employment) had adopted the profit-sharing law. Although this covered only 10 per cent of the number of industrial enterprises, most of the remainder were too small to need schemes, being mostly partnerships or individual craftsmen.

The great majority of the individual factories and workshops which had joined the scheme, 684 out of 1,101, were in the Tehran area. Isfahan and Gilan came next, each with 81, and Khorassan with 44. Every province had half a dozen schemes or more, however, and it is fair to say that the concept of profit-sharing has spread throughout the country. The concentration in Tehran reflects mainly the heavy concentration of industry inevitable in a metropolis.

Over half the workers involved, 54,656 out of 103,046, were employed in 219 concerns in the textile industry, which apart from its importance in the industrial structure is particularly easy to adapt for profit-sharing, since piece-work is relatively easy to calculate, and there is now a relatively large number of modern factories big enough to warrant adoption of a profit-sharing scheme.

The food processing industry, which is a smaller scale activity on average, contributed 355 schemes, employing 16,695 workers, followed by the metal-working industry with 136 schemes and 7,574 workers, many of them craftsmen. The construction industry included 144 schemes and 6,895 workers, and the relatively highly capitalised chemicals industry only 66 schemes but 5,306 workers.

The type of scheme operating varies appreciably from one sector of industry to another, according to the average size of unit and the type of process used. In the textile industry, with a strong showing of large modern plants, the incentives are keyed to quality as well as quantity production. Just under 30 per cent were based on gross production alone, 10 per cent on increases in output above a set norm, 7 per cent on reduced wastage or spoilage, just over 10 per cent on net profits, and no less than 42 per cent on a combination of two or more approved methods of calculation.

In the food packaging and processing industry, where the average size of unit is much smaller, just over half the schemes are based on gross output. More than 14 per cent were based on increased output above a norm, 29 per cent on reduced wastage or spoilage. Profit-sharing based on the distribution of a share of the net profits accounted for less than one case in 20. But other methods accounted for 9 per cent and a combination of methods for 13 per cent of the cases.

In metal-working, over a third were based on gross production, a sixth on net profits, nearly a quarter on other methods and 14 per cent on a variety of methods combined. In the chemicals industry a third of the agreements were based on gross production and another third on reduced wastage and spoilage.

The sums paid out in the early stages of the movement have not been spectacular by western wage standards. They average about 2,600 rials a year. But this represents a bonus of upwards of 10 per cent on the wages of the average industrial worker, and can be considerably more in cases where productivity is rising fast and high bonuses can be won.

Statistics are still incomplete because of the time lag which elapsed between the introduction of the law, the acceptance of agreed systems, the earning of the first bonuses and the time taken to calculate and distribute them. Between March 1966 and January 1967, however, a sample 112 enterprises in Tehran had paid a little more than 39 m. rials to just under 15,000 workers for a period of less than a full year.

The breakdown of payments by industry showed that only 18 factories in the metal-working sector, employing 2,628 workers, had paid nearly

$12\frac{1}{2}$ m. rials or nearly 5,000 rials per head. In the textile sector, 19 businesses with 6,721 workers had paid nearly $13\frac{1}{2}$ m. rials, or 2,000 rials a head. In the chemicals industry, 28 businesses had paid 3,469 workers nearly $8\frac{1}{2}$ m. rials, or 2,500 rials a head; and 36 concerns in the food industry had paid 1,668 workers a total of nearly $4\frac{1}{2}$ m. rials, representing a similar rate of bonus.

Plans are in hand to introduce profit-sharing and participation schemes in the additional range of industries which are now being developed or surveyed in Iran, including the steel and petrochemical industries, the new mining developments, and the engineering, vehicle and tractor building industries. Such schemes are of course implicit in the country's fast growing co-operative structure, covering large sectors of the distributive trades, small craft industries, and a large and rising share of the new agricultural producers' co-operatives.

The Three Corps

THE Literacy Corps, sixth principle of the revolution of the Shah and people, was both the pioneer of and prototype for the Health Corps and the Reconstruction and Development Corps, points 7 and 8 respectively.

One of the first laws passed in the reign of Mohammad Reza Shah had been concerned with the introduction of free and compulsory education. Because of the continuing lack of schools and shortage of teachers, this necessarily represented more a statement of intent than an immediate solution to Iran's grave education problems. To express an intention, however, is often the most important early step in its realisation — and certainly the number of primary and secondary schools in the country increased more rapidly thereafter than ever before.

Despite the political and economic problems of the early years of the Shah's reign, the number of schools of all types rose from 2,700 in 1941 to 6,700 in 1953, and total enrolment of students increased from less than 400,000 to 870,000 over the same period. It was, however, during the second decade of the Shah's reign that the educational expansion programme really began to snowball. Huge appropriations were allocated to educational development. By the end of 1962, the number of primary, secondary and vocational schools in Iran had risen to more than 14,000, while the total enrolment of students exceeded 2 million. Over this period higher education also developed rapidly and, by the time of the Sixth of Bahman referendum, the number of students pursuing higher education courses was about 25,000.

Despite the great efforts, and considerable achievements, of previous decades the harsh fact remained that in 1963 illiteracy in Iran still stood at a stunning 80 per cent, a reduction of only 5 per cent on the 1956 figure. If the position was to be remedied in the foreseeable future — and unless it was remedied there could be little hope for the rapid social and economic development of the country — a massive new initiative had to be launched. With the Ministry of Education already fully extended, it was by no means

clear where such an initiative could be found. It emerged in the sixth
principle of the revolution of the Shah and people.

The sixth principle involved the complete mobilisation of the literate
minority of the country to bring literacy to the majority — in traditional
terms a return to the educational precepts of Zoroaster and the Prophet.
Because of the scarcity of university places there had been for some time a
surplus of secondary school graduates who were unable to pursue their
education further. Because of their relatively high educational training,
these young men would have been wasted in unskilled jobs. Although they
were all eligible for military training the army could not absorb every one
of them. Nor were there sufficient white collar openings for all of them in
government service, business or the professions.

Under the law of January 1963, by which the Literacy Corps was created
in its present form, young men of conscript age were enabled to serve in the
Corps in lieu of their normal military service. Twice yearly, secondary
school recruits are sent to training centres in the provinces where they
receive four months intensive training in military and non-military subjects.
Military subjects occupy about one-third of the training period. They
include basic weapon and tactical training from drill and map reading up to
the role of the individual in atomic war. Meanwhile two-thirds of the training period is devoted to non-military subjects. These include conventional
teacher training programmes in classroom procedure ; methods of teaching
Farsi, arithmetic and science ; and educational psychology. The purpose
of this training period, however, is to equip the Corpsmen not only to fight
illiteracy by the teaching of reading and writing but to act as all-purpose
village workers and messengers of the revolution in every sector of village
life affected by the Sixth of Bahman reforms. To help the Corpsman in this
vital role his training programme also includes such elementary but important subjects as health education and sanitation ; first aid ; agricultural
education ; community development ; rural sociology and village law.

The Corpsman, then, has as his first duty the formal education of
children. Auxiliary to this are the teaching of adults in evening classes ;
the setting up of small village libraries and circularisation of reading material
amongst the literates ; the organisation of recreational and youth groups
including the teaching of games and physical education ; and the establishment of boy scout troops.

The Corpsman's second, and main duty, is to act as general adviser,
teacher and helper to his village in matters of health, agriculture and community projects. In practice no formal distinction exists between these
two roles. The elementary textbooks used by the Corpsman, for example,
have a strong emphasis on the practical knowledge needed to improve
village life. Typical titles are *The Home and Health* ; *Poultry and Livestock* ;

The Three Corps

General Village Health and *Trees, Forest and Orchard.*

Health education and sanitation are of primary importance in rural Iran, where life expectancy is low and infant mortality high. Practical measures which the Corpsman can undertake include the purification of drinking water, construction of shower baths and conversion of old pools into showers, the conversion of open latrines, the construction of mortuaries, the separation of livestock from living quarters and the institution of classes for village midwives. He takes along with him to his village a kit of posters, pamphlets and other health publications and can call on mobile cinema units with films on health to reinforce his message.

A vital part of the Corpsman's task is to acquaint the farmers in his village with the organisation and functions of the Ministry of Agriculture — how to obtain help from the proper part of the ministry and how to get information on such subjects as insecticides, fertilisers, agricultural implements, soil studies and livestock breeding. The farmers also need to be taught the rudiments of marketing. Most important, they must learn to appreciate the theory and practice of the Agricultural Co-operative Movement.

An essential function of the Corpsman is to promote and encourage group action and group participation in village affairs. Through the formation of Parent Teacher Groups, the Corpsman keeps in constant touch with the parents of children in his care. These help encourage students to attend his classes and, at the same time, encourage more adults to follow their example. Each Corpsman is expected to deal easily with a class of 20 to 25 boys and girls. If the number in a class rises to more than 35, one or more additional Corpsmen are sent to his assistance.

Every 20 village schools are grouped under an education supervisor, who is a graduate of the College of Education with at least five years' experience in elementary school supervision. Supervisors visit schools regularly in order to help the Corpsmen. Other regular visitors are the district Agricultural Extension, Health and Co-operative experts who give the Corpsmen specialist assistance.

The actual achievements of the Literacy Corps in its first four years of operation have fully justified the high hopes held for it and the immense amount of work put into its development. Due to the work of the Corpsmen the number of rural elementary schools in Iran has risen from 7,000 to 22,000. Since 1963 some 130,000 girls, half a million boys, 12,000 adult women and a quarter million adult men have been taught to read and write by the Literacy Corps, in day and evening classes in the villages. Some 1.5 million students are now enrolled in rural schools—and a large proportion of this increase may be attributed directly to the efforts of the Literacy Corps.

In the villages it is the girls who have benefited most from this teaching.

Document Five

Before the Literacy Corps was formed there were 438 girls at school in the towns for every thousand boys, while in village schools the proportion of girls was only 225 to every thousand boys. While the ratio of girls to boys in city schools has now increased by 8 per cent, in the village schools it has increased by 26 per cent.

It is difficult to measure the impact of the Literacy Corps in its capacity as harbinger of the revolution in cold statistics. However, a few figures taken at random may give some idea of the achievements that its guidance has made possible for the villagers. By 1967 more than 11,000 schools had been built, 60,000 kilometres of roads linking villages to highways had been laid, more than 10,000 *qanats* — underground irrigation systems — had been repaired and nearly 2½ million trees had been planted.

Like the Literacy Corps, the Health and the Development Corps were the revolutionary solutions to problems which neither the conventional efforts of the government nor the Shah's initiative alone could hope to rectify satisfactorily within the forseeable future. According to the law relating to the formation of the Health Corps, it consists of doctors, dentists, pharmacists, engineers, medical assistants, graduates with first and second degrees, and secondary school graduates. After completing a four-month training similar to that of the Literacy Corpsmen, they are sent to various rural districts of Iran where their duties are to promote public health by treating the sick, preventing disease, developing sanitary arrangements, providing maternity and child health care, teaching the principles of nutrition and dietary science, and guiding the people generally towards a more hygienic way of life. The long term objectives of the Corps are to improve the state of the economy by augmenting the nation's manpower resources through the development of a healthy population, and to raise the educational level of the people through the provision of tuition in public health.

The structure of the Health Corps is made up of four main levels : organisational headquarters, provincial divisions, regional bases and local teams. The two top levels are concerned primarily with planning and administration. To ensure co-ordination, and to facilitate the supply of mobile teams, there is one regional base for every 8/12 teams. Each base comprises an administrative section, a laboratory section, a dentistry unit, a sanitary engineering group, a health education group, a statistics unit and a transportation section. This organisation serves as a base for the mobile health teams and its special facilities are at their disposal as required. Thus, when a sanitation improvement scheme is decided upon in a village the team concerned contacts its base and the sanitary engineering group is sent out.

The most dynamic units of the Health Corps are the mobile teams. Medical teams are led by a physician and include two or three secondary school graduates as medical aides, a driver with transportation, and the necessary supply of medicines. Revolving around their bases, each team moves into the villages of its prescribed area according to a timetable as tightly planned and scheduled as a military operation. Each base has sub-centres in two or three other villages, placing under medical protection the inhabitants of 30/40 adjacent villages — amounting to 20,000 people.

To enable the medical teams and other Health Corps units to carry out their programme, they have been provided with comprehensive transportation, medical and living facilities. Taking into account the rough road conditions in the far-flung rural areas of Iran, the headquarters organisation provides each mobile team with one cross-country vehicle. Additionally, each base is allocated one ambulance for emergency cases and a van for the transportation of medical and sanitation equipment to wherever the mobile teams requiring it are located. As well as providing the medicines required by mobile teams, the headquarters organisation supplies ophthalmic, dental, laboratory and clinical equipment, and instruments for minor surgery. Mobile teams are also provided with such living facility equipment as beds, sleeping-bags, blankets, sheets, oil lamps, primuses, stoves, hurricane lamps, torches, flasks, ice chests and watersacks.

By May 1967, four groups of Health Corpsmen, totalling 1,700, had completed their two year service period and a further two groups, representing 1,600 Corpsmen, were still active in the field. At present there are altogether five hundred medical units at work in the villages. Allowing for the fact that each mobile unit is capable of looking after between thirty and fifty villages with a total population of between ten to fifteen thousand, this means that the Health Corps is at present catering for some 14,000 villages with a total population of more than five million.

The Reconstruction and Development Corps was created by a decree issued by the Shah on September 23, 1964. One of the first duties of the Development Corpsman is to conduct a survey of each village — a sort of 20th Century Domesday Book — covering such subjects as the villages' natural features, economic characteristics, social structure, educational facilities and degree of agricultural advancement. The purpose of obtaining this information is to gain a clearer idea of the condition of each village served by the three Corps, so that an operational plan can be made which takes into account the difficulties and problems of the village and its inhabitants in the various fields of agriculture, stockbreeding and development.

Every member of the Reconstruction and Development Corps is required, during the period of his service in the region to which he is sent, to conduct training programmes for the villagers in agriculture and stockbreeding, and to try to raise the general level of knowledge of the farmers and their families. In order to accomplish this, every Corpsman must see that the villagers themselves create a small experimental farm of at least 1,000 square metres, using seed supplied by the Ministry of Agriculture. This farm must serve to demonstrate the best ways of preparing the ground, sowing the seed and harvesting the crop, including the use of the best seed, chemical fertilisers, irrigation and pest control.

The Corpsman must also show the villagers how to make a model orchard, from which they will learn the correct way to plant and graft fruit trees, and prepare an orchard nursery. He must also vaccinate at least two hundred head of cattle and sheep against diseases prevalent in the locality, and must give instruction in the improvement of the ventilation, lighting and sanitation of stables. In regions suitable for bees, he must introduce modern hives in place of existing old-fashioned ones and teach the correct principles of apiculture. For the protection of crops and livestock against disease, each Corpsman is supplied with various kinds of pesticides and veterinary products, the uses of which he must demonstrate to the villagers. In order to demonstrate the advantages of chemical fertilisers for crop improvement, each Corpsman must use such fertilisers on an area of at least 1,500 square metres of farmland and pasture.

Finally, in order to instruct young villagers in problems of social life, every Corpsman must establish at least one club consisting of fifteen to twenty-five young farmers and train them by carrying out selected small-scale agricultural, social and community projects.

Since its inception some 3,500 members of the Development Corps have worked or are working in the villages. The list of their achievements is formidable : model seed farms, model market gardens and model orchards have been established ; more than a million head of livestock and poultry have been vaccinated or treated ; thousands of orchards have been pruned, stables disinfected, gardens and poultry farms pest controlled ; village street systems have been relaid, village water systems installed and, in several cases, water towers constructed.

However, the real achievement of the Development Corps, like the real achievements of the Literacy Corps and of the Health Corps, cannot be measured in cold statistics. What these three organisations have achieved, individually and collectively, is the blazoning of the message of the revolution across every village in the land. The young men and women of Iran have been mobilised in a manner which makes the achievements of such western mutations as the Peace Corps and VSO pale indeed by comparison. Most important of all, the common people of Iran have been brought to realise that responsibility for the success of the revolution lies in their own hands. If any one lesson has been taught by the three Corps more firmly than any other it is the lesson of self help. It is a lesson which the people of other countries, in the west as well as in Afro-Asia, would do well to learn.

374

Bibliographical Notes

THE primary sources for a work of this nature are to be found not so much in the documents, but in the memories of men and women who participated in the events which constitute the history of Iran for the last fifty years. However, there is considerable documentation available in the following two works by the Shah : *Mission for my Country* and *The White Revolution of Iran*. These are indispensable studies. A documented record, *Iran in the reign of His Majesty Mohammed Reza Shah Pahlevi*, prepared by Ali Asghar Shamin, is now available in an English translation by Dr Aladin Pazargadi of the Tehran University. Finally, I have relied upon General Hassan Arfa's *Under Five Shahs*, described as 'a dramatic account of the evolution of Iran by one who took part', whenever I was in doubt about the chronology of events.

al-Mulk, Nizam. *The Book of Government or Rules for Kings*. Translated from the Persian by Hubert Darke. London, 1967.

Arberry, A. J. *Sufism*. London, 1950.

Arfa, General Hassan. *Under Five Shahs*. London, 1964.

Avery, Peter William. *Modern Iran*. London, 1965.

Balfour, James M. *Recent Happenings in Persia*. Edinburgh, 1922.

Banani, Amin. *The Modernization of Iran, 1921–1924*. Stanford University Press, California, 1961.

Barnett, Clifford R., and others. *Iran*. Ed. Herbert H. Vreeland. (Country Survey Series.) Human Relations Area Files, New Haven, 1957.

Bémont, Frédy. *L'Iran Devant le Progrès*. Institut d'étude du développement économique et social de l'université de Paris. Paris, 1964.

Benedick, R. E. *Industrial Finance in Iran*. Harvard University Press, 1964.

Binder, Leonard. *Iran : political development in a changing society*. Cambridge University Press, 1962.

Bozorg, Alavi. *Kaempfendes Iran*, Berlin, 1955.

Bibliographical Notes

Browne, E. G. *The Persian Revolution of 1905-1909*. London, 1910.

Campbell, John C. *Defense of the Middle East, Problems of American Policy*, Council of Foreign Relations. New York, 1958.

Christensen, A. *Les Gestes Des Rois Dans Les Traditions de L'Iran Antique*. Paris, 1936.

Churchill, Sir Winston. *The Second World War*, vol. 6: War Comes to America. Cassel paperback edition. London, 1965.

Curzon, Hon. George N. *Persia and the Persian Question*. 2 vols. London, 1892.

Deborin, G. *The Second World War, a Politico-military Survey*. Ed. Major-General I. Zubkov. Moscow.

Eagleton, William J. R. *The Kurdish Republic of 1946*. Royal Institute of International Affairs, London, 1963.

Elwell-Sutton, L. P. *A Guide to Iranian Area Study*. American Council of Learned Societies. Michigan, 1952.

Modern Iran. London, 1941. (Reprinted 1942, 1943 and 1944.) Persian translation i. by Ali Javeher Kalam, Tehran, 1947: ii. by Abdol Azim Saburi, Tehran, 1957.

Persian Oil: A Study in Power Politics. London, 1955. (A Russian translation of this publication was issued in Moscow, 1956: a Chinese translation was issued in Peking, 1958.)

Engler, Robert. *The Politics of Oil. Private Power and Democratic Directions*. First Phoenix edition, Chicago, 1967.

Essad-Bey, Mohammed. *Reza Shah*. Prepared with the aid of Paul Maerker Branden and Elsa Branden. London, 1938.

Fatemi, N. S. *Oil Diplomacy: Powderkeg in Iran*. New York, 1954.

Ferdowsi, *The Epic of the Kings, Shāh-nāma, The National Epic of Persia*. Trans. Reuben Levy, London, 1967.

Ford, Alan W. *The Anglo-Iranian Oil Dispute of 1951-1952: A Study of the Role of Law in the Relations of States*. Berkeley, 1954.

Frazer, Lovat, *India Under Curzon*. Second Edition. London, 1911.

Frye, Richard N. *Iran*. London, 1954; second edition, 1960.

Ghirshman, R. *Iran from the Earliest Times to the Islamic Conquest*. Harmondsworth, Middlesex, 1961. (French version published in Paris, 1951: English version first published 1954, with a reprint in 1961.

Gregory, Lois (Mrs Lois Darab Khan). *The Shah and Persia*. London, 1961.

Gupta, Raj Narin. *Iran: An Economic Study*. Indian Institute of International Affairs, New Delhi, 1947.

Haas, William S. *Iran*. New York, 1946.

Halpern, Manfred. *The Politics of Social Change in the Middle East and North Africa*. Princeton, New Jersey, 1963.

Bibliographical Notes

Harnack, Curtis. *Persian Lions, Persian Lambs: an Odyssey in Iran.* London, 1965.

Huot, Jean Louis. *Implementation of Iran's Land Reform Program, March 12, 1962.* Tehran.

Iran Plans for the Future. A Summary of Activities (of) the Plan Organisation of Iran. Tehran, 1958.

Issawi, Charles, and Yegeneh, Mohammad. *The Economics of Middle Eastern Oil.* London, 1963.

Jackson, A. V. W. *Zoroaster, the Prophet of Ancient Iran.* New York, 1919.

Labour Conditions in the Oil Industry in Iran. International Labour Office, Geneva, 1958.

Lambton, Ann K. S. *Landlord and Peasant in Persia: A Study of Land Tenure and Land Revenue Administration.* London and New York, 1953.

Laqueur, Walter Z. *The Soviet Union and the Middle East.* London, 1959.

Lenczowski, George. *Russia and the West in Iran,* 1918–1948. Ithaca, New York, 1949. (Supplement 1954.)

Malek-Mahdavi, Ahmed. *Manpower. Third Plan Frame.* Division of Economic Affairs, Plan Organisation. Tehran, 1961.

Marlowe, John. *Iran, a short political guide.* London, 1963.

The Persian Gulf in the Twentieth Century. London, 1962.

Millspaugh, Arthur C. *Americans in Persia.* The Brookings Institution, Washington, D.C., 1946.

The American Task in Persia. New York and London, 1925.

Nehru, Jawaharlal, *Discovery of India.* Bombay, 1948.

O'Connor, Harvey. *The Empire of Oil.* New York, 1962.

Pahlavi, Mohammad Reza Shah, Shahanshah of Iran. *Mission for My Country.* London, 1961.

Biography of Reza Shah, in *Self-Made Man* (a collection of biographies). Tehran, 1956.

The White Revolution of Iran. The Imperial Pahlavi Library. Tehran, 1967.

Pannikar, K. M. *The Foundations of a New India.* London, 1963.

Rajput, A. B. *Iran To-day.* Third edition. Lahore, 1953.

Rashidian, Seiffullah. *A Plan for Economic Well-being.* London, 1967.

Rice, Cyprian. *The Persian Sufis.* London, 1964.

Roosevelt, Kermit. *Arabs, Oil and History, The Story of the Middle East.* London, 1949.

Sahebjam, Freidoune. *L'Iran des Pahlavis.* Paris, 1966.

Sanghvi, Ramesh ; German, Clifford, and Missen, David, Gen. Eds. *The Revolution of the Shah and the People.* London, 1967.

Shamim, Ali Asghar. *Iran in the Reign of His Majesty Mohammad Reza Shah*

Bibliographical Notes

Pahlavi's Central Council, Celebrations of the 25th Century of the Iranian Empire. Trans. Dr Aladin Pazargodi, Tehran, 1966.

Shuster, W. Morgan. *The Strangling of Persia: Story of the European Diplomacy and Oriental Intrigue that Resulted in the Denationalization of Twelve Million Mohammedans. A Personal Narrative.* New York, 1912.

Siassi, Ali Akbar. *Silver Jubilee, 16th September 1965: Iran, a quarter century of historic progress, 1941–1965,* with a foreword by His Excellency Mr Ardeshir Zahedi, Iranian Ambassador to the Court of St. James's. London, Imperial Iranian Embassy, 1965.

Skrine, Sir Clarmont. *World War In Iran.* London, 1962.

Stark, Freya. *Statistics. Third Plan Frame.* Division of Economic Affairs, Plan Organisation. Tehran, 1937.

Stevens, Sir Roger. *The Land of the Great Sophy.* London, 1962. Reprinted with minor corrections, 1965.

Sykes, Sir Percy. *A History of Persia.* 2 vols. Third edition, 1930; London: New York, 1963. Reprinted 1951, 1958 and 1963. *Persia.* Oxford, 1922.

Tehrani, Alexander. *The Plan Organization of Iran: Historical Review, September 25, 1955–March 20, 1958.* Tehran, 1958.

Upton, Joseph M. *The History of Modern Iran: an interpretation.* (Harvard Middle Eastern Monographs, II.) Cambridge, Mass., 1960.

Wilber, Donald N. *Contemporary Iran.* New York and London, 1963. *Iran — Oasis of Stability in the Middle East.* Headline Series, No. 137. Foreign Policy Association. New York. *Iran Past and Present.* Princeton, New Jersey, 1948. Further editions issued in 1950, 1955, 1958 and 1963.

Wilson, Sir Arnold T. *Persia.* London, 1932. *Persian Gulf.* Oxford University Press, 1928.

Yeselson, Abraham. *U.S.–Persian Diplomatic Relations, 1883–1921.* New Brunswick, 1956.

Index

379

Index

Index

Index

Iran (*contd.*)

in, 236-7 ; receives American aid, 244, 247, 257 ; resumes diplomatic relations with Britain, 247 ; signs agreement with Russia, 247-8 ; joins Baghdad Pact, 249 ; reduction of American aid to, 263 ; land reform in, 280-281, 290-91 ; industrial revolution in, 292-5, 359-63 ; profit sharing in industry in, 294-5, 364-8 ; women receive the vote in, 301 ; Literacy Corps in, 305-306, 307-8, 369-72 ; Health Corps in, 309, 372-3 ; Reconstruction and Development Corps in, 309, 373-4 ; Houses of Equity in, 309, 310, 311, 312 ; economic success of, 323-324, 334

Iran, a short political guide, 17, 169, 173, 268

Iran from the Earliest Times to the Islamic Conquest, xviii

Iran, in the reign of His Majesty Mohammed Reza Shah Pahlavi, 61

Iran Novin Party, 287

Iran : Political Development in a Changing Society, xxiii, 161, 222

Iran, Shah of, xvi, xvii, xxiii, xxiv, xxv, 4 ; reforms of, xxv, 139-41 ; birth of, 3, 26 ; influenced by his father, 26, 31-2 ; becomes Crown Prince, 30 ; education of, 31, 36-7, 38-46 ; writes an appreciation of his father, 33 ; religious awakening of, 34-5 ; religious experiences of, 35-6 ; goes to school in Switzerland, 36-7 ; a keen sportsman, 39 ; academic interests of, 39 ; effect of Western Europe on, 39-40 ;

as a student of history and current affairs, 41-2, 44-5 ; political ideology of, 42-3 ; religious dedication of, 44 ; returns to Tehran from Switzerland, 46 ; enters Military College in Tehran, 47 ; becomes inspector in the army, 48 ; absorbs lessons of his father's government, 53-4 ; his views on the invasion of Iran by Britain and Russia, 70, 71 ; sees his father for the last time, 73 ; becomes Shah, 75 ; takes the oath of loyalty, 77 ; his early problems as ruler, 81-2, 87-9 ; initiates Tripartite Treaty, 83 ; declares war on Germany, 87 ; proclaims Iran a constitutional democracy, 90 ; results of his proclamation, 93-6 ; fears return of spheres of influence after Second War, 103 ; host to ' Big Three ', 103 ; gains important success at Tehran Conference, 108 ; broadcasts to people at end of Second War, 114 ; calls on Western Powers for aid against Russian occupation, 119-20 ; takes Iran's case against Russia to Security Council, 120-21 ; in dispute with Prime Minister Qavam, 124-6 ; orders Qavam to dissolve cabinet, 127 ; orders new elections, 128 ; moves his army against rebels in Azerbaijan and Kurdistan, 130 ; threatened by Soviet Ambassador, 131 ; defeats rebels in Azerbaijan and Kurdistan, 132-3 ; creates Industrial and Mineral Bank, 141 ; his Seven Year Plan, 141, 151, 152, 166, 168, 215, 230, 239 ;

Index

Index

Index

Index